Teaching Unity

**A Guide for Parents and Teachers
with Learning Activities for Ages 8-12**

Dr. Randie S. Gottlieb

Free Downloads

Four colorful PowerPoint programs designed to illustrate these lessons are included with your purchase, along with printable student handouts, craft patterns, fillable forms, editable Word documents, a certificate, and a color-pack of photographs and illustrations.

To download: Go to **www.TeachingUnity.com.** On the right side, under Unity Community, click "Register" or Login with Facebook. Then on the homepage, click on Free Downloads. You will be asked to login if you haven't already done so. Then click any "Login to Download" button and follow the instructions. **You will need your book to locate the secret code!** The files are large and will require a laptop or desktop computer. We recommend downloading the files to your computer desktop so they are easy to find.

For bulk discounts, contact: Books@unityworks.org
or visit: <u>www.unityworks.org</u> > Bookstore > Information

Teaching Unity

ISBN 978-0-9828979-9-7

© 2013 UnityWorks LLC, rev. 2018

<u>All rights reserved</u>. No part of this book may be reproduced or transmitted in any form or by any means without prior written permission from the publisher.

<u>Handouts</u>: UnityWorks hereby grants permission to the purchaser to copy student handouts as needed for their own educational activities with children. The copyright information must clearly show on all copies. Scanning, large-scale reproduction or distribution, and inclusion in commercial publications are not permitted.

<u>Disclaimer</u>: It is the responsibility of the user to determine the suitability of the materials and activities in this book, and the associated downloaded items, to meet the user's particular needs and the needs of the teachers, children or students involved. The user therefore agrees to hold the author and UnityWorks, along with its personnel, employees, agents, contractors or volunteers, harmless from any claims and/or litigation arising from or related thereto. Reasonable caution and adult supervision of children is recommended at all times.

<u>Bulk Purchase</u>: Please contact us with your request: info@TeachingUnity.com.

If you find these items useful, please let others know about them.

Thank you!

www.TeachingUnity.com

Special thanks to my husband, Steven E. Gottlieb, M.D. for his ongoing support.

Edited by Steven Gottlieb and Denise Tronstad
Cover photo by Steven Gottlieb
Cover design by Jordan Gottlieb and Kate Sansom
Musical transcription by Jonathan Gottlieb

Artwork on the back cover and on p. v courtesy of: www.clipsahoy.com

Quotations from the Bahá'í writings reprinted with permission of
the National Spiritual Assembly of the Bahá'ís of the United States
and the Bahá'í Publishing Trust of Wilmette, IL.

Clip art images taken or adapted from:
The Big Box of Art from www.Hemera.com

All websites and references listed
are correct at the time of publication.

Published by UnityWorks, LLC
Yakima, Washington, USA

What People Are Saying

From school teachers, parents and kids

"Wow! I love the subject matter—the Power of Unity—it speaks across lines of race, religion, gender and all the other divisions that we use to separate ourselves. Really wonderful work." (Beth Shevin, Los Angeles)

"I love the great variety of approaches. Parents impressed and happy!" (Lani Diessner, Oregon)

"A human being cannot describe how much you guys did for me. Thank you from the bottom of my heart." (Zia, age 11, Washington State)

"I really love the book—easy to follow, easy to use, creative and wonderful." (Juli Redson-Smith, Colorado)

"Love your *Unity* book and used some of the ideas for the art curriculum at the school in Haiti." (Judy Rector)

"This book is phenomenal—an incredibly useful teaching tool! All the activities reinforce concepts that are so crucial for people today." (Barry Tronstad, Ventura)

"It's perfect for ELL classes too!" (Denise McMillan, Ventura)

"What a wonderful new resource to look forward to. I'm already excited about it and I hope we can use it down here in New Zealand." (Cyndy Pratt)

"For those of us who home-school our kids, we have the bounty of LOTS of time to work with them and the challenge of almost no available curriculum. So each family is left to make things up, which isn't necessarily a bad thing, but it's exhausting trying to be creative every day. It is such a relief to have a nicely laid out, flexible and systematic curriculum to work through. So thank you, thank you for your efforts." (Genesta Zarehbin, Oakland)

"Thank you so much for the lessons and PowerPoints on Unity! This is going to help more than you can think." (Alem Hamzic, high school student, Bosnia)

"*Teaching Unity* is a high, waving banner being raised in the name of the oneness of mankind—not optional learning, but the very path of human destiny." (James Williams, Virginia)

What if all the children in the world were born without prejudice?

They are!

Preface

As I was growing up in Southern California, racial tensions in Los Angeles erupted in the Watts riots of 1965, resulting in dozens of deaths, thousands of injuries and arrests, and millions of dollars in property damage. Martial law was declared and enforced by 15,000 members of the National Guard and local police. Newspapers described the area as a war zone. Watts was 25 minutes from my home.

Almost 30 years after the Watts uprising, Los Angeles exploded in violence once again in 1992 when a jury acquitted several police officers who were accused of brutally beating Rodney King, a Black motorist, following a high-speed chase. On the first day of rioting, Reginald Denny, a White truck driver passing through the area, was pulled from his cab by an angry mob of African-Americans and beaten nearly to death. Appealing for calm, King famously asked, *"Can't we all get along?"*

Despite apparent progress made since that time, including the historic election of the first Black president of the United States in 2008—which some celebrated as the moment when America's racial divide was a thing of the past—racial mistrust, suspicion and hostility continue to plague our nation.

More recent echoes of the Rodney King incident can be found in the Florida shooting death of Trayvon Martin in early 2012 and the response from all sides. While in Chicago for a convention shortly after that tragic and controversial event, I was somewhat encouraged to see people of diverse backgrounds and colors marching together in the street, some holding signs with the same question: *"Can't we all get along?"*

My response is this book:

Teaching Unity
We *Can* All Get Along.

Table of Contents

PART I: Introduction 1
    About this Book 3
    To Parents and Teachers 5
    One Teacher's Experience 7
    Teaching Tips and Tools 9

PART II: Lessons and Materials 11
    Warm-up Activities 13
    Unit 1: The Light of Unity 21
    Unit 2: Unity in Diversity 35
    Unit 3: The Colors We Are 59
    Unit 4: Overcoming Prejudice 77
    Music 113
    Handouts 125

PART III: Additional Activities 145
    Warm-ups 149
    Craft Projects 150
    Outdoor Games 168
    Skits, Demonstrations and Puzzles 177
    Speaking, Reading, Writing and Research 193
    Further Reading and Research 200

PART IV: Children's Performance 203
    Children's Performance 205
    Materials Needed 206
    Sample Agenda 207
    Rehearsal Groups 208
    Rehearsal Notes 209
    Sample Program for Audience 211
    Scripts and Instructions 212
    Closing Activities 219
    Follow-up Ideas 220

PART V: Planning a Children's Retreat or Camp 221

- Planning Committee 223
- Participants 223
- Teachers 224
- Special Role of Youth 224
- Other Personnel 225
- Facility 225
- Finances 226
- Schedule 226
- Publicity 231
- Registration 235
- Materials 238
- Site Preparation 239
- Check-in Process 240
- Meals and Snacks 242
- Signs and Certificates 243
- Opening Activities 244
- Orientation Program 244
- Event Guidelines 245
- Videos on Unity 247
- Volunteer Orientation 248
- Planning Checklist 249

PART VI: Appendices 253

- A. Words of Wisdom 257
- B. Memorization Techniques 268
- C. Help with Reading 271
- D. Think-Pair-Share 273
- E. Speed Discussions 275
- F. Sample Letter from Sponsor 276
- G. Additional Resources 277
- H. Bibliography 280
- I. About the Author 281

PART VII: Index of Activities 283

- List of Activities in Each Unit 285
- Index of Activities by Category 289

PART I

Introduction

About this Book

This book is about hope. It is intended as a resource for parents and teachers. Its purpose is to help prepare our children for life as citizens in a global society—recognizing our interdependence, respectful of our differences, and working together towards a prosperous and peaceful world.

The book is based on the principle of the oneness of humankind. An emerging consciousness of our oneness is a hallmark of the present age and a prerequisite for achieving the well-being, peace and security of all the earth's inhabitants. We come in different shapes, sizes and colors. We speak different languages and have different cultures, ethnic backgrounds and religious beliefs. But we live on one planet, breathe the same air and walk upon the same ground. It is time to recognize that we are one human race. There is no *us* or *them*; it's all *us*!

Oneness, however, does not mean sameness. Along with a recognition of our oneness comes an understanding of the value of diversity and the need for unity. It is not enough to celebrate Black History Month, International Women's Day or Cinco de Mayo. We need a new holistic vision of ourselves as diverse human beings.

While considering various types of diversity, the primary focus of this book is on race and skin color. Racism is perhaps the most appalling and one of the most deep-rooted features of our nation's heritage. We cannot just ignore it and hope it will go away. Ignorance only serves to reinforce the many walls of prejudice that persist as barriers to the unity of humankind. We need to address race directly in ways that our students and children can understand.

Many books describe what is wrong with our society in great detail but stop short of offering clear, practical solutions. It is hoped that this easy-to-use teacher's guide will serve as a valuable starting place in helping children to not only understand some of the challenges we face, but to identify potential solutions, to develop an increasingly multicultural perspective, to build skills and capacity, and to become empowered to act as a positive force for justice and harmony in the world.

The following pages are filled with fun, hands-on, kid-tested learning activities designed for ages 8-12. Many of the activities can be adapted for older and younger students as well. Parents and teachers will need to decide which activities are most appropriate for their particular group.

Using an integrated approach, the lessons incorporate a variety of teaching and learning strategies including storytelling, demonstrations, group discussion, memorization, felt lessons, crafts, music, outdoor games, student presentations and more. The material is organized in a sequential, step-by-step format with each activity building on the previous one. Each activity can also stand alone.

If used for an intensive program such as a summer school, holiday camp or weekend retreat, you will need to select activities to fit within the time allotted. If used as part of an ongoing program such as a daily academic class or weekly after-school club, one or more activities can be selected for each session, until the entire curriculum has been completed. The index makes it easy to find exactly what you need.

The suggested time for each activity is noted in parentheses after the heading. However, if children need additional time to practice a skill, or if the group is engaged in a fruitful discussion and wishes to continue, the time can be extended and the remaining activities saved for a future session.

Written in plain language, the lessons are complete, easy-to-use and require little outside preparation. Essentially everything is included, with the exception of craft supplies and common household items. In addition to detailed lesson plans, there are simple patterns for making instructional materials, copy-ready student handouts, song sheets, music scores, plans for a children's performance, and a comprehensive planning guide for organizing a weekend retreat or week-long Unity Camp.

Participants from one of our many children's retreats.

As long as there are children, there is hope. Each generation brings a fresh opportunity to renew the world. *Teaching Unity* provides parents and teachers with the tools they need to get started.

* * * * *

To Parents and Teachers

Parents are the first educators of the child. In addition to providing physical care and protection, ongoing love and encouragement, we impart to them our beliefs and values, shape their character and teach them how to relate to other people.

When our children reach school age, we entrust them to the care of teachers who provide them with the knowledge, skills and tools to help them realize their potential as human beings, and to contribute to their families, their communities and the larger society.

Whether as parents or teachers, we are often challenged to counteract the destructive standards of a world in disarray—with its deeply-entrenched prejudices, its all-pervasive materialism and glorification of violence—a world where injustice is tolerated, where economic exploitation is commonplace, where apathy is widespread, and where dishonesty and political corruption seem to be the norm.

Especially damaging is racial prejudice. Although great strides have been made, it still permeates the institutions of our society and holds a strong grip on individual hearts and minds.

Prejudice, an irrational negative prejudgment about another group, has been passed down for generations. It is learned from our families and friends, from the media, and even from our religious communities and schools. Many young children already hold negative stereotypes of other racial and ethnic groups by the time they enter first grade.

These attitudes are reflected in their everyday behavior. Children might begin with simple teasing, which may seem harmless, or the refusal to play with others from certain groups. Teasing and exclusion can lead to name-calling, harassment, bullying and worse. Even the smallest denial of one person's rights and dignity, plants seeds of hate that affect us all.

In a comprehensive survey conducted by the author in 2002 at four middle schools, 85% of the students reported hearing hateful words (about race, weight, gender, etc.) on a regular basis. With regard to race in particular, 30% of the students said they heard 11 or more racial slurs every single day. Most of this is not reported for fear of retaliation and a self-imposed code of silence. These statistics mirror that of the nation as a whole.[1]

How then do we move beyond people-made barriers to create a society where all feel welcome, where differences are valued, and where people are treated with dignity and respect?

---

1. http://nces.ed.gov/programs/crimeindicators/crimeindicators2011/ind_10.asp
   http://en.wikipedia.org/wiki/School_bullying#Statistics
   http://nces.ed.gov/pubs2011/2011316.pdf

Research shows that the best way to reduce prejudice is through purposeful interaction among people from different groups. Parents and teachers can encourage children to work side-by-side with those from other backgrounds. We can serve as role models. We can give them the tools and strategies needed to form healthy attitudes and relationships, and we can plan specific activities that foster cooperation and understanding.

For example, one of the alternative high schools that I worked with was successful in reducing conflict between two rival groups through an innovative art program. Students from both groups were paired up, and each was asked to paint a portrait depicting the other person's life story. In order to complete the assignment which was a large part of their final grade for the class, the students were forced to learn about someone who had previously been considered an enemy. The final portraits were then incorporated into a mural painted on an outside wall of the school. Several business owners in the community were so impressed that they commissioned these same students to paint additional murals on buildings around town.

While it is easy to transfer a lot of information through abstract verbal explanations, lectures and books, this has little impact on attitudes and behavior. Rather, children learn best through concrete experiences that engage their senses and emotions. This book includes many such activities, for example: Tug of Peace, Unity Bingo and Cooperative Musical Chairs. While these games may seem like play, the children are actually learning valuable lessons about cooperation and justice.

Learning about unity should not be considered optional, an add-on to the curriculum. It should be viewed as a critical part of the education of every child.

Teaching unity requires wisdom, patience, humility and courage. It calls for persistent effort by women and men of diverse backgrounds and colors. We need to purge our own hearts from all traces of racial superiority and inferiority; actively work to undo 500 years of racial conditioning; and teach our children directly about the oneness of humanity, the value of diversity and the need for unity. We may not be responsible for the past, but together we can take responsibility for our common destiny. In a world torn by injustice, hate and war, our homes and classrooms can become models of hope for the future.

Write to Me!

I would appreciate hearing about your experience using the activities in this book. Feel free to send me your comments and questions, your stories and photographs, and the responses of your students and children.

< *rg@unityworks.net* >

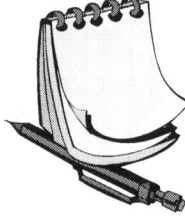

One Teacher's Experience

From Dr. Susan Walker, Seattle

I shared the first PowerPoint last week with two fourth-grade classes—along with the donkey example, the gym shoe discussion and the word puzzles. It was a great lesson! The kids were engaged and interested.

We were talking about how we really <u>are</u> one human family, about the science and genetics, and one girl said, "But people don't treat each other like we are one family." It was very poignant from a rather disruptive kid who is pretty impulsive and unthinking. She stopped and was really thinking about this!

With the word puzzles, I made the kids work silently alone at first for a few minutes. Some were so angry, frustrated and confused, but I wouldn't let them even ask a question. Then when they were told that they could work together to solve the problems, they were so excited, going from pairs to small groups, then around the classroom getting ideas from everyone. They all figured everything out except the *pair of dice* or *paradise*. I gave them a hint (what if it said "shoe shoe") and they went from *pair of shoes* to *paradise*! Then we talked about what it was like to work alone versus together and the differences were dramatic. It was a great illustration of the power of unity!

For the donkey problem, two kids were tied with yarn. I had the rest of the class brainstorm ideas then present the ideas to the "donkeys." The donkeys had to decide what they were going to do, and they talked and selected one of the ideas and carried it out. We spoke about how great ideas come from teamwork, decisions are made through discussion and cooperation, and things get done well when people work together. Another great illustration of unity!

I finished lesson two yesterday. One of the other fourth-grade teachers was listening in and she told me she couldn't believe how engaged the kids were (this is a very difficult group). She said, "How amazing these lessons are. They've caught the kids' imagination and curiosity completely!"

We did the machine lesson—how the different parts of the machine work together in unity. They really get this idea of unity in diversity, and it was so wonderful to hear these kids, each one, explain what the concept is to the whole class.

With the small group discussion questions, I put the kids in pairs and did a speed discussion.* I read the question and gave them one minute to discuss it. After each pair reported back, we switched partners for the next question. They loved it! They were engaged and involved, each one focused on discussing the question with their partner and then taking turns reporting their ideas back to the whole class.

---

* See Appendix E for a brief description of this instructional strategy.

Each student in both classes interpreted the question, "Is it possible to fight with someone and still be unified?" in relation to disagreements or arguments with their friends, classmates or family. None of them thought of the destructive fights that lead to war. They said that disagreements don't have to destroy a relationship, and they emphasized how important different views are in discovering truth—in fourth-grade language. Oh, and they emphasized the idea of how important diversity is to brainstorming and getting new ideas to solve problems.

Also, after watching the PowerPoint last Friday, we read the corresponding handout to review the concepts. The kids wanted to see another PowerPoint that same day, but I told them we would see the next one after the break. One girl said, "The PowerPoints are awesome!"

Lesson three went great! I showed pictures of the faces on the screen using the download pack and held up the colored paper to the screen. It was very easy—just a few minutes of prep time! What a graphic, visual way of showing that we are all shades of tan/brown. The kids (and I) were really taken by this concept. It was so clear. The book [*All the Colors We Are*] was perfect for this age level. It reinforced and explained the comparisons of the colored paper to the pictures. I can see it being used with all elementary grades. I'll stop at a paint store this weekend and get paint chips for the Class Features activity, so kids can pick out their own skin colors.

Oh, I also got out the globe because the kids had lots of questions about why we are all shades of tan and how we are all related. We compared places at the equator to northern and southern regions, and I told them the story of how the first humans started in Africa and slowly traveled outward populating the planet, and how our skin color relates. Great discussion!

This is really a powerful curriculum! It is easy to pick and choose what works with this group and what I have time for, as well as to adapt the specific activities to the needs of the kids. We aren't doing the art projects because I just don't have the time. Maybe when I'm done with the whole unit we can sneak in a few of them.

Teaching Tips and Tools

Preparing for Class

In order to present these lessons effectively, you will need to read through each lesson plan and become familiar with the objectives and the concepts to be taught. Practice the presentation until it feels smooth and comfortable.

Explanatory notes to the teacher are not meant to be read as a script but are intended only as a guide. Key phrases and highlights from these notes can be written on the board before or during the lesson.

All instructional materials should be made or obtained in advance. Make a sample of each craft, so you know how to do it and can easily explain it to others.

Group Discussions

During class discussions, all students should be encouraged to participate, not just the ones who speak first or loudest. A child who is silent can be asked, "Maria, what do you think about this?" Have students raise their hands rather than shouting out the answer. A simple comment like "I'm happy to see so many of you raising your hands quietly" will reinforce this rule.

If a student's answer is incorrect, rather than saying, "No, that's wrong," it is better to respond with, "Good try. You're on the right track," or "That's an interesting thought!" Then ask another question or give a small hint that will help the child succeed. Be patient and enthusiastic. Encouragement is generally more motivating than criticism. Do not allow the children to laugh at or tease each other.

With a larger group, you may find it useful to ring a bell or develop a hand signal to bring the children back to order after a discussion or other class activity. Raising your hand while standing quietly in front of the class can be very effective. As soon as one person notices the teacher, that person should stop talking and raise his/her hand. As others notice, they should join in. Teach children the signal and practice it a few times before starting the discussion.

Assistants

Youth and adults can be invited to assist you with the learning activities and classroom management. Assistants can be put in charge of discussion groups. They can help with craft projects, lead the singing, teach one of the classes, work one-on-one with students who need extra assistance, and remove a disruptive child if necessary. Discipline is easier to maintain if assistants are spaced throughout the room during the lesson.

Handouts

Most of the handouts are included with the lesson plans, and all are grouped in the handout section of the book for convenience in photocopying. They are also available for downloading from: **www.TeachingUnity.com**. Handouts can be copied one at a time as needed for a particular class, or all at once as part of the handout packet for a summer camp or weekend retreat. Provide handouts for any assistants as well.

The 17-page packet on The Light of Unity (from the title page through the song sheet) can be photocopied, stapled and included in students' folders. This packet will be used in several lessons. Copying on both sides of the page will save paper. If each item is copied on a different color, it will be easier for children to find.

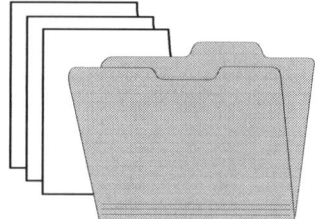

PowerPoints

Four colorful PowerPoint programs have been developed to illustrate the themes in this book. These slide shows can accompany the readings, or they can be used in place of them for students who would have difficulty with the text. The PowerPoints are available free to purchasers of this teacher's guide. You can download them from: **www.TeachingUnity.com**.

- Unity (Unit 1, activity #7)
- Unity in Diversity (Unit 2, activity #4)
- The Colors We Are (Unit 3, activities #3-5)
- Review of Units 1-3 (Unit 4, activity #1)

Thought for the Day

For each theme in the book, we have included a quotation or thought-for-the-day for students to memorize. This will focus their thinking and help them to better remember the lesson. Some of the quotes have been simplified for use with children.

The exact wording and the authors' names are included in Appendix A: Words of Wisdom, along with additional quotes drawn from different cultures and religious traditions, from scientists and philosophers, statesmen and women, poets and Nobel laureates, writers, musicians and others.

You can choose to use the exact quote, the simplified version found in the text, a different quote from the compilation, or another passage of your own choosing. Appendix B describes a number of effective memorization techniques.

PART II
Lessons and Materials

Warm-up Activities

Before introducing the first lessons in this curriculum guide, you may wish to take the class through some of the warm-up activities described below.

1. Unity Bingo (20-30 min.)

This is a fun mixer which has become a favorite activity at all of our children's events. A sample Bingo sheet (based on some of our own participants) is included on the next page, followed by a blank form that can be filled in with your own set of questions.

You will also need pencils or pens and small prizes for all. An assistant can be put in charge of checking completed Bingo pages and handing out the prizes.

> Note: A blank Bingo form is also available online as part of the download packet for this book at: **www.TeachingUnity.com**. Download the file, save it to your desktop, and type your questions into each square. The completed form can then be saved, changed as needed, and printed out for each group.

Instruct the participants to:

- Walk around the room, introduce yourself, and obtain one signature per square.
- Each square should be signed by a different person. If there are fewer than twenty people, some will need to sign twice.
- You can put your own name in one of the squares.
- Fill in all the squares to get a prize.
- Everyone wins!

Cicily completes her Bingo sheet

– Sample Bingo Sheet – Name: _____

# Unity Bingo

Walk around the room, introduce yourself, and obtain one signature per square.
Each square should be signed by a different person. You can put your own name in one of the squares.
If there are fewer than twenty people, some will need to sign twice.
Fill in all the squares to get a prize. Everyone wins!

Find someone who . . .

Who is attending their first children's retreat?	Who drove more than 2 hours to get here?	Who has a brother or sister attending this retreat?	Who is under 10 years old?
Who is over 50 years old?	Who plays a musical instrument?	Who speaks Spanish?	Who can say a Tongan prayer?
Who has been to a PowWow?	Who has lived in another country?	Who can say hello in 3 languages?	Who has eaten frogs legs before?
Who lives in Washington?	Who lives in Oregon?	Who lives on the Yakama Nation Reservation?	Whose first or last name starts with "S"?
Who likes to sing?	Who likes to dance?	Who likes to read?	Who plays soccer?

Name: _____

 # Unity Bingo

Walk around the room, introduce yourself, and obtain one signature per square.
Each square should be signed by a different person. You can put your own name in one of the squares.
If there are fewer than twenty people, some will need to sign twice.
Fill in all the squares to get a prize. Everyone wins!

Find someone who. . .

2. Room Mixer (10-15 min.)

Ask everyone (children, youth and adults) to walk around the room, and as you call out each item below, they should gather with others who have the same characteristic, then introduce themselves.

For example, for the first item, everyone with very short hair will be in one group. People with medium-length hair will be in another, and those with very long hair will be in a third group. If someone doesn't have an exact match, they should come as close as they can. Give them a minute or two to introduce themselves before calling out the next item. You can vary the list to fit the participants. After the activity, point out that we can always find something in common with people from around the world.

a. The same length hair	c. The same type of shoes	e. The same birth month
b. The same color shirt	d. The same height	f. (your item here)

3. Group Match (10-15 min.)

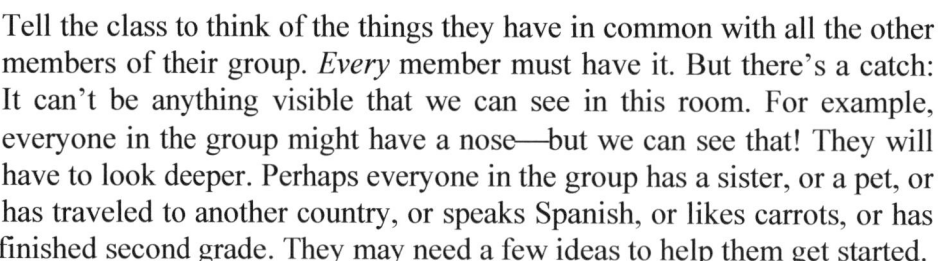

Divide the participants into groups of approximately equal size. Small groups of 4–5 work best. Each group will need a reporter with a pencil, paper and a hard surface (such as a table or clipboard) to write on.

Tell the class to think of the things they have in common with all the other members of their group. *Every* member must have it. But there's a catch: It can't be anything visible that we can see in this room. For example, everyone in the group might have a nose—but we can see that! They will have to look deeper. Perhaps everyone in the group has a sister, or a pet, or has traveled to another country, or speaks Spanish, or likes carrots, or has finished second grade. They may need a few ideas to help them get started.

Give the groups about five minutes to work and offer small prizes to the team with the longest list. Of course, they will have to read their list out loud before receiving their reward.

4. Circle Diagram (10-15 min.)

Ask participants to pair up with someone they don't know well and to make a circle diagram of some of their favorite things. (Draw an example on the board.)

Section A will include things only Person "A" likes. Section B will include things only Person "B" likes. Section C, where the circles overlap, will include things they both like (see below).

Each pair will need a blank diagram (on the following page) and something to write with. Give them about five minutes to work. When finished, ask for a few volunteers to share. A blank form is also available online as part of the download packet for this book: www.TeachingUnity.com.

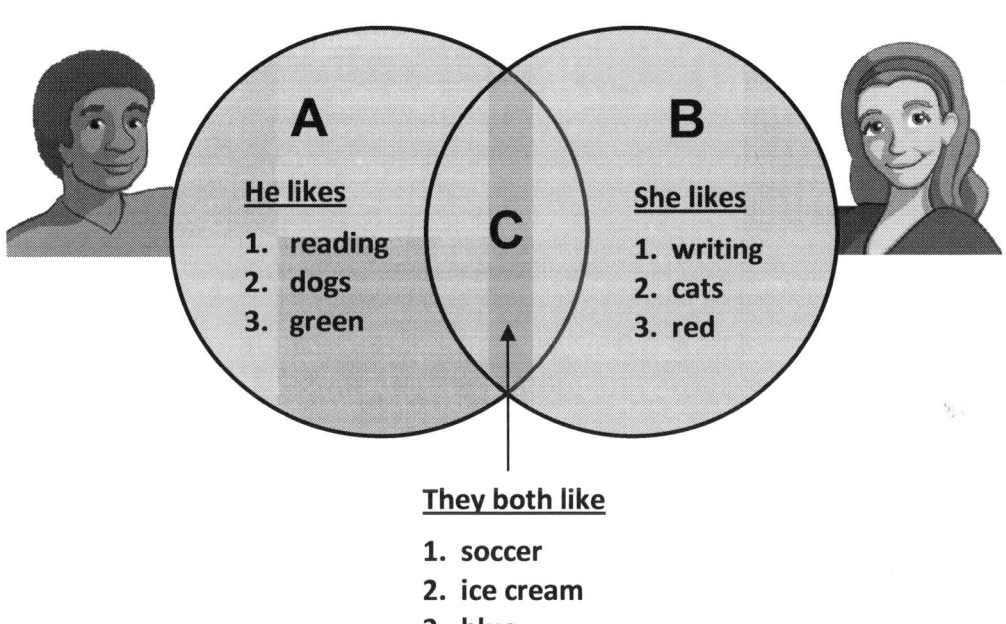

Note to teachers: This circle diagram, also known as a *Venn Diagram*, is made up of two or more overlapping circles. It is used to show relationships between sets (different groups of things). Here we are using it to explore similarities and differences between two people. The Venn diagram was developed in 1880 by English mathematician John Venn.

Circle Diagram: Work with your partner to make a list of some of your favorite things. List things that only one person likes in the left outer circle, and things only the other person likes in the right outer circle. List things that you both like in the middle section where the circles overlap.

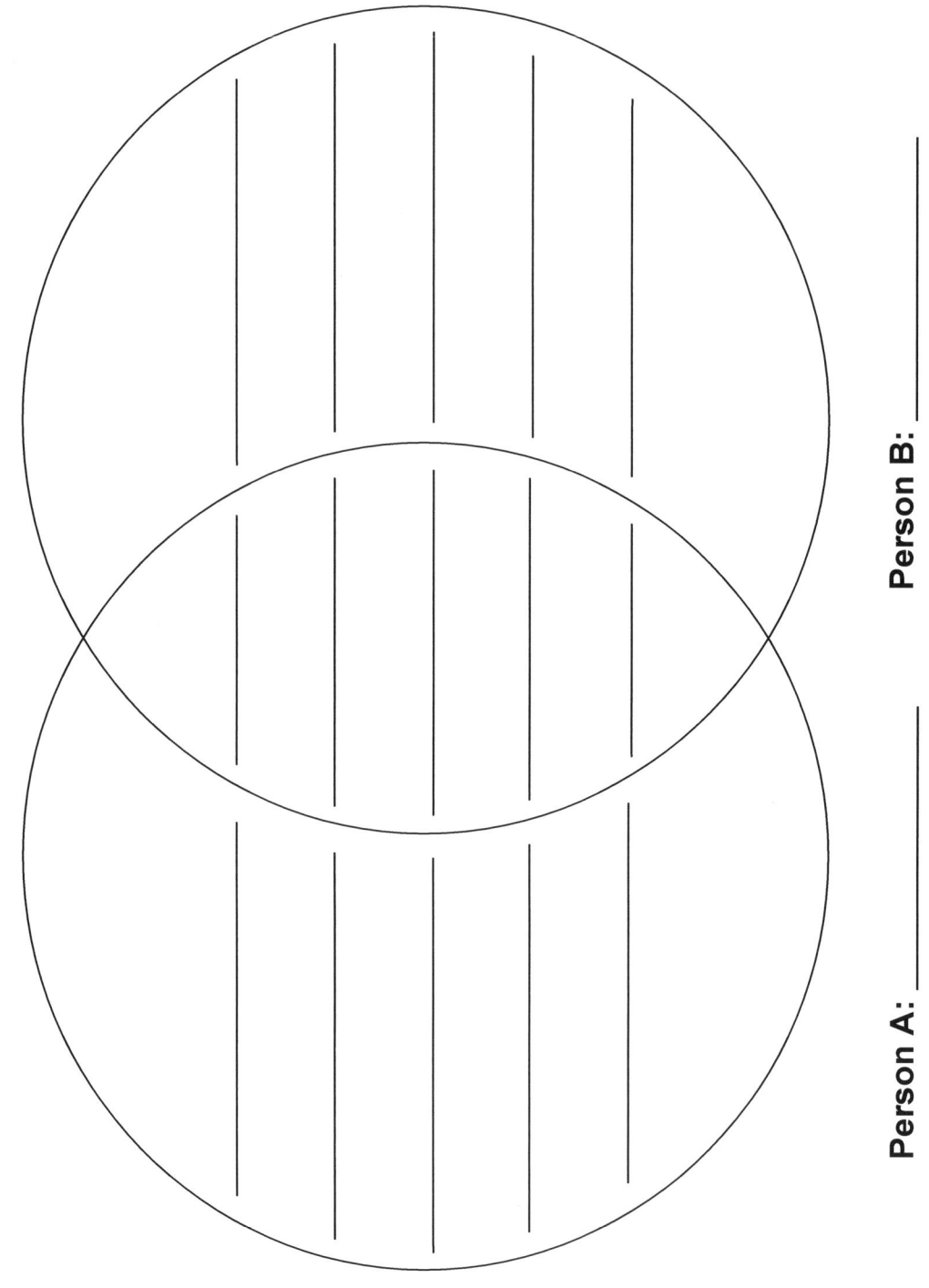

Person A: _____

Person B: _____

5. Getting to Know You Chart (15-20 min.)

Divide the participants into small groups of 4–5 people, and ask each group to fill in a "Getting to Know You" chart (see sample below). There will be some similarities and many differences as well. The group charts can then be posted on the wall, giving people an opportunity to learn more about their classmates. The categories in the left column can be modified to fit the participants. If a digital camera and printer are available, a photo of each person can be glued to the top of the chart. A blank form is also available online as part of the download packet for this book: www.TeachingUnity.com.

– Sample Chart –

"Getting to Know You"

NAME	Jesse	Carmel			
Photo					
Age	10	8			
Special talent	drawing	gymnastics			
Favorite subject	science	math			
Favorite place	ocean	my room			
Favorite song	Silent Night	Raindrops			
Favorite color	blue	blue			
Favorite food	tacos	peanut butter			
Favorite animal	Buddy (my dog)	horses			
Favorite game	soccer	chess			

"Getting to Know You"

NAME					
Photo					
Age					
Special talent					
Favorite subject					
Favorite place					
Favorite song					
Favorite color					
Favorite food					
Favorite animal					
Favorite game					

Copy this page to make one chart for each group.

Available from: www.TeachingUnity.com

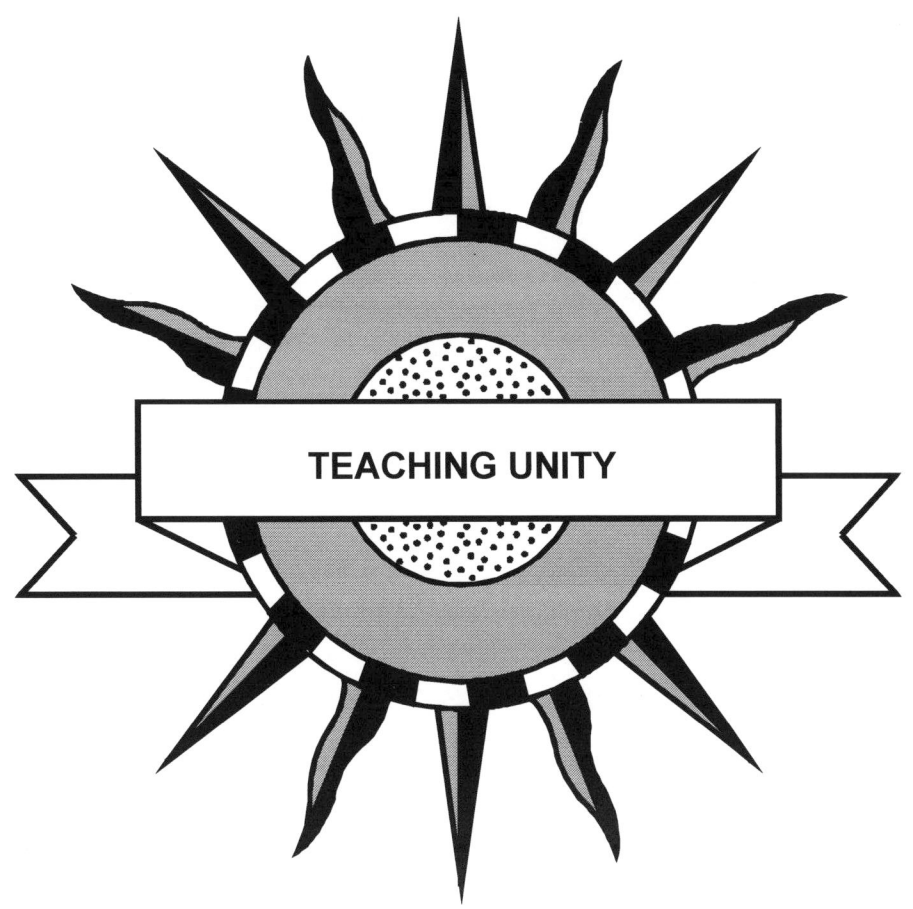

UNIT #1

The Light of Unity

The Light of Unity

Objectives: Students will be able to:
- Identify unity as one of the most important needs in the world today.
- Define unity and disunity, and give examples of each.
- List some of the benefits of unity.
- Explain that people have many similarities and differences, but there is only one human race, and we are better off working together in unity.

---

*Before class, prepare all instructional materials on the list at the end of this lesson.
Post pictures of people. Arrange the flowers. Orient any assistants.
Distribute pens and folders with handouts to all.*

---

1. INTRODUCTION (2 min.)

Tell the students:

- Today, we will learn about one of most important needs in the world today: **UNITY**.
- Unity can help us to solve many of the world's most difficult problems and can lead to greater peace, prosperity and happiness for us all.
- First, let's learn a song about unity, and then we'll talk about what unity means.

2. SONG: "One Planet, One People" (5-10 min.)

Have students locate their song sheets and teach them the song.
See music section for teaching ideas and musical score.

3. DEFINITIONS (10 min.)

Using large print, write the words **unity** and **disunity** in two columns at the top of a second whiteboard—or on chart paper which can be posted and left up on the wall. Have students write these same headings at the top of the notebook paper in their folders. Then ask them to find a partner and quickly brainstorm examples or definitions for each word.

Give students a few minutes to work, then have them share. Take one suggestion from each person so everyone has a chance to participate, and list their ideas on the board. Then read each column out loud.

unity	disunity
harmony	fighting
work together	shouting
living in peace	name-calling
making friends	criticizing
encouraging	blaming

4. READING: "Unity / Disunity" (5-10 min.)

Have students locate "Unity is / Disunity is" (in their handout packet and on page 29). Ask your assistants or capable students to read the items in the first box *(Unity is...)*, and the second box *(Disunity is...)*. Choose people with expressive voices who read well. Less fluent readers can also be called on if given an opportunity to rehearse the parts beforehand.

Then ask the class:

- How do we feel when we are unified?
  (Happy, friendly, peaceful...)
- How do we feel when we are disunified?
  (Angry, sad, frustrated...)
- Do you think the world is unified now?
  (Accept all opinions.)

Have the children raise their hands to answer.

5. PANTOMIME (10-20 min.)

Explain to the students that they are going to demonstrate what unity and disunity look like—using movements but no words. Divide the class into an even number of small groups of about 3-5 students each. Ask half of the groups to illustrate **unity**, and the other half, **disunity**.

Allow the groups a few minutes to prepare—giving them hints if necessary. (No offensive gestures, please.) Then ask them to share their dramatizations, one group at a time. When finished, ask the class: *Which groups would you rather join? What kind of world would you rather live in?* Allow time for discussion.

6. THE BENEFITS OF UNITY (5-10 min. for each activity)

Depending on the time available, select one or more of the following activities to demonstrate some of the benefits of unity. After each activity, ask the class what they have learned.

A. <u>Bundle of Sticks</u>: Give one child a thin stick to break. *(This should be easy.)* Then give the child a lot of thin sticks tied together in a bundle. *(The bundle should be impossible to break.)* What can be learned from this? *(There is strength in unity.)* Explain that now we are going to play some games that require unity in order to succeed.

B. <u>Chair Lift</u>: Have one child sit in a sturdy chair at the front of the room. Four other children enter and, one by one, each tries to lift the chair without success. (They can flex their muscles, struggle, grunt, wipe the sweat from their brow, look discouraged—really hamming it up, to show how difficult it is.)

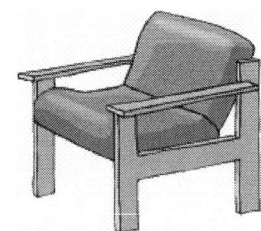

After each child has tried it alone, have them huddle together and quietly consult on a solution. Then have them stand at the sides and back of the chair. One child can say aloud "1, 2, 3!" and together they lift the chair and its occupant, carry it a few steps, then gently set it down. What can be learned? *(There is strength in numbers. We can do it together!)*

C. <u>Donkey Tug o' War</u>: Select two children of similar size and strength to be hungry donkeys. Tie them together with one end of the rope around each donkey's waist. Set out two food bowls filled with plastic food, leaves or colored paper, about 10-15 feet (3-5 meters) apart.

Tell the class that the donkeys are very hungry and each wants to eat from its own bowl, but they may not remove the rope. (Quietly remind the donkeys that they are only acting and shouldn't be too forceful.) Give the signal, and let the donkeys pull against each other, each trying to get to its own bowl without success.

Let them struggle for a few moments, then stop the action and ask them to consult with each other. The rest of the class can also brainstorm ideas and suggest strategies to the donkeys. How can they both eat without removing the rope? *(They will need to take turns.)* Ask the class what was learned. *(Problems can be solved through teamwork, discussion and cooperation.)*

Make sure there is sufficient space for this activity, a thick rope or tie that won't cut at the waist, and a bell to stop the action if necessary.

Drawing courtesy of Phil Bartle, Ph.D.
www.scn.org/cmp/ex-illu.htm - #13

D. <u>Hot and Cold</u>: Show the class a small object, then ask for a student volunteer to leave the room. Hide the object. Then invite the volunteer to return and search for it, while the rest of the class says "warm, warmer, hot…" or "cold, colder, freezing…" as the student gets closer or farther away from it. Once the object has been found, ask what can be learned from this demonstration. *(The value of cooperation; we need help; working together we can achieve the goal.)*

Note: The children often ask to repeat this demonstration with additional volunteers.

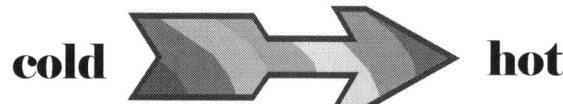

E. <u>Shoe Demo</u>: As a demonstration of human interdependence, call on one of the children to hold up his or her shoe. Choose someone with a shoe made up of at least three materials (rubber, canvas, leather, plastic, metal, cotton, velcro, etc.), and have a suitable backup shoe or other item with you just in case.

- Ask the class what the shoe is made of and list the materials on the board.
- Then mention the first item (e.g., rubber), and ask where it comes from. *(Rubber trees.)*
- Where do rubber trees grow? *(In the Amazon jungle, Southeast Asian rainforest, etc.)*
- How do we get the rubber from the trees? *(A cut is made in the tree bark, which allows the "latex" to flow out into a bucket. It is then collected and processed.)*

> *See the following websites for a brief description of rubber tapping:*
> * www.youtube.com/watch?v=BhFqYc4sPvI
> * www.kepu.ac.cn/english/banna/tropic/tro418_01.html
> * youtube.com > enter "rubber tapping process" in the search box

- Who made the rubber harvesting tools and what are they made from?
- How does rubber get from the tree to the shoe factory?
- Who drives the trucks? What are trucks made of?
- Who designed and built the trucks? Where do we get fuel for the trucks?
- Who made the roads for the trucks to drive on? What are roads made of?

Continue with this type of questioning for each material composing the shoe—or at least until the children understand the point: that we depend on many other people for even the simplest of things. Ask how many individuals they think might be involved in the making of one shoe and bringing it to market. *(Thousands)*

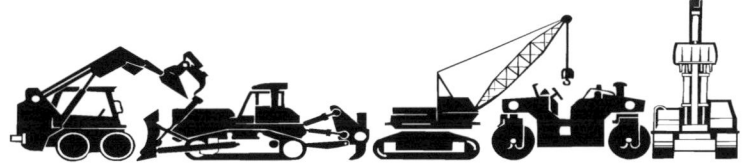

<u>Ask</u>: What can we learn from this? *(We learn the importance of cooperation. We depend on others, and they depend on us. This is called interdependence. Our civilization requires many types of knowledge and skills, which requires a division of labor. We need each other.)*

F. <u>Word Puzzle</u>: Give each student a copy of the word puzzle (in the handouts section of this book) and ask them to determine the common word or phrase illustrated in each box. Do the first one with them so they understand the task (see puzzle with answers below). Then give them a few minutes to finish the entire page, each working alone. No talking!

Then let them work in pairs for a few minutes; then in groups of four; and finally, allow them to consult with anyone else in the class. When done, review the entire page together. Usually, as more people work together, more answers are found. Ask the students what was learned. *(The value of diverse experiences and perspectives; some problems are easier to solve in groups; two heads are better than one.)*

	sandbox	**man overboard**	**I understand**	**pair of dice** (or) **paradise**
	1 SAND	2 MAN / BOARD	3 STAND / I	4 DICE DICE
	5 WEAR / LONG	6 R O ROADS D S	7 RIGHT TIME	8 CYCLE CYCLE CYCLE
	long underwear	**crossroads**	**right on time**	**tricycle** (or) **recycle**

G. <u>Summary</u>: Ask students to think about what they have learned about the benefits of unity. Give them a minute, then have them pair up with the nearest classmate and share their thoughts. Then call on volunteers to share one of their insights. Write their answers on the board. (See Appendix D for a description of this "Think-Pair-Share" technique.)

7. READING: "Unity" (15-20 min.)

Have students locate the reading on "Unity" in their handout packets. (See page 30 for teacher's version.)

Along with or instead of this reading, you can show the PowerPoint on "Unity," available as a free download from our website.

Read the first paragraph out loud, then ask:

- How many races of people are there in the world?
  (That's right! Only one.)

- What is it called?
  (The human race.)

Then call on capable student volunteers to read each remaining paragraph out loud, make up one or two questions about their paragraph and invite other children to answer—just as you did. If necessary, encourage them to call on someone who hasn't yet had a chance. If you select some of the more capable students first, the others will more readily understand how this method of student questioning works.

8. THOUGHT FOR THE DAY: "So powerful is the light of unity…" (10-15 min.)

Write the passage neatly on the whiteboard, one phrase on each line. Read the words aloud slowly.

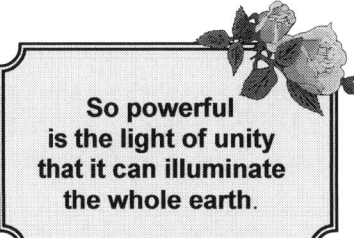

So powerful is the light of unity that it can illuminate the whole earth.

A. <u>Understanding</u>: Ask the students:

- What does "illuminate" mean?
  (To make lighter or brighter.)

> Hold up a light bulb, flashlight or candle as a memory aid.
> You can use a picture if the actual object is not available.

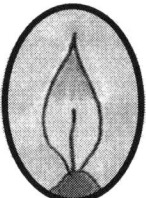

- What do you think the whole sentence means?
  *(Unity is like a bright light in the darkness.
  It has the power to bring peace and progress to the world.)*

B. <u>Repetition</u>: Read the words again slowly and have students repeat after each phrase. Read them again, faster. Then read two phrases at a time as students repeat. (You can also use gestures as a memory aid. Flex your arm when saying the word *"powerful,"* clasp your hands together when saying *"unity,"* spread your fingers wide with palms out for *"illuminate"* and move your hand in a wide arc to indicate *"the whole earth."*)

C. <u>Backwards Buildup</u>: Read the last phrase and have students repeat until it is memorized. Then add the previous phrase and read through to the end. Continue in this manner until you have reached the beginning. By that time, most children will have the entire passage memorized.

"… the whole earth."
"… that it can illuminate the whole earth."
"… is the light of unity that it can illuminate the whole earth."

D. <u>Disappearing Act</u>: Next, using an eraser, swipe a narrow diagonal path through the entire passage on the board. This will leave a blank space on each line. Ask for student volunteers to read the passage again. Let everyone take a turn. Then make another eraser swipe and ask for another round of volunteers. Continue until the passage has completely disappeared. (See illustration on page 268.)

E. <u>Card Queue</u>: Have each word printed on a separate large card. Give one card to each student. If there are more students than words, two students can hold the same card. If there are fewer students than words, some can hold two cards. Mix the students up and tell them to arrange themselves in order without speaking. Then have each child read his or her word in order, holding up the card up as they speak.

F. <u>Recitation</u>: Ask for volunteers to recite the whole quote from memory. Call on the most capable students first, so they serve as models. End with a recitation by the whole class.

9. CLOSING QUESTIONS (2 min.)

Ask the students:

- What is one of the most important needs in the world today? *(Unity.)*
- Why is unity so important? *(For our own happiness; for the peace, progress and security of the world.)*

10. CLOSING SONG: "One Planet, One People" (5 min.)

Have students locate their song sheets and close with the song learned earlier.

Collect all folders and pencils.

11. CRAFT: Lanyards (30-60 min.)

Craft activities are designed to reinforce the material presented during class. We saw that sticks couldn't be broken when they were tied together. A braided lanyard is another concrete example of the strength that comes from unity. Children can make a variety of lanyard projects including key chains, bike streamers, shoe bobs, bracelets, barrettes and zipper pulls. Instructions and ideas are included at the end of this lesson.

Demonstrating unity – activity #5

Unity is:

- Knowing that we are part of one human family
- Treating all people with respect
- Valuing diversity
- Serving others
- Consulting together
- Making sure everyone is included
- Listening and trying to understand
- Working to make things better for all
- Solving conflicts peacefully
- Being kind to others even when they aren't perfect
- Showing cooperation and teamwork
- Forgiving people
- Making friends

Disunity is:

- Being selfish
- Insisting on your own way
- Not getting along with others
- Thinking you are better than everyone else
- Showing prejudice and hatred
- Shouting at people
- Telling lies about others
- Leaving people out
- Name calling and putdowns
- Laughing when someone makes a mistake
- Arguing or fighting
- Hurting other people
- Not caring about others
- Backbiting

Reading for activity #4

Teacher's version of reading for activity #7

 UNITY

One Human Family: There is only one race of people in the world. Do you know what it is called? That's right! It's the human race, and we all belong to it. We come in different shapes, sizes and colors, but we are one human family.

> Show pictures of people from around the world.

> Aloha
> Bonjour
> Hello
> Hola
> Jambo
> Shalom

We may be young or old, tall or short, male or female, rich or poor. We may have dark skin, light skin or a color in-between. Some of us were born in China, South Africa, Canada, India or Brazil. We may speak English, Spanish, Arabic or Japanese. Some of us are good at sports, others at math, music or art. Some are Christians or Jews. Others are Hindus or Buddhists, agnostics, Muslims or Bahá'ís. We are alike and different in many ways. But we all share one planet—our common home.

> **Ask**: * Do you know how many countries there are in the world? *(Almost 200)*
> * How many languages? *(Over 5,000)*
> * How many races? *(One. Scientists tested blood samples from people all around the world, and they discovered that we are all related!)*

The Importance of Unity: Our world will be a better place when people learn to live and work together in unity. How can the human race make progress if we are each thinking only of ourselves? Without unity, how can we solve the world's most difficult problems like war, poverty, hunger, pollution and disease? Wouldn't it be better if we stopped fighting and worked together for peace, if we treated each other with justice and love, if we were united with our brothers and sisters from all around the world?

> Show globe or photo of the earth from space.

Like a Human Body: The human race is like a human body. The body has many different parts (eyes, ears, heart, lungs), and each part plays an important role. They all work together, so the person can be healthy and function well. What would happen if the different parts of the body refused to cooperate—if the mouth decided not to eat, the heart decided not to beat, or the left and right hands were always fighting with each other? In the same way, human beings (whether we are part of a family, a classroom, a neighborhood or village, a nation or the entire world) must learn to get along.

We Are Connected: People who understand unity know that everything in the whole universe is connected. Everything depends on something else to live. Animals must eat other animals or plants in order to survive. Plants need sunshine and rain to grow. Human beings are also connected to each other like links in a chain. Everything we do affects our planet and the other people on it. Every link is important. You are one of the links in that chain.

The Power of Unity: Unity is a powerful force that can connect us all. It can connect families, communities and countries. Unity gives us strength. We are more powerful working together than alone. Unity is like medicine for the world's sickness. Unity can bring peace, progress and light to the world.

LANYARDS

A lanyard is a concrete example of the strength that comes from unity.

Materials
- Lanyard (flat plastic lacing, also called craft lace, gimp or boondoggle)
- Scissors
- Ruler or tape measure
- Lanyard hooks, swivels or key rings
- Nails or pushpins (optional)
- Paper clips

Lanyard supplies can be found at craft stores or online, e.g., www.guildcraftinc.com > type "boondoggle" in the search box; or www.tandyleatherfactory.com > search for "craft lace."

Projects
Children can make a variety of lanyard projects including key chains, bike streamers, shoe bobs, bracelets, barrettes and zipper pulls. Different stitches can be used to make the project: a square, circle, butterfly, triangle, spiral, braid, diamond, brick, twist, corkscrew, chain link and more. Children should start by learning a basic box or square stitch.

Lanyard earrings

Online Instructions
- www.youtube.com > enter "boondoggle square stitch" in the search box
- www.boondoggleman.com > click on "square stitch" from the bottom menu

The Boondoggle Man also describes more advanced stitches and shows photos of completed projects. Click on "Some Ideas."

Tips
1. For most beginning projects, you will need two strands of lanyard the same length.
2. Use 12 inches (30 cm) of lanyard for each inch (2.5 cm) of final project. For example, a 3-inch (7.5 cm) key chain would need two 3-foot (1 meter) strands of lanyard.
3. Measure carefully to avoid wasting material or running out in the middle of a project.
4. Warm the plastic lace in the sun to make it more flexible and easier to work with.
5. Loop both strands through a paper clip, key ring or lanyard hook before you begin.
6. Find the centers and make a starter stitch (see instructions online).
7. Hook the lanyard around a nail or pushpin to hold it while you work.
8. Pull stitches tight, with the same amount of tension for each stitch.
9. Don't pull too tight or the lanyard could break.
10. If you stop before your project is completed, attach a paper clip after the last stitch to keep the ends in place.
11. End the project with a finishing stitch so it doesn't unravel.

MATERIALS NEEDED – UNIT 1

> Note to Teachers: Most of the handouts are included with the lessons and are grouped in the handout section of this book for ease of photocopying. They are also available for download from our website (below). The remaining items, once obtained, can be re-used for many years. The wide variety of activities and materials allows for diverse learning styles. It also increases understanding and retention of the concepts, and it makes the lessons more memorable and enjoyable for the students.

Downloads available from: www.TeachingUnity.com

- ❑ **General Items**
    - White board, easel, markers, eraser
    - Folders and song sheets for each student
    - Paper and pens / pencils for all
    - Dictionary, globe and/or large world map
    - Packet of readings on "The Light of Unity" for each student [A]
    - Pictures of diverse people from around the world [B]
    - Flowers [C]

- ❑ **Unity / Disunity** (activity #4, p. 23)
    - Handout on "Unity is / Disunity is"

- ❑ **Benefits of Unity Skits** (activity #6, p. 23-26)
    - <u>Bundle of Sticks:</u> One thin stick, plus 20-30 more sticks tied in a bundle [D]
    - <u>Chair Lift:</u> Sturdy moveable chair
    - <u>Donkey Tug o' War:</u> A bell, two bowls with pretend food for the donkeys, a rope, yarn or long strip of cloth (approx. 5 yards or 5 meters) to tie them together
    - <u>Hot and Cold:</u> Any small object that can be hidden
    - <u>Shoe Demo:</u> Backup shoe for the interdependence demo
    - <u>Word Puzzle:</u> Copies of the puzzle for each student

- ❑ **Unity** (activity #7, p. 26)
    - Handout on "Unity"
    - Teacher's version of the handout (included with lesson)
    - Photo of the Earth from space [E]

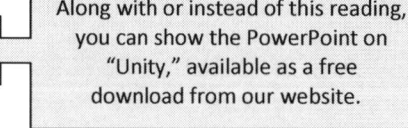

Along with or instead of this reading, you can show the PowerPoint on "Unity," available as a free download from our website.

- ❏ **Thought for the Day** (activity #8, p. 27)
  - Light bulb, flashlight or candle as a memory aid
  - Small cards with one word from the passage printed on each card

- ❏ **Lanyards** (activity #11, p. 28)
  - Craft samples and instructions
  - Craft supplies (see separate list)

A. The download pack includes full-page color illustrations designed to accompany the lessons in this book. The illustrations can be posted on the wall during class as an aid for visual learners and to help bring the readings to life.

B. Photographs of people can be found on the National Geographic website (www.nationalgeographic.com), on Flicker.com, in the social studies section of teacher supply stores, from educational textbook publishers under classroom posters, and in clip art software. We have also included a selection of faces in the download packet. The images can be laminated and posted around the room.

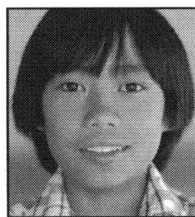

C. Real or artificial flowers can be arranged around the classroom or taped next to the photographs of people to embellish them. Large, vivid pictures of flowers can be found in gardening magazines and seed catalogs, available from many hardware stores and online. A selection of flower photos is also included in the download color-pak for this book.

D. Wooden skewers from the grocery store meat department are inexpensive and perfectly suited for this activity. Cut off the sharp points before giving them to younger children.

E. This image is in the public domain and may be used freely with acknowledgment to NASA.

Download and print it from:
<http://nssdc.gsfc.nasa.gov/image/planetary/earth/apollo17_earth.jpg>.
Posters and prints are also available from teacher supply stores and science museums, by emailing NASA at: <request@mail630.gsfc.nasa.gov>, or by calling (301) 286-6695.

✶ ✶ ✶ ✶ ✶

UNIT #2

Unity in Diversity

Unity in Diversity

Objectives: Students will be able to:
- List some similarities and differences among human beings.
- Explain why diversity is important.
- Distinguish between unity and sameness.
- Describe the concept of unity in diversity using concrete examples.

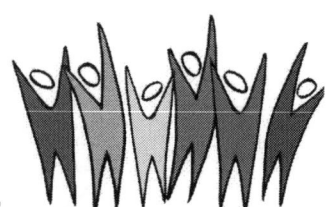

Before class, prepare all instructional materials on the list at the end of this lesson. Set up craft activity centers. Orient assistants for discussions and craft projects. Make space for activity #2. Set up felt board. Distribute folders and pencils to each student.

---

1. INTRODUCTION AND REVIEW (15-20 min.)

Tell the class that we have been learning about unity, and today we will begin our study of a new concept—unity in diversity—after a short review:

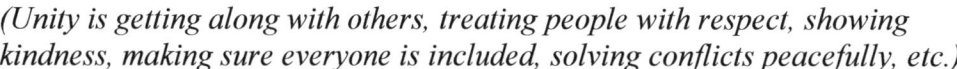

- Who can explain what is meant by *unity* and *disunity*, and give some examples of each?

    (Unity is getting along with others, treating people with respect, showing kindness, making sure everyone is included, solving conflicts peacefully, etc.)

    (Disunity is not getting along with others, being selfish, name calling, backbiting, leaving people out, fighting, telling lies, arguing, etc.)

- What are some of the benefits of unity?

    (Added strength; together we can do things we can't do alone; division of labor; power to solve large problems; two heads are better than one; our own happiness; the peace, progress and security of our family, our neighborhood and our world.)

- Why is unity so important to the world today?

    (Without unity, how can we solve the world's most difficult problems: war, poverty, hunger, disease, etc. Like the parts of a human body, the human race must work together if we want to be healthy and productive.)

- Who can recite the thought-for-the-day from our previous lesson?

    (Hold up a candle as a visual reminder and call on several volunteers. Then have the entire class recite the words in unison).

    So powerful is the light of unity that it can illuminate the whole earth.

- Ask the students to take out their song sheets and sing "One Planet, One People."

Teaching Unity, Unit 2: Unity in Diversity, p. 36

2. SIMILARITIES AND DIFFERENCES (15-20 min.)

Ask the class:

- What is one of the most important needs in the world today?
  (That's right. Unity! But unity doesn't mean sameness.)

- Look around at the people in this room. Are we all exactly the same?
  (We're alike in some ways and different in others.)

- Let's look at some of the similarities. How many things can you name that <u>all</u> humans have in common? Let's start with physical characteristics.
  (Obviously barring an accident or medical condition.)

Write their answers on the board.

> a. Physical characteristics? *(bellybutton, arms, legs, eyes, skin...)*
> b. Feelings? *(sadness, joy, anger, fear, hope...)*
> c. Physical needs? *(air, water, food, shelter, clothing, sleep...)*
> d. Spiritual or emotional needs? *(faith, hope, love, justice, family, friends...)*
> e. Other commonalities? *(all live on the same earth, breathe the same air, speak a language, have parents, talents, a body, a mind...)*

- Look around again. What are some of the differences? *(We all have noses, but they are different shapes. We all need to eat, but we like different foods....)*

- Let's look at some other similarities and differences:

Have all the children stand up in a tight group in the center of the room. Ask them to move left (all the way to one side of the room) if they are the oldest child in their family, or to move right (all the way to the other side) if they are <u>not</u> the oldest. (Adopted children can consider their biological or adoptive family.) Continue down the list below.

Have children move to the left or right as you call out each characteristic:

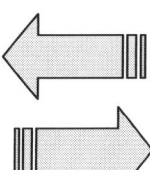

- Oldest child in family
- Born in our town
- Under the age of ten
- Can do a cartwheel
- Have pierced ears
- Like pizza
- Have a pet
- Can multiply 12 x 12
- Like to do art
- Like to sing or dance
- Like to play sports
- Speak more than one language
- Have been to another country
- Are girls
- Are boys
- Belong to the human race

If there is not enough room to move back and forth, you can take the children outside or have them stand up and sit down instead. You can also modify the list to suit the children in your group.

When finished, have children return to their seats and ask what we can learn from this demonstration. *(We are alike and different in many ways.)*

Let children know that it's okay to have similarities and differences. We're all human, but no one in the world is exactly like you!

3. DISCUSSION: Leaves of One Tree (5-10 min.)

Show the class a tree branch with leaves, or a living tree, and ask:

- Are all the leaves on this branch exactly the same? *(No. They are similar but they have different colors and sizes.)*

- What do all the leaves share in common? *(All are leaves; all are attached to the same branch which gives them life; all need sun and rain to grow.)*

- What happens to a leaf that is separated from the branch—like this? **Pull off a leaf.**  *(It dies.)*

- We can compare people to the leaves of one branch or the fruits of one tree.

- What does this mean to you? *(Encourage the children to share their thoughts. For example, we are all leaves and branches on the tree of humanity, and we need each other in order to live.)*

4. READING: "Unity in Diversity" (15-20 min.)

Have students locate the reading on "Unity in Diversity" (in their handout packets and on page 42). Read the title. Then call on capable student volunteers to read each paragraph out loud, except for the bulleted list of questions in the middle section. This list should be read by the teacher and answered by the class.

After they read, have each volunteer make up one or two questions about their paragraph and call on other children to answer. (Demonstrate if necessary.) Encourage them to call on those who haven't yet had a chance. Remind the children to raise their hands.

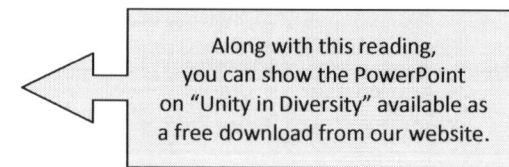

Along with this reading, you can show the PowerPoint on "Unity in Diversity" available as a free download from our website.

5. MUSICAL DEMONSTRATION (5-10 min.)

A. Hum a single musical note and ask the class to hum it with you. *(Hmmm……)* Then sing with the children *"Row, row, row your boat"* or *"Happy Birthday"* or other common song—using only that one note. The song will sound rather dull. Explain that this is a demonstration of **sameness**. Bo-ring!

B. Next, tell the children that when you give the signal, they should loudly make as many different noises as they can. You should hear squawking, hooting, hissing, howling, barking and other discordant sounds. Stop the children after a few seconds and explain that this demonstrates **diversity without unity**. It's what we have in the world today.

C. Then quickly divide the class into three groups (approximately equal in size), and give each group one note of a chord. Have each group hum its note separately, then have all sing together for (hopefully) a pleasing sound. Explain that this is a demonstration of **unity in diversity**—and it takes a lot of practice.

6. FELT LESSON: "The Eye" (10-15 min.)

Present the felt lesson on "The Eye" (see patterns and instructions at the end of this lesson). Invite the children to try the same presentation in front of the class. Ask for volunteers.

7. MACHINES IN MOTION (30-40 min.)

Divide the children into small groups of 3-4, and give each group a different machine to analyze. You can use the pictures on the following page, or your own examples of machines appropriate to the local culture and level of technology. Allow children to choose a different item if the one they are given seems too difficult. Give them copies of the "Machines in Motion" handout (page 48), and have them work in groups to answer the following questions:

- What does the machine do?
- What are the different parts that make up the whole?
- What is the function of each part?
- How do the different parts move?
- How do they work together?
- How is the machine an example of unity in diversity?

(Each part has a different but important role in the functioning of the machine. It also has to work in harmony with all the other parts in order to get the job done.)

Give the groups about ten minutes to work. When ready, bring them together to share.

> As a follow-up activity, some children may wish to visit this website for a description of basic machines: www.mos.org/sln/leonardo/inventorstoolbox.html

Machines in Motion: *This page can be photocopied onto cardstock, and the pictures cut out and distributed, one to each group for activity #7. The images will help children visualize the functions of each machine. Laminate the cards for greater durability.*

Note: *If desired, you can put the cards in a box and allow each group to pick one at random.*

8. DISCUSSION: Unity in Diversity (20-30 min.)

Divide the class into the same small groups and ask an assistant or capable student to lead each group. If there aren't enough helpers, you can form larger groups.

Give each assistant a copy of "Unity in Diversity: Discussion Questions" (page 49). As group facilitators, they should ask the questions and encourage the students to share their thoughts. Groups can move to another room or outside if desired.

Allow about 15 minutes for them to work. Walk around to observe the discussions. Then bring the children back together to share their thoughts. Ask each group to contribute one insight from their discussion. Write these on the board. Go around again until all the ideas have been shared.

This activity can also be done as a speed discussion with students in pairs. See description of the technique in Appendix E and in "One Teacher's Experience" (starting at the bottom of page 7).

9. THOUGHT FOR THE DAY: "We are all the fruits of one tree..." (10-15 min.)

Write the passage on the board with one phrase on each line.
Read the words aloud slowly, then ask students:

- What do you think this sentence means?
  (Don't see each other as strangers. We are all like fruits growing on the same tree. We are also diverse, like beautiful flowers in the garden of humanity, and we are part of one unified body, like the ocean waves.)

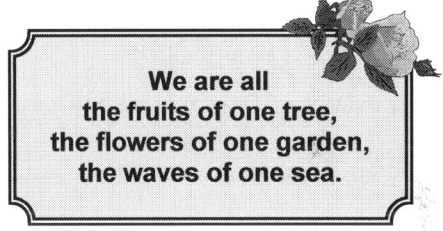

**We are all
the fruits of one tree,
the flowers of one garden,
the waves of one sea.**

Continue with the memorization process outlined on page 27, this time holding up a piece of fruit as a memory aid. You can also use gestures to help children remember the words. For example, when saying *"We are all,"* indicate everyone in the room with a sweep of your hand, hold an imaginary flower to your nose and sniff, and curve your hands up and down to indicate the waves of one sea.

10. SONG: "Hawaiian Unity Song" (5-10 min.)

Have students locate their song sheets and teach them the song.
See music section for teaching ideas and musical score.

11. CRAFT ACTIVITIES (45-60 min. each)

Craft activities are designed to reinforce material presented during class. Instructions for the craft projects are included at the end of this lesson.

★ ★ ★ ★ ★

Reading for activity #4

UNITY IN DIVERSITY

The Flowers of One Garden: Imagine the flowers in a garden. Each flower has a different shape, its own special color and sweet-smelling perfume. But they all grow from the same earth, the same sun shines upon them, and the same clouds give them rain. Each flower is pleasing by itself, but when the different flowers are all together, the garden is even more beautiful.

It is the same with people. We are like beautiful flowers growing in a garden. We each have a different shape and our own special color. We speak different languages, wear different clothing, enjoy different music and eat different foods. Our diversity adds beauty to the garden of humanity.

The Value of Diversity

- Think of all the colors in nature. Can you name some of them?
- Can you imagine if the entire world were all <u>one</u> color? Which color should it be?
- Would a rainbow be as beautiful if all the bands were the same shade?
- Could you bake a cake with only one ingredient?
- What if all the musical instruments in an orchestra made the same sound?

Just think how dull it would be if all people everywhere looked and acted and thought and talked and dressed exactly the same! What if you had to eat the same food every day, wear the same clothes, read the same books and think the same thoughts for the rest of your life? What if you never, <u>ever</u> got to try anything new? And what if all your friends were exactly like you?

Diversity is important because it gives us beauty, variety, choices and new ideas. Fresh ideas and different points of view are valuable as they can help us find creative solutions to the problems that confront us.

Unity Is Not Sameness: Unity does not mean sameness. Unity means respecting our differences and working together in harmony. It means knowing that each part has something valuable to contribute to the whole. Each member of the human family has something special to offer to the human race.

When we have **unity in diversity**, there is harmony, like the sound of different notes joined together in a perfect chord. We are showing unity in diversity when we all work and play and live together in peace.

"The Eye"

Teacher's Guide, Script, and Patterns for Felt Lesson

TO THE TEACHER: This packet contains instructions, a script and patterns for making a felt lesson on "The Eye: An Example of Unity in Diversity." In order to present the lesson, you will need either a felt board or carpet board (see instructions on following pages). A carpet board is more durable and has a more finished look. After preparing the board and cutting out the pattern pieces, read through the script and repeat the actions until you can present the lesson smoothly. The objectives of the lesson are listed below. The children will be able to:

(1) **Depict the eye as a concrete example of unity in diversity.**

(2) **Give specific examples of why diversity is important.**

(3) **Explain the difference between unity and sameness.**

– Script for felt lesson –

"The Eye"

	NARRATION	ACTION	
1	The eye is an example of unity in diversity.	Place large white eye in center of felt board.	
2	Each part of the eye has a different job, but they all work together for the same goal.	Place blue circle in center of eye; then add black circle on top.	
3	For example, the pupil is the black opening in front of the eye that admits light, so we can see.	Point to black pupil.	
4	The iris opens and closes, changing the size of the pupil to let in just the right amount of light.	Point to blue iris.	
5	What would happen if all the parts of the eye were the same?	Place white circle over other circles.	

Questions for the class

1. What are the different parts of the eye?
2. What is the function of each part?
3. What would happen if one part didn't work or didn't want to cooperate with the others?
4. What can we learn about unity in diversity from this example?

The parts of the eye are different, but they all work together, and all are necessary for sight.

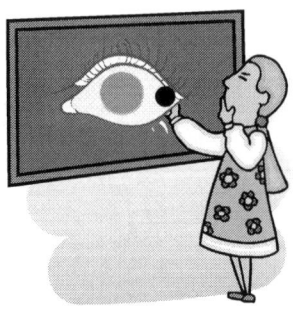

Instructions for Making Felt or Carpet Board

A felt board can be purchased at a teacher supply store, or one can be constructed by gluing a large piece of felt onto a stiff backing such as heavy cardboard, thin plywood or masonite. Spray glue gives the best results. A carpet board is constructed in the same way. Felt and glue are available at yardage and craft supply stores.

Materials

- Sharp scissors
- Large piece of felt or indoor-outdoor carpet*
  (choose beige or other neutral color,
  approx. 24 x 36 inches or 60 x 90 cm)
- Backing board (same size as felt or carpet)
- Spray glue or white craft glue

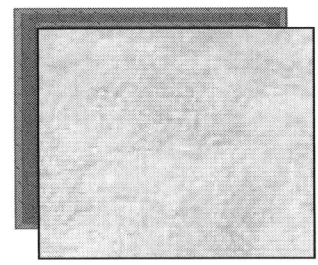

  * If using carpet, test a piece of felt to be sure it sticks.
  Some types of carpeting may work better than others.

Instructions for Making Felt Pieces

1. Photocopy the pattern pages.

2. Using the copies, cut around each shape outside the line.*

3. Use tape or large paper clips to attach each pattern to the correct color of felt.

4. Carefully cut out each felt piece, using the pattern as a guide.

5. Store the script and felt pieces in a zip-lock plastic bag for ease of use.

Materials

- Pattern pieces (on following pages)
- Sharp scissors
- Pieces of black, white and light blue felt
- Double-stick or regular tape

* **Tip:** If making more than one set of felt pieces, you can make a more durable pattern by first laminating the paper copy. Then cut out the pattern along the lines, and trace it onto the felt.

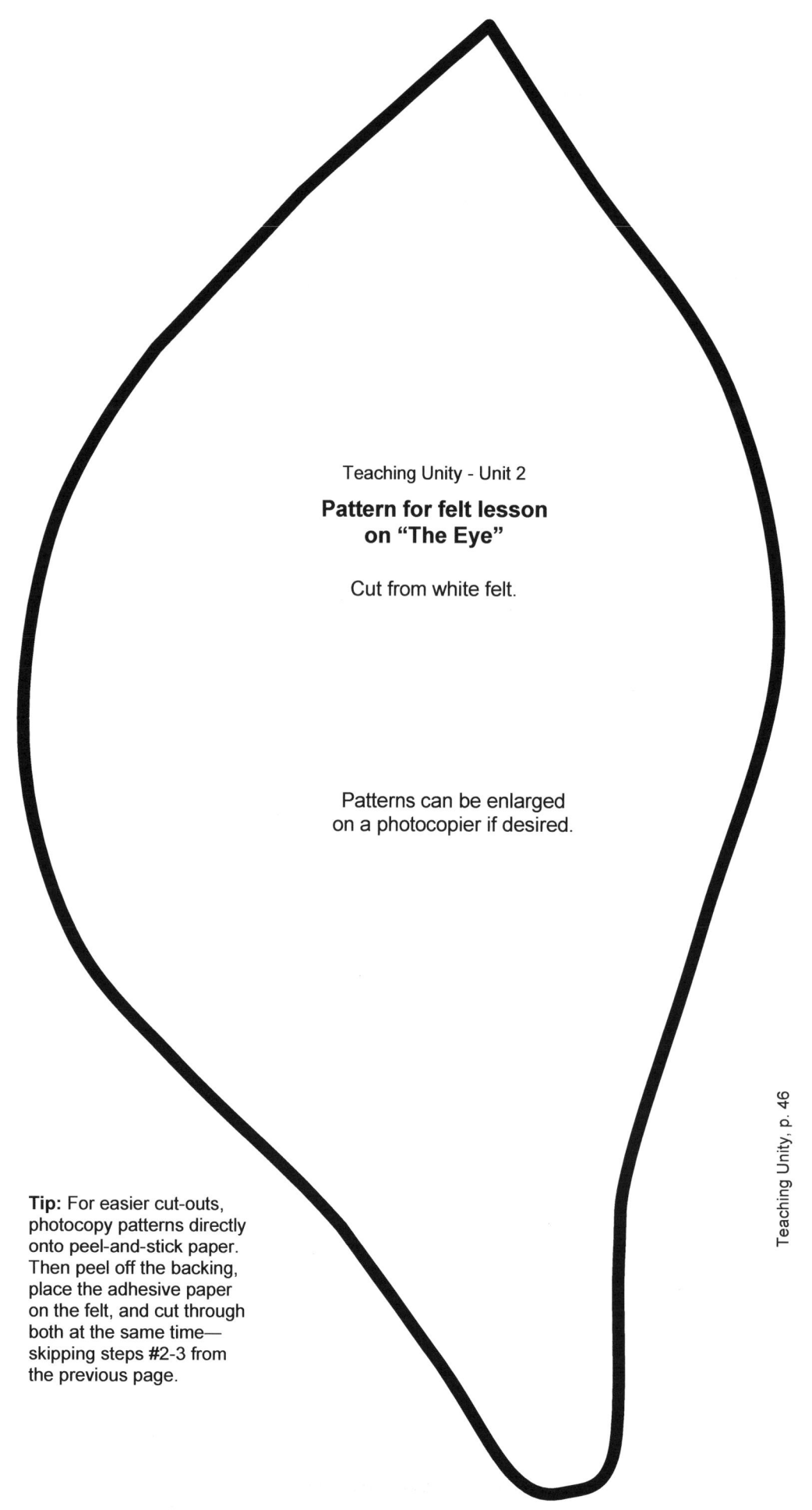

Teaching Unity - Unit 2

Pattern for felt lesson on "The Eye"

Cut from white felt.

Patterns can be enlarged on a photocopier if desired.

Tip: For easier cut-outs, photocopy patterns directly onto peel-and-stick paper. Then peel off the backing, place the adhesive paper on the felt, and cut through both at the same time—skipping steps #2-3 from the previous page.

Patterns for felt lesson on "The Eye"

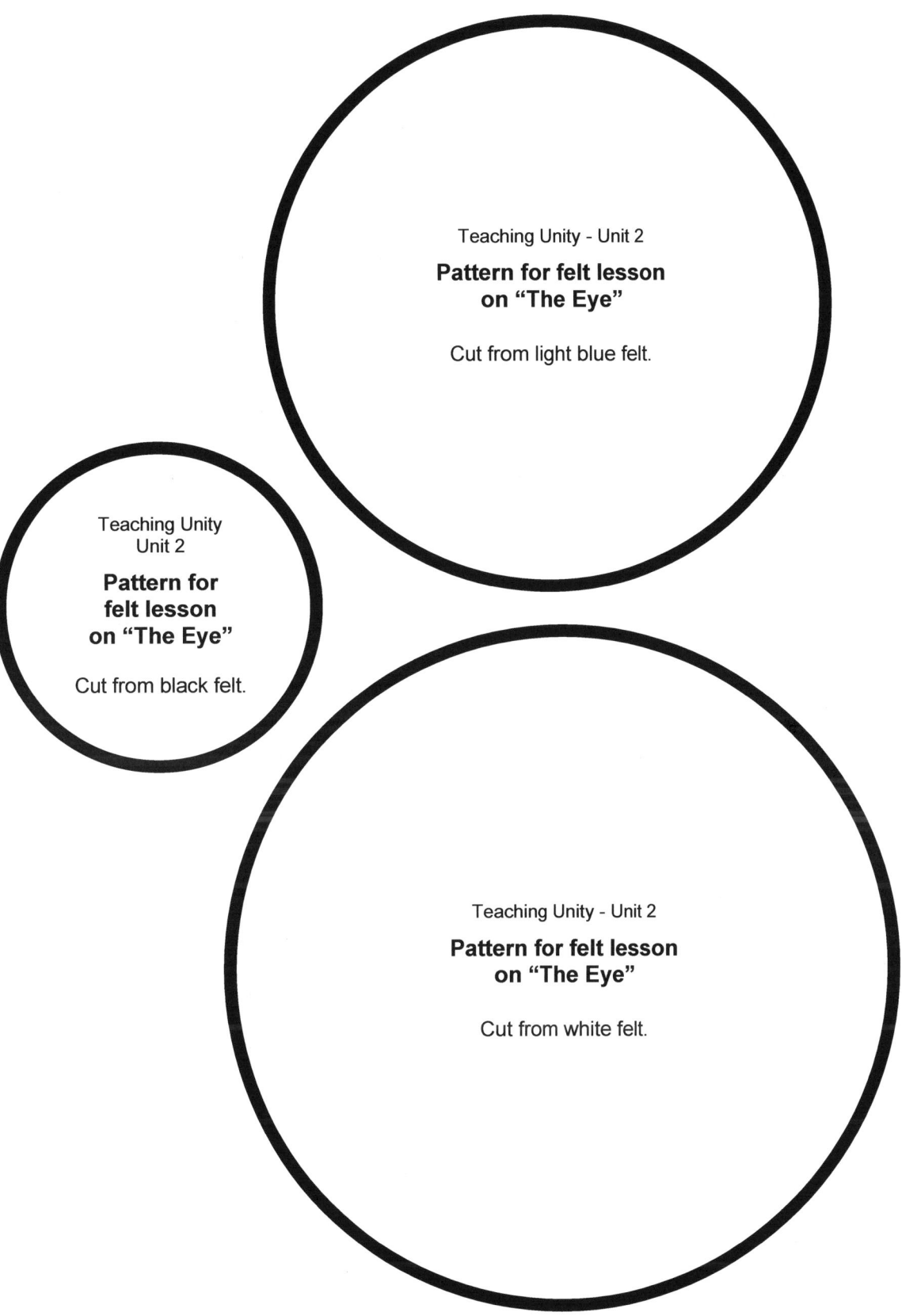

Teaching Unity - Unit 2
Pattern for felt lesson on "The Eye"
Cut from light blue felt.

Teaching Unity Unit 2
Pattern for felt lesson on "The Eye"
Cut from black felt.

Teaching Unity - Unit 2
Pattern for felt lesson on "The Eye"
Cut from white felt.

Machines in Motion

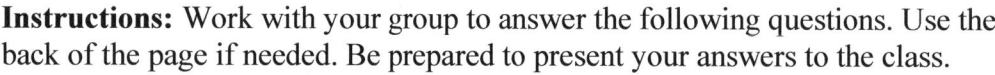

Discussion Questions

Instructions: Work with your group to answer the following questions. Use the back of the page if needed. Be prepared to present your answers to the class.

> **Your machine:**

1. What does the machine do?

2. What are the different parts that make up the whole?

3. What is the function of each part?

4. How do the different parts move?

5. How do they work together?

6. How is the machine an example of unity in diversity?

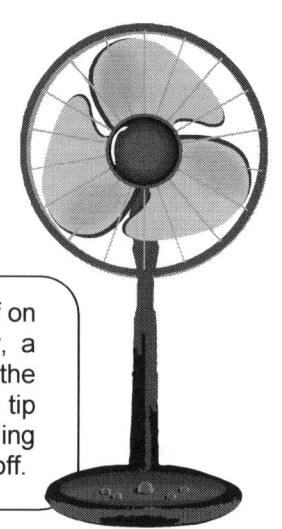

> **For example:** An electric fan is used to cool people off on a warm day. It has rotating blades to move the air, a motor to turn the blades, an electric cord to connect the motor to a power source, a wide base so it doesn't tip over, a cage to protect people's fingers from the turning blades, and controls for high speed, medium, low and off.

UNITY IN DIVERSITY

Discussion Questions

> **Instructions for group facilitator:** Gather your small group and find a quiet place to work. Your job is to ask the questions below and encourage all of the children to share their thoughts. A child who is silent can be asked, "What do you think about this?" Do not allow the children to laugh at or tease each other. Take notes below and prepare the children to share their answers. You will have about 15 minutes for this activity.

1. What does unity in diversity mean?

2. What is the difference between unity and sameness?

3. Why is diversity important?

4. Is it possible to fight with someone and still be unified?
   (No. Fighting is an example of disunity.)

5. Is it possible to disagree with someone and still be unified?
   (Yes. People can have different opinions and still consult with courtesy.)

6. Should contact sports (football, soccer, rugby, ice hockey, karate, boxing, wrestling), which often involve aggression and violence, be considered examples of disunity?

7. Can people live far apart and still be unified?
   (Yes. Family and friends might live in different parts of the world.)

8. It is possible to be unified with people we don't even know?
   (Yes. People around the world can be working together for the same goals—like ending poverty or protecting the environment.)

9. No two people are exactly alike. Why do you think that is?

CRAFT ACTIVITIES

Craft activities are designed to reinforce material presented during class. For a weekend retreat, there may only be time for one or two crafts. For an ongoing class, you might choose a different craft each time. Another option is to prepare a separate table for each craft and have each child choose one to start. If their first choice is full, they can select another station. When they have completed a project and cleaned up their work area, they may assist others who need help or move on to the next station. Remind children to label all projects with their names. Quiet music can be played in the background if desired.

(A) FLOWERS OF ONE GARDEN

(B) LEAF LAMINATES

(C) DIVERSITY STREAMERS

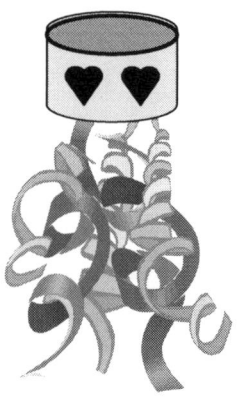

FLOWERS OF ONE GARDEN

Materials

- ☐ Scissors
- ☐ Glue sticks
- ☐ Old National Geographics or other magazines with photos of people
- ☐ Construction paper (¼ sheets and full sheets in different colors)
- ☐ White poster board (approx. 11 x 14 inches or 28 x 36 cm) (Four can be cut from 22 x 28-inch standard poster board.)
- ☐ Circle patterns in different sizes (e.g., small plastic lids or ribbon spools to trace around)
- ☐ Sponge pieces cut into 1-inch (2.5 cm) squares about ¼-inch (6 mm) thick (optional)
- ☐ Pencils, colored markers and black permanent markers
- ☐ Yarn in different colors (optional)

Instructions

1. Search through the magazines and tear out 5-6 pages with photos of diverse human faces.

2. Using one of the circle patterns, trace a circle around each face. Then carefully cut out the circle.

3. Glue each face in the center of ¼ sheet of construction paper. Use a different color of paper for each face.

4. Draw flower petals around each face and cut out the flower.

5. Glue the flowers onto the poster board, or for a 3-D effect, first glue the flowers onto the sponge squares, so the photos stand out from the background.

6. Add your name, and decorate the page if desired:
    - Add a quote or heading.
    - Draw leaves and stems.
    - Glue a ring of yarn around each face circle.

Teaching Unity, Unit 2: Unity in Diversity, p. 51

Samples of the "Flowers of One Garden" collage

Teaching Unity, Unit 2: Unity in Diversity, p. 52

LEAF LAMINATES

Begin by taking the children outside to gather leaves, suggesting that they search for leaves of different sizes, shapes and colors. For best results, select flat leaves with interesting edges and without bulky stems. Allow 15-20 minutes for the leaf hunt.

Materials for Laminate

- ❑ Newspaper
- ❑ Wax paper sheets, pre-cut to fit frame (approx. 8½ x 10 inches or 22 x 28 cm)
- ❑ Fresh leaves (gathered by the children)
- ❑ Confetti, glitter, bits of colored paper (optional)
- ❑ Iron (2 or more irons will speed the process)
- ❑ Scissors

Materials for Frame

- ❑ Construction paper
- ❑ Ruler
- ❑ Pencil
- ❑ Craft knife or scissors
- ❑ Cutting board (optional)
- ❑ Clear tape
- ❑ Permanent marker
- ❑ Glue stick
- ❑ Yarn (optional)

Instructions

1. Spread two sheets of newspaper on table and place one sheet of wax paper on top.

2. Arrange the leaves and any glitter, confetti or other items on the wax paper.

> **Important:** Do not place leaves near edge. Leave a one-inch margin to obtain a good seal.

3. Place another sheet of wax paper on top of the leaves and cover this with two more sheets of newspaper.

4. Press the top of the newspaper with a warm iron (polyester setting) until the wax paper melts together. An iron that is too hot may damage the leaves and prevent the wax paper from sticking. Children should be carefully supervised for this step, or an adult should use the iron.

5. Remove the wax paper "sandwich" and trim any rough edges with a scissors. The sandwich should be just a little larger than the frame window.

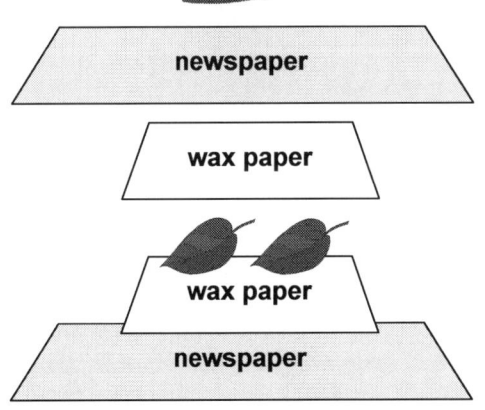

Teaching Unity, Unit 2: Unity in Diversity, p. 53

Making a Frame

1. Select two sheets of construction paper (any color), and stack them one on top of the other.

2. Using the ruler and pencil, draw lines about ¾-inch (2 cm) in from the bottom and side edges of the construction paper, and about 2½ inches (6 cm) from the top.

3. Place both sheets of paper on the cutting board, and using the craft knife, carefully cut out a rectangle along the lines just drawn. Cut through both sheets of paper at once. Be careful not to cut through to the edges. (Children will need careful supervision or assistance.)

> Note: A scissors can be used instead of the craft knife and cutting board. If using a scissors, start by poking a hole in the center of the paper, then cutting out to the lines.

4. Remove the inner rectangles, and tape the leaf sandwich inside the resulting window. Put tape on the side of the frame with the pencil lines. ⟶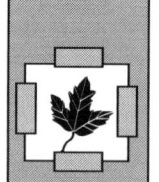

5. Attach the back of the frame using the glue stick.

6. On the front side, use the marker to write a quote or heading. For a more finished look, neatly print the heading on a separate piece of paper and glue it onto the frame.

7. Punch two holes at the top and add a yarn hanger if desired. Display the finished project in a window and watch the light shine through.

You may wish to pre-cut frames for younger children. A simple frame can also be made by gluing strips of construction paper along the edges of the wax paper.

Sample leaf laminate with frame

DIVERSITY STREAMERS

Materials

- ☐ Clean, empty tin can
- ☐ Awl (or hammer and large nail)
- ☐ Ribbon in different colors and widths
- ☐ Scissors
- ☐ Masking tape
- ☐ Duct tape
- ☐ Contact paper (solid color or woodgrain)
- ☐ Assortment of stickers
- ☐ Thin chain, thick yarn, or strand of plastic beads for hanging the can (approx. 1 yard or 1 meter)
- ☐ Paper clip, pipe cleaner or small piece of wire for attaching chain

Instructions

1. Using the awl, punch a hole in the <u>center</u> of the can bottom. See < www.mathopenref.com/constcirclecenter2.html > for help. If the hole is off to one side, the can will not hang straight.

2. Cut a strip of contact paper large enough to cover the can. It should be a rectangle a little longer than the can's circumference, and a little taller than the can's height.

3. Carefully apply the contact paper to the outside of the can, slowly peeling off the backing and smoothing out bubbles as you go. Overlap edges around the side, and trim off excess paper at the top with a scissors.

4. Cut about 10 lengths of ribbon, each approx. 18 inches (46 cm.)

5. Trim one end of each ribbon into a "V" shape.

6. Using a small piece of masking tape, tape the straight edge of one ribbon to the inside of the can.

7. Continue adding ribbons all around the inside of the can. Ribbons should touch each other side-to-side with no gaps. When finished, reinforce with strips of duct tape.

8. Decorate the can with stickers if desired.

9. To hang, thread a length of yarn or chain up through the hole in the bottom of the can. Hold it in place with a knot, a paper clip, pipe cleaner, short piece of wire or tape.

Kierra with her diversity streamer

MATERIALS NEEDED – UNIT 2

> Note to Teachers: Most of the handouts are included with the lessons and are grouped in the handout section of this book for ease of photocopying. They are also available for download from our website (below). The remaining items, once obtained, can be re-used for many years. The wide variety of activities and materials allows for diverse learning styles. It also increases understanding and retention of the concepts, and it makes the lessons more memorable and enjoyable for the students.

Downloads available from: www.TeachingUnity.com

- ☐ **General Items**
    - White board, easel, markers, eraser
    - Folders and song sheets for each student
    - Paper and pens/pencils for all
    - Dictionary, globe and/or large world map
    - Candle and fruit as memory aids (activity #1, #9)

- ☐ **Leaves of One Tree** (activity #3, p. 38)
    - Tree branch with leaves (or a picture of one)

- ☐ **Unity in Diversity** (activity #4, p. 38)
    - Handout on "Unity in Diversity"

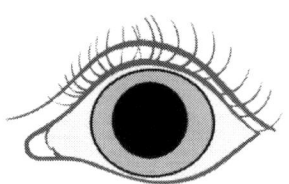

Along with this reading, you can show the PowerPoint on "Unity in Diversity," available as a free download from our website.

- ☐ **The Eye** (activity #6, p. 39)
    - Felt board and easel
    - Felt lesson (script and patterns included)

- ☐ **Machines in Motion** (activity #7, p. 39)
    - Picture cards or list of machines

- ☐ **Unity in Diversity** (activity #8, p. 41)
    - Handout of discussion questions for group leaders

- ☐ **Crafts** (activity #11, p. 41, 50-57)
    - Craft samples and instructions for flower collage, leaf laminates and diversity streamers
    - Craft supplies (see separate lists)

★ ★ ★ ★ ★

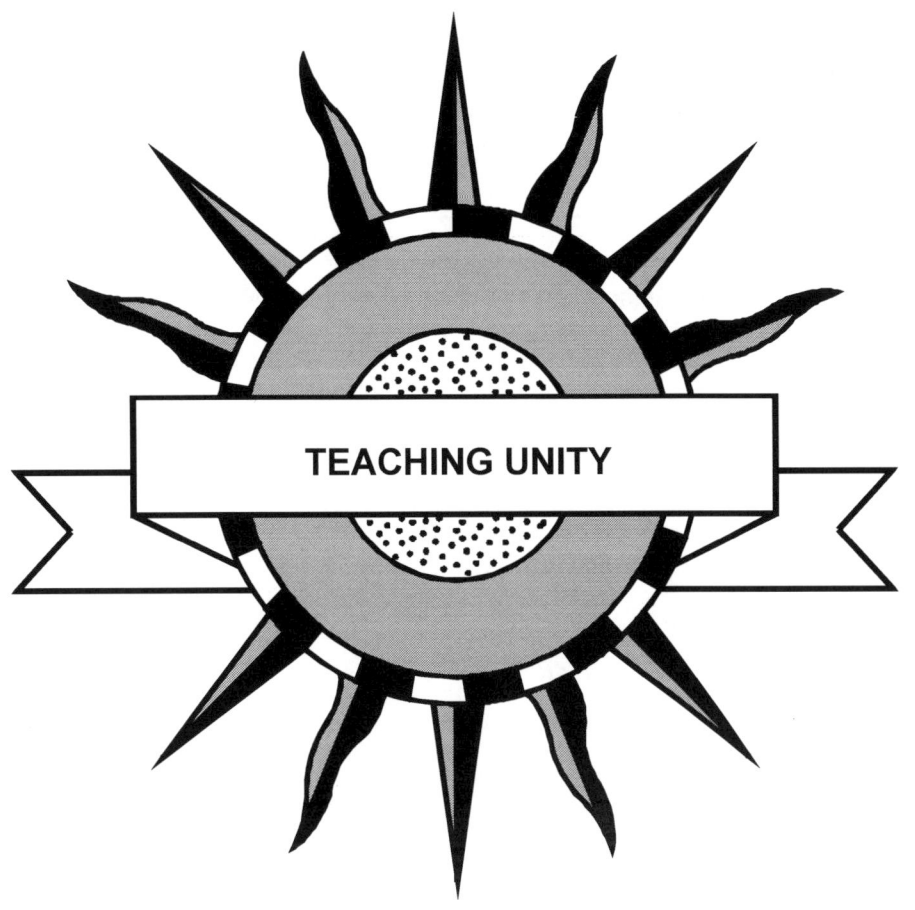

UNIT #3

The Colors We Are

The Colors We Are

Objectives: Students will be able to:
- Explain why we need skin and how we get our skin color.
- Recognize that our system of labeling people by color is not correct.
- Choose a more accurate name for their own skin color.
- Recognize that we are each special in different ways.

Before class, prepare all instructional materials on the list at the end of this lesson. Write the thought-for-the-day neatly on the board, one phrase on each line. Set up craft area. Orient any assistants. Distribute folders and pencils to each student.

---

1. INTRODUCTION AND REVIEW (15-20 min.)

Tell the class that we have been learning about unity and unity in diversity. Today we will learn about the colors we are—after a short review:

- Are all people exactly the same?
  (No. We have many similarities and many differences.)

- What are some of the things we have in common?
  (Physical characteristics, feelings, emotional needs, etc.)

- What are some of our differences?
  (Talents, likes and dislikes, language, skin color, etc.)

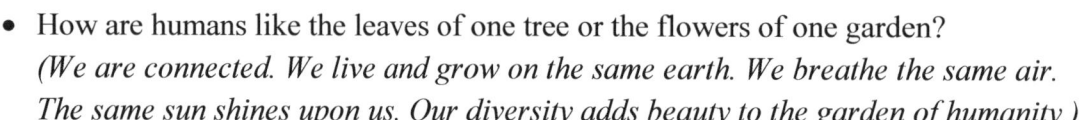

- How are humans like the leaves of one tree or the flowers of one garden?
  (We are connected. We live and grow on the same earth. We breathe the same air. The same sun shines upon us. Our diversity adds beauty to the garden of humanity.)

- Why is diversity important?
  (Variety, choices, new ideas, each has something different to offer the whole.)

- What is the difference between unity and sameness?
  (All are the same vs. respecting our differences and working together in harmony.)

- Give some concrete examples of unity in diversity.
  (Flowers, musical chord, body, eye, machines, orchestra, cake, rainbow, etc.)

- Have students take out their song sheets to sing "One Planet, One People" and the "Hawaiian Unity Song" learned during previous classes.

2. THOUGHT FOR THE DAY: "What should it matter…" (10-15 min.)

Ask for several volunteers to recite each of the passages learned previously. Hold up the candle and the fruit as reminders. Then have the whole class recite each quote in unison:

So powerful is the light of unity that it can illuminate the whole earth.

We are all the fruits of one tree, the flowers of one garden, the waves of one sea.

Today's quote should be on the board, with one phrase on each line. ⟶

Read the quote aloud slowly, then ask students:

- What do you think these words mean?
  *(If something fulfills its purpose,
  it doesn't matter what color it is.
  For example, a bowl is used to hold food.
  If it does the job well, we shouldn't care if the bowl is dark or light.
  It's the same with people.)*

> **What should it matter
> that one bowl is dark
> and the other is pale,
> if each is of good design
> and serves its purpose well?**

Continue with the memorization process outlined on page 27, holding up a bowl (or two bowls of different colors) as a visual memory aid.

3. SKIN COLOR DEMO (15-20 min.)

Ask the class:

- How many human races are there? *(That's right, only one!)*

- Just because we're part of one human family, it doesn't mean we all have the same color hair, eyes or skin. Can you name some common skin colors?
  (Accept all reasonable responses, including red and yellow which are discussed below.)

  A. Have five volunteers line up in front of the room each holding up a large, close-up color photograph of a face (see list of materials at end of lesson).

  B. Give five sheets of colored construction paper to a sixth volunteer and have her/him match one sheet to each face according to the colors we commonly use for people (see chart below). The sixth volunteer should give the matching paper to the person holding the relevant photo. Have them hold it next to the face in the photograph, so it can easily be compared to the actual skin color.

Teaching Unity, Unit 3: The Colors We Are, p. 61

> black ...... African
> white ...... European
> red .... American Indian
> yellow ..... Asian
> brown ..... Hispanic/Latino

C. For each photograph, ask the children if the paper color truly matches the skin color. *(Guide them to recognize that American Indians are not really red; people of Asian descent are not really yellow; people of European descent are not really white, etc.)*

D. Then take the light brown ("tan") construction paper and hold it next to each face, one by one. Ask the class which is closer to the actual skin color—tan or the shade assigned by society? *(While some of us have very dark or very light skin, most people come in different shades of tan.)*

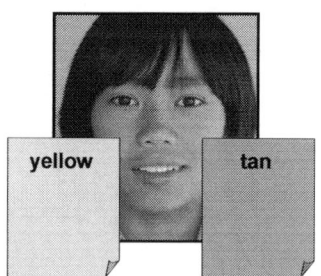
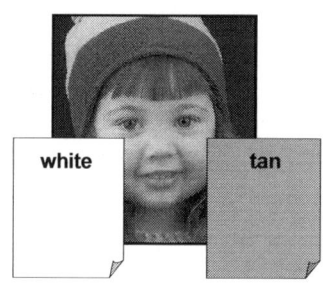

> Tip: Use light brown for a better match.

E. Ask the children what we can learn from this demonstration. *(Our system of labeling people by color is not accurate!)*

> Instead of the demo, you can use "The Colors We Are" PowerPoint, which also includes concepts from activities #4 and #5 below. See list of materials at end of this unit.

4. COLORS OF OUR WORLD (5 min.)

Explain to the class that today, we're going to find out what colors we really are. Write the words "pigment" and "melanin" on the board.

- There are many types of pigments or colorings that brighten our world.
- **Carotene** pigment makes carrots and pumpkins orange.
- **Chlorophyll** pigment makes leaves and grass green.
- **Hemoglobin** pigment makes our blood red.
- And **melanin** pigment makes our skin brown. All people have melanin in their skin.* Melanin protects us from the sun's harmful rays.

> * Note to teacher: People with a rare form of albinism are unable to produce melanin.

While speaking, hold up a large color picture of each item. See examples below.

5. HOW WE GOT OUR SKIN COLOR (30-40 min.)

Using the book, *All the Colors We Are*, read the story while showing children the pictures. (See ordering information at the end of this lesson.)

As you read, have children suggest answers to the questions in the text:

- *What color is your skin?*
- *How do you think we got our own special color of skin?*
- *Do you think your ancestors came from a very warm, sunny place?*
- *Or did they come from a cooler place with less sunshine?*

Write their answers on the board. The words "pigment" and "melanin" should already be on the board so children can see how they are spelled.

After reading the story, ask the following questions:

A. Can skin change its color?
(Yes, in the sun it can get darker, turn pink or red, or burn.)

B. Long ago, when groups of people lived in the same part of the world for thousands of years, what happened to their skin in places like Kenya or Nigeria—places in Africa close to the Equator—which receive a lot of direct sunlight? *(Their skin gradually became darker.)*

C. Why? *(To protect people by blocking the sun's rays.)*

D. What happened to peoples' skin in places like Sweden or Russia, where the sun is much less intense? *(It gradually got lighter to let in more of the sun's rays.)*

Using a flashlight to represent the sun, shine it on the globe to show that the light is more direct, and thus more intense, near the equator and less intense near the poles.

E. Where do you think the ancestors of these people may have lived? And these people? *(Show photos of people whose ancestors came from very warm and very cold areas.)*

Teaching Unity, Unit 3: The Colors We Are, p. 63

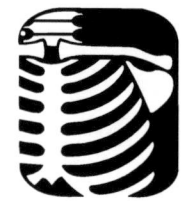

F. What happens if we get too much sun?
   (Sunburn, heatstroke, skin cancer.)

G. Too little sun? *(Our body won't produce enough vitamin D, so we can't absorb calcium, leading to rickets* and weak bones.)*

H. In order to be healthy, humans need just the right amount of sun. The pigment in our skin helps us adapt to the sun's rays. Because of obvious differences in skin color, many people think we are separate races. Recently, however, scientists have proven that we are all members of one human race.

> * <u>Teacher's Note</u>: Rickets is a severe and prolonged vitamin D deficiency that leads to softening and weakening of the bones in children. Vitamin D helps the body absorb calcium which children need to build strong bones. Rickets can be caused by lack of exposure to sunlight, which stimulates the body to make vitamin D. Signs and symptoms of rickets include bowed legs, leg fractures and impaired growth. (www.mayoclinic.com)

6. CLASS FEATURES CHART (30-40 min.)

Be sure group leaders are ready with their instructions and blank charts (pages 66-67), paint chip samples, pencils and mirrors.

Hold up a "pigment poster" depicting various skin shades and explain that we are going to learn about our own individual colors of skin, eyes and hair by finding color chips that match. Divide the class into small groups of four or five, and assign an assistant to each group. Groups can move to another room or outside if desired. Give them about 15 minutes to work. Then call them back together and post their charts on the wall. Share a few of the descriptions, then ask:

- What do we need skin for?
  (It covers our bones and muscles, keeps germs out, protects us from the sun, allows us to give off heat by sweating, contains our sense of touch, pain, etc. And as one child explained it, "So we don't leak!")

- What does this activity tell us about the way we look?
  (We all have the same basic parts, with some variations.)

> Note: If the teacher shows enthusiasm for this activity, the children will likely feel excited as well and will be eager to begin their investigations. If the teacher is uneasy or anxious, the children will receive a negative message about skin color, and may be more hesitant.

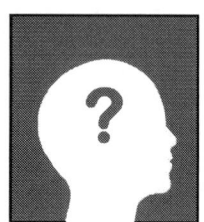

7. HOORAY FOR SKIN POEM (15-20 min.)

Have children locate the poem (in their handout packet and on page 68). Read the poem aloud while the children follow along. Ask what they think the poem means, then practice reading it in unison.

8. SONG: "Good Neighbors Come in All Colors" (5-10 min.)

Have students locate their song sheets and teach them the song. See music section for teaching ideas and musical score.

9. PERSONAL POSTER (45-60 min.)

This project (pages 69-72) is designed to reinforce material presented during class and to encourage children to celebrate their diversity. The children will be making individual posters by tracing their own hands, painting the drawing to match their skin color, and writing a short personal description. Show them a sample poster beforehand and display their work after they have finished.

Extension Activities and Alternatives

A. If there is time and interest, the children can share *"What my picture means to me,"* and *"What I learned about my classmates"*—either in small groups or as a whole class.

B. If you wish to do a group project or if the children in your class are all very similar in looks and coloring, you might make a class poster instead. Prepare a large poster board with the thought-for-the-day. Have the children paint directly onto their own hands using various colors of the rainbow, then press their hands onto the poster, making a design around the words. Have soap and water ready for cleanup.

C. As an alternative project, rather than just painting their hands, students can paint their personal portraits—mixing paint to match their skin and eye colors and adding yarn to match their hair. You can prepare a simple head pattern (p. 76) for students to cut out and color. (See Starting Small video described on page 247 for an example of this project.)

Instructions for activity #6

Class Features Activity

Materials needed: Mirrors, paint chip samples, class features chart, pencils

> **Instructions for group leaders:** Gather your small group and find a quiet place to work. Your job is to encourage all the children to participate. Do not allow them to laugh at or tease each other. You will have about 15 minutes to work.

1. Ask children to study the paint samples and to choose the one that most closely matches their own skin color. Practice saying the colors out loud.

   (Children can decide to use the labels on the paint samples as their skin color names, or they can choose other names. This activity focuses on the beauty of skin color. It helps the children to realize that they each have their own special color, and it empowers them to decide how they wish to be called. As the group leader, you should participate too.)

2. Work with students to fill in the features chart (see sample below).

Name	Eye color	Skin color	Hair length, color, texture
Maria	brown	gingersnap	long, reddish, straight
Marcus	black	caramel	short, black, curly
Lua	blue	peach	medium, blonde, wavy

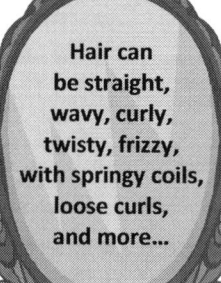

Hair can be straight, wavy, curly, twisty, frizzy, with springy coils, loose curls, and more...

3. After completing the chart, ask the children: "What do we need skin for?"

   _____

   _____

   _____

4. Return to the classroom with your group and post your chart on the wall.

For activity #6

Class Features Chart

Name	Eye color	Skin color	Hair length, color, texture

HOORAY FOR SKIN
by Susan Engle

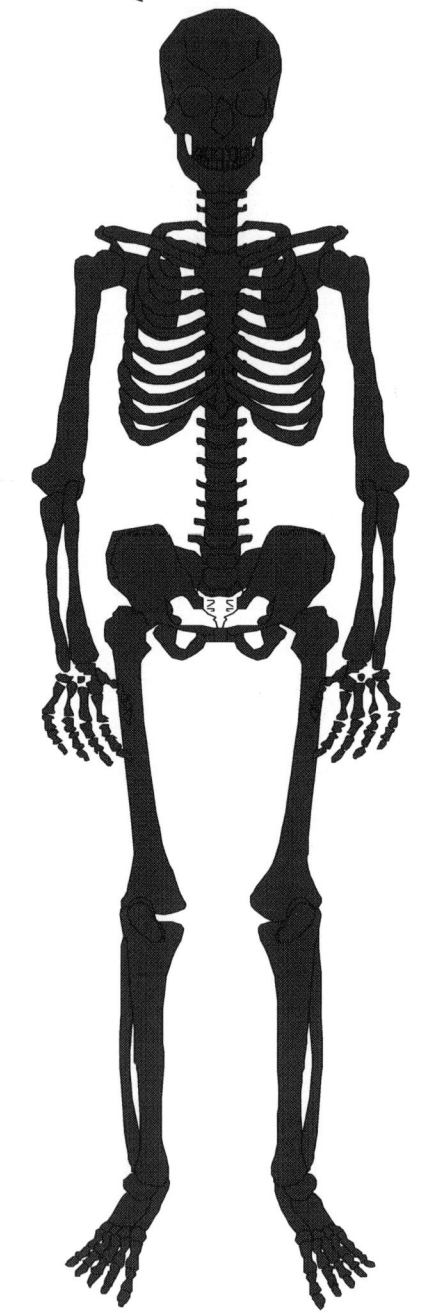

Rejoice and celebrate the skin
That keeps the veins and muscles in,
That keeps the cold and germies out.
That is what skin is all about.

Suppose that when you got your skin,
You found the skin side outside-in.
So when you talk to Mrs. Jones,
Your eyes meet over fat and bones,
And tissues, blue and white and red,
That stretch from toe to hand to head.
It makes me glad to have a skin
To keep the outside boneside-in.

Now there are folks who would be mad
If our insides were all they had
To tell all kinds of folks apart.
Maybe they'd learn to read the heart
Instead of judging from a hue
If one man's false and one man's true.

Let's all join hands and feast our eyes
On skins of every shape and size,
Of every tone of gold or white,
Of luscious black, of dark or light,
Of every shade that folks come in.
Rejoice and celebrate the skin.

© 1986, Susan Engle. Used with permission.

Personal Poster
A Celebration of Our Diversity

The children will be making individual posters by tracing their own hands, painting the drawing to match their skin color, and adding a short personal description.

> *Have children finish the writing and tracing activities before you set out the paint at each table. When done, they should clean up the workspace and hang up their posters for display. They will have about 45 minutes to work.*

Materials for Writing and Tracing

- ❑ Blank "I Am…" form
- ❑ Lined paper (trimmed to same size as form)
- ❑ Marker for printing first name
- ❑ Pens and pencils
- ❑ Cardstock or watercolor paper
- ❑ Scissors
- ❑ Glue sticks
- ❑ File folders in various colors (these can be turned inside out to hide brand names), or use poster board (approx. 12 x 17 inches or 30 x 44 cm)

Instructions for Writing and Tracing

1. Fill in the "I Am…" form or write your own text on lined paper.

2. Trace your hand and wrist on the cardstock, then carefully cut out the drawing.

3. Glue the text page onto one side of the folder.

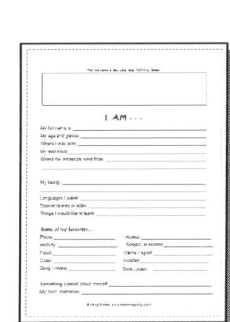
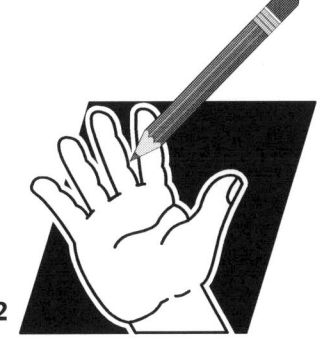

Painting the Hand
for Your Personal Poster

Materials for Painting

- ❑ Newspaper or tarp to protect table
- ❑ Extra sheet of paper to place under each painting
- ❑ Hand cutouts from tracing activity (above)
- ❑ Tempera or acrylic craft paints, preferably in squeeze bottles (black, white, red, yellow, blue – or order multicultural paints from a teacher supply store.)
- ❑ Sturdy paper or plastic bowls for mixing colors
- ❑ Paint brushes
- ❑ Water cups for rinsing brushes
- ❑ Paper towels for cleaning up
- ❑ Tacks or clothesline to hang pictures for display

Tip: Have the children experiment but don't do it for them. Provide guidance by letting them start with one color, then ask: Do you need to add a lighter or darker color to match your skin? Do you think it needs more red or more blue?

Instructions for Painting

1. Set paints out in center of table and give each child a mixing bowl, brush and water cup.

2. Put small dabs of various colors in each child's bowl and assist them to mix the colors until they find one that closely matches their skin.

   Tip: Red + yellow + blue = brown.

3. The matching color should be used to paint their hand cutout.

4. When dry, glue the cutout onto the folder and hang in the craft display area.

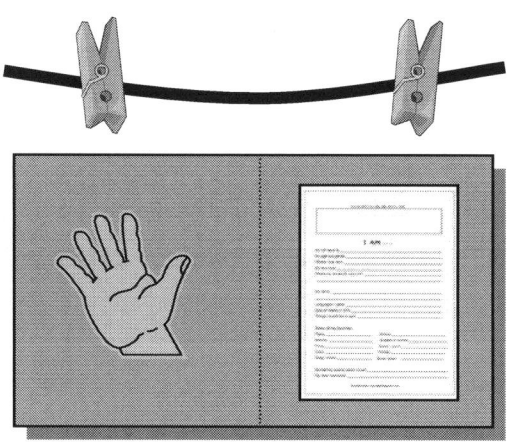

Sample Group Project

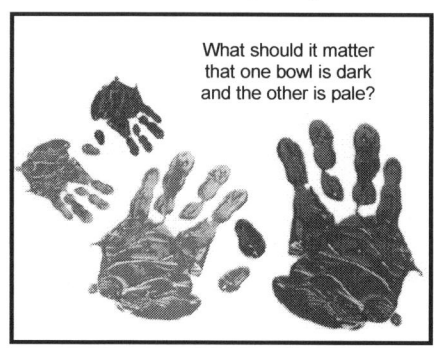

What should it matter that one bowl is dark and the other is pale?

Image courtesy of IdeaGo/FreeDigitalPhotos.net

Sample form for personal poster – activity #9

Print first name in box using large CAPITAL letters

MARIA

I AM...

My full name is: __Maria Elena Garcia__
My age and gender: __9 years old, female__
Where I was born: __Yakima, Washington__
My skin color: __Ancient gold__
Where my ancestors were from: __Bolivia – Sweden – France – USA__

My family: __Teresa, Manuel, Juan, Lily, Lilita, me (Maria Elena)__

Languages I speak: __English and Spanish__
Special talents or skills: __Music (flute)__
Things I would like to learn: __French and guitar__

Some of my favorites...

Place: __Chuck-E-Cheese__   Animal: __Romeo & Juliet (my parakeets)__
Activity: __soccer__   Subject in school: __recess__
Food: __ice cream__   Game / sport: __soccer__
Color: __red__   Holiday: __Christmas__
Song / music: __rock music__   Book / poem: __The Lorax__

Something special about myself: __I can curl my tongue__
My best memories: __When I visited my cousins in California__

Teaching Unity, Unit 3: The Colors We Are, p. 71

Print first name in box using large CAPITAL letters

I AM...

My full name is: _____

My age and gender: _____

Where I was born: _____

My skin color: _____

Where my ancestors were from: _____
_____

My family: _____
_____

Languages I speak: _____

Special talents or skills: _____

Things I would like to learn: _____

Some of my favorites...

Place: _____   Animal: _____

Activity: _____   Subject in school: _____

Food: _____   Game / sport: _____

Color: _____   Holiday: _____

Song / music: _____   Book / poem: _____

Something special about myself: _____

My best memories: _____

© UnityWorks, www.teachingunity.com

Make one copy of this page for each student, and trim on dotted lines.

Teaching Unity, Unit 3: The Colors We Are, p. 72

MATERIALS NEEDED – UNIT 3

Note to Teachers: Most of the handouts are included with the lessons and are grouped in the handout section of this book for ease of photocopying. They are also available for download from our website (below). The remaining items, once obtained, can be re-used for many years. The wide variety of activities and materials allows for diverse learning styles. It also increases understanding and retention of the concepts, and it makes the lessons more memorable and enjoyable for the students.

Downloads available from: www.TeachingUnity.com

❑ **General Items**
- White board, easel, markers, eraser
- Folders and song sheets for each student
- Paper and pens/pencils for all
- Dictionary, globe and/or large world map

❑ **Thought for the Day** (activity #2, p. 61)
- Candle, fruit and bowl for use as memory aids
- Optional poster of different colored bowls (in the download color-pak)

❑ **Skin Color Demo** (activity #3, p. 61-62)
- Five sheets of construction paper (black, white, red, yellow, light brown)
- Five large close-up color photos of diverse people to symbolically match the construction paper colors above (African, European, Native American, Asian, Hispanic/Latino)[A]

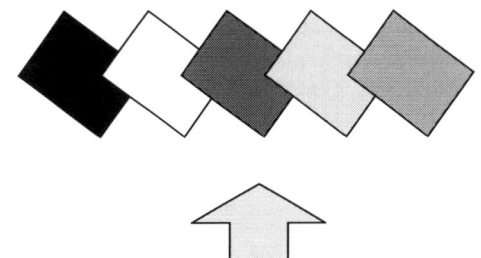

Along with or instead of this demonstration, you can show the PowerPoint on "The Colors We Are," available as a free download from our website. The PowerPoint also includes concepts from activities #4 and #5.

- ❑ **Colors of Our World** (activity #4, p. 62)[B]
    - Four large color pictures: bright orange pumpkin, dark green leaf, red heart, and photo of people with different skin colors (in the download color-pak)

- ❑ **How We Got Our Skin Color** (activity #5, p. 63-64)
    - The book, *All the Colors We Are.* [C]
    - Page of questions (included with the lesson)
    - Bright flashlight and globe
    - Photos of people whose ancestors came from very warm climates and very cold climates (a few of each)[A]

- ❑ **Class Features Chart** (activity #6, p. 64)
    - Instruction page and blank features chart for each group leader
    - Flesh-tone paint chip samples (one set per group)[D]
    - Small hand mirrors (one for every 2-3 students)
    - Tape or tacks for posting class features charts on the wall
    - Pigment Poster[E]
    - Optional book: *I Love My Hair,* by Natasha Anastasia Tarpley, 1998 (ISBN: 978-0316523752).

> **For photographs of different hair types**
> - www.curls.biz/curly-hair-type-guide.html
>
> **For a discussion of the term "nappy hair"**
> - www.nappyhairaffair.com
> - www.adversity.net/special/nappy_hair.htm
> - www.carolivia.org/nappyhair

- ❑ **Hooray for Skin** (activity #7, p. 65)
    - "Hooray for Skin" handouts

- ❑ **Personal Poster** (activity #9, p. 65)
    - Craft samples and instructions
    - Craft supplies (see separate list)
    - Blank "I Am…" forms (one per student)
    - Skin color reference charts (optional)[F]

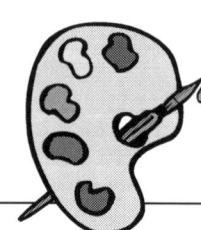

A. Some of these photographs may have already been obtained for a previous class. (See the list of materials for Unit #1, page 33.) They are also available in the download color-pak. The images can be laminated and posted around the room.

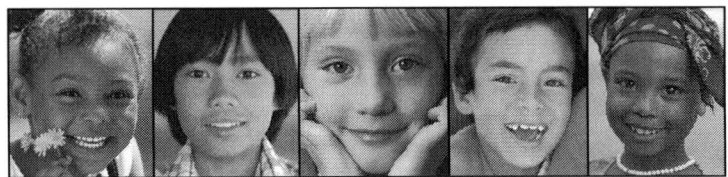

B. The above pictures are available in the download packet. Similar images can be found in clip art programs or online. For example, visit **www.google.com**, click on "Images" and type "pumpkin" in the search box. A variety of pumpkins will appear. Double-click on the image you wish to use. Next, click on "Full-size image," right-click on the image, then "Save Picture As." Give the file a name and save it to your desktop or other location. It will then be available for editing and printing. Images can be enlarged, mounted, laminated or displayed in a plastic page protector.

C. *All The Colors We Are / Todos los Colores de Nuestra Piel: The Story of How We Get Our Skin Color,* by Katie Kissinger, photographs by Wernher Krutein, published by Redleaf Press, MN (www.redleafpress.org), ISBN: 0-934140-80-4. It should be available through your local library or bookstore, and on www.amazon.com.

D. Bring the above book, *All the Colors We Are,* to the paint store and ask for free paint chip samples to match the various skin tones. Choose paint samples with inviting, kid-friendly names, such as *peachy cream, cinnamon swirl* and *sunny gold*, rather than *Tagsdale Linen* or *Rio Grande Mud*. You may need to select samples from different brands. Choose 15-20 colors to make a complete set, and make a separate set for each group of students.

E. A sample *Pigment Poster* can be found in the download packet for this teacher's guide. If preferred, you can make your own poster by cutting up extra paint samples and arranging the pieces in a design to illustrate the beauty of our diverse skin tones. Glue your design onto tag board or laminate for durability. Students can also make their own posters (see instructions on p. 154).

F. Skin color reference charts from the book, *How to Paint Skin Tones,* are available online at: < http://slappingpaint.net/JN_creatingfleshtones.htm >. The charts show how to blend different paint colors to create specific skin tones.

* * * * *

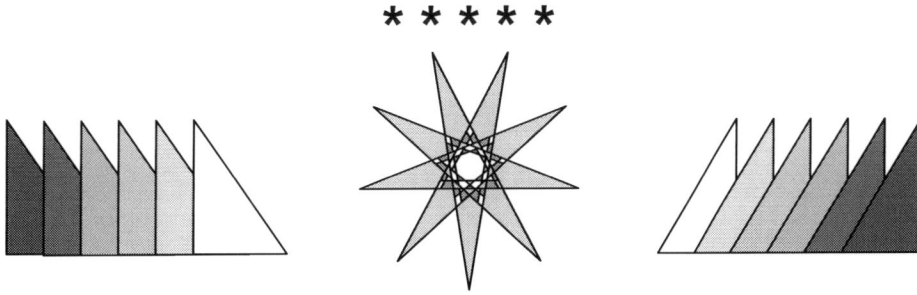

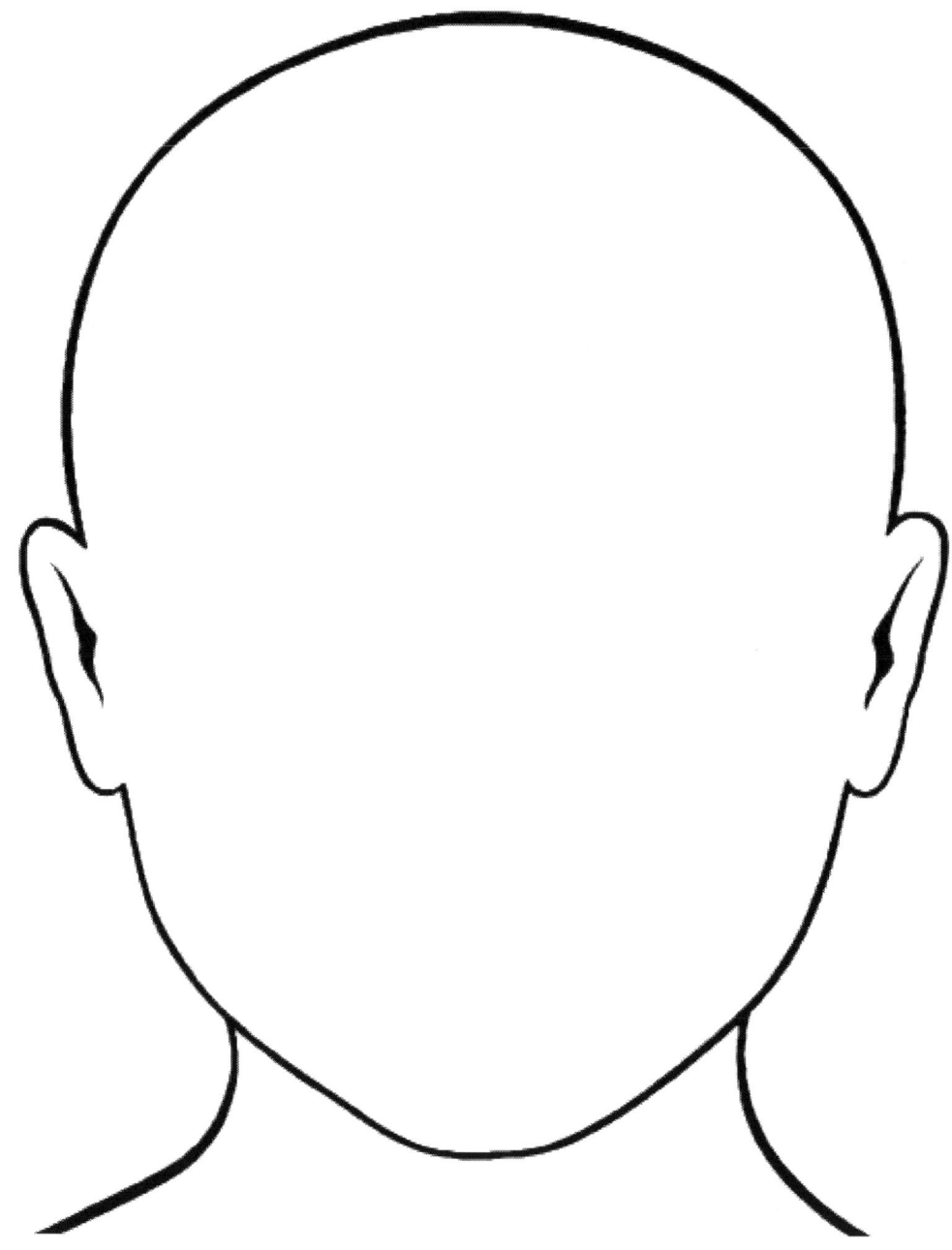

Head template for personal portrait, activity 9C on p. 65.

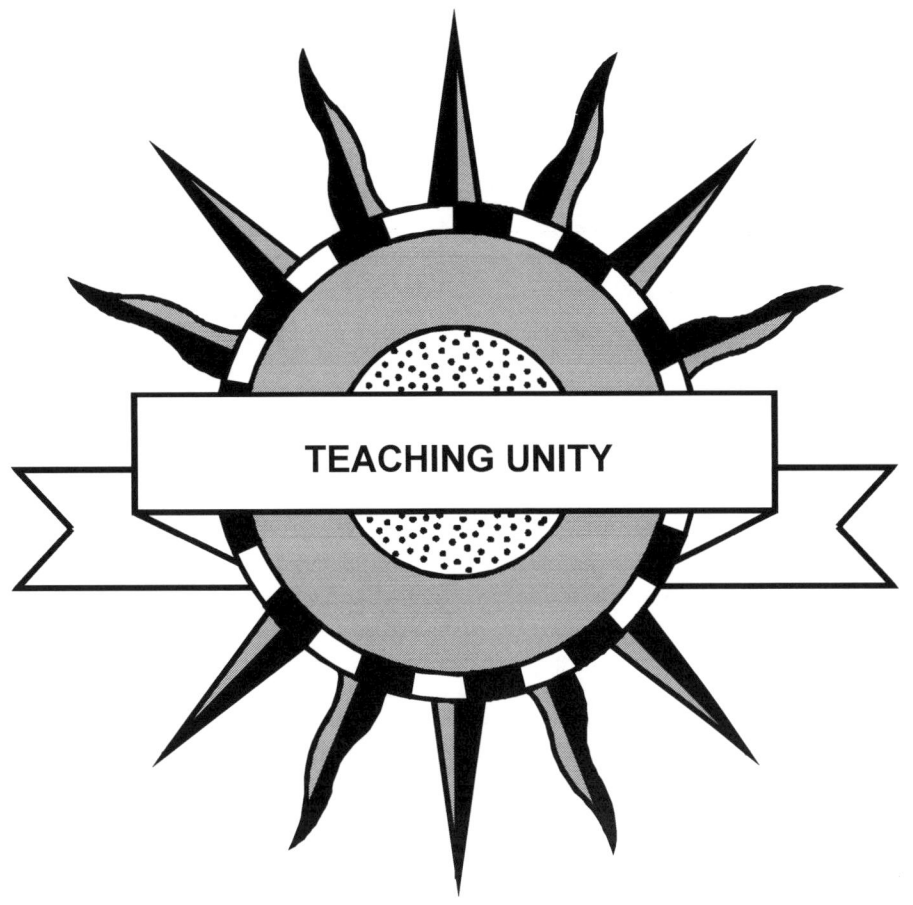

UNIT #4

Overcoming Prejudice

Overcoming Prejudice

Objectives: Students will be able to:
- Name some of the barriers to unity, including prejudice.
- Define prejudice and describe some of its effects.
- Demonstrate positive responses to putdowns and biased remarks.
- Work together to develop and practice various approaches to creating unity in their own families, schools and communities.

Before class, prepare all instructional materials on the list at the end of this lesson. Write the questions for activity #7 on a separate board or poster for ready reference. Set up felt board. Orient assistants. Distribute folders, markers and pens.

---

1. **INTRODUCTION AND REVIEW** (20-30 min.)

   Tell the class that we have been learning about unity, unity in diversity, and our skin colors. Today we will learn about one of the barriers to unity, called prejudice, and how to get rid of it—after a short review:

   - What is unity? What is disunity?
   - Give some examples of each.
   - What are some of the benefits of unity?
   - Why is unity so important to the world today?
   - What are some of the things all people have in common?
   - What are some of our differences?
   - Why is diversity important?
   - What is the difference between unity and sameness?
   - Can you give some concrete examples of unity in diversity?

   > These questions are also found in the PowerPoint review of Units 1-3, available as a free download from our website.

   (See pages 36 and 60 for sample responses to the questions above.)

   - Why do we need skin?

     (To cover our bones and muscles, to keep germs out, to protect us from the sun, for our sense of touch, to give off heat by sweating, etc.)

   - How do we get our skin color?

     (From our parents and our ancestors—relatives who lived long ago, from the sun, and from melanin.)

Teaching Unity, Unit 4: Overcoming Prejudice, p. 78

- What is melanin and what does it do?

    (Tiny grains of pigment or color in our skin. It makes our skin brown and protects us from the sun's harmful rays.)

- Why do some people have more melanin in their skin, and some have less?

    (It depends on whether their ancestors lived in very warm climates with a lot of sun, or very cool ones. More sun meant that more melanin was needed to protect their skin.)

- Are people really black, white, red, yellow and brown?

    (Some do have very dark or very light skin, but we are mostly different shades of tan or brown.)

- How many races are there?

    (One human race.)

- How are people like the flowers of a garden?

    (We live and grow on the same earth. We breathe the same air. The same sun shines upon us. Our diversity adds beauty to the garden of humanity.)

- Who can recite one of the memorized passages from our previous lessons?

    (Hold up the candle, fruit and bowl as visual reminders. Call on several volunteers for each quote and then have the entire class recite it in unison.)

So powerful is the light of unity that it can illuminate the whole earth.

We are all the fruits of one tree, the flowers of one garden, the waves of one sea.

What should it matter that one bowl is dark and the other is pale, if each is of good design and serves it purpose well?

- Ask students to take out their song sheets and sing the songs learned previously:

    "One Planet, One People"   **"Hawaiian Unity Song"**   **"Good Neighbors"**

2. BRIDGES AND BARRIERS (15-20 min.)

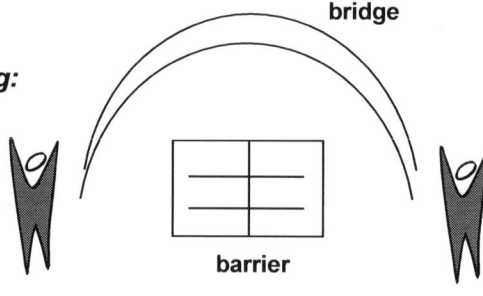

Draw on the whiteboard as you explain the following:

Sometimes our words and actions can be **barriers** to unity—like walls keeping people apart. And sometimes our words and actions can be like **bridges** of understanding—bonds connecting people's hearts.

A. Give each child a red card and a green card. Explain that red means *stop* and it represents a brick in the wall. Green means *go* and represents a piece of the bridge.

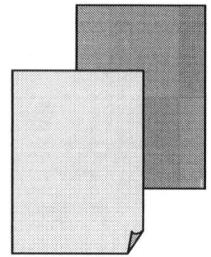

Note: Use 3x5 index cards or heavyweight paper. If red and green are not available, use two other colors.

B. On the red cards, ask students to write one thing that is a barrier to unity (backbiting, gossiping, prejudice, name calling, disrespect, lying, criticizing, frowning, sarcasm, blaming, etc.). They should print legibly using large letters. Have them first check with their neighbors to be sure they are not all writing the same words. Offer to assist with spelling as necessary.

C. On the green cards, have students write one thing that builds bridges between people (honesty, kindness, cooperation, sharing, helpfulness, fairness, service, love, listening, friendliness, patience, telling the truth, keeping your promises, etc.).

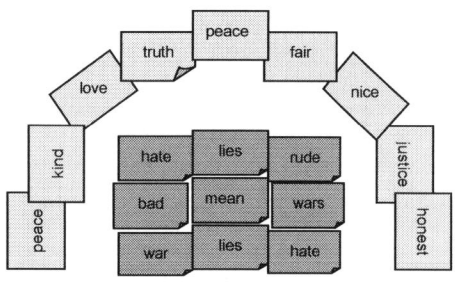

D. Help students tape their barrier words onto the classroom wall in the shape of a brick wall. (See illustration at left.)

E. Next, have them tape their bridge words in an arc passing over the barrier wall.

F. Call on two volunteers to read the cards out loud, then invite children to share any thoughts they might have.

If wall space is not available, use chart paper or a large bulletin board with pushpins.

3. DISCUSSION: Prejudice (10-15 min.)

Write the word "prejudice" on the board. Then ask students the following questions and write their answers on the board:

- One of the biggest barriers to unity is **prejudice**. Does anyone know what prejudice is?
  (Not liking people before you even meet them; prejudging people in a bad way.)

- It's easy to remember if you separate the word into two parts: **pre · judice** (which means to prejudge).

- Some people think that their skin color or race is the best, and they don't like people of a different race or color. That's called racial prejudice. They don't understand that we have different skin colors to protect us from the sun, or that there is really only one human race. Prejudice isn't very logical, is it!

- In addition to racial prejudice, what other types of prejudice can you think of?
  (Sex, age, religion, height, weight, language, accent, disability, nationality, how much money someone has, education, type of job, clothing, etc.)

- How do you think people feel when others treat them with prejudice?
  (Sad, hurt, left out, angry, frustrated, etc.)

- How do you think people feel who <u>are</u> prejudiced?
  (Superior, better than others.)

- How do they act toward people they don't like?
  (Unkind, rude, unfair, mean, ignore them, etc.)

- How does prejudice stop people from reaching unity?
  (It's a barrier that breaks trust and keeps people apart.)

- Do you think prejudice is a problem in the world today?
  (Encourage children to share their thoughts.)

- Can you think of any examples of prejudice in your school or community?
  (Encourage children to share examples, but without naming individuals.)

Explain that later we will share some personal stories about what it feels like when someone is prejudiced against you or isn't treating you nicely, and we'll practice ways to respond.

4. READING AND DISCUSSION: "The Sneetches" (15-20 min.)

This classic Dr. Seuss story-poem is about prejudice and discrimination. It is available on Amazon.com. A summary of the story can be found at: < **wikipedia.org** >. Enter "*sneetches*" in the search box.

Briefly, Sneetches are yellow bird-like cartoon creatures. Some of them have green stars on their bellies, while others do not. The stars become a symbol of privilege and an excuse to discriminate. In the end, the stars no longer matter, and all of the Sneetches become friends.

An excerpt from the poem is included in the handout section of this book and on page 90. You can show students a picture of the Sneetches (visit **www.Google.com/images** and type "*sneetches*" in the search box). Then read the excerpt out loud with feeling while the children follow along on their handouts. You may need to explain that words like "thars" are used instead of "theirs" for humor and to maintain the rhyme.

> As an alternative, there is a 6-minute reading of the complete story with illustrations online. Visit < **www.youtube.com** > and type "*sneetches strain*" in the search box.
>
> If the children would like to see a 12-minute animated cartoon version of The Sneetches, visit < **www.youtube.com** > and type "*sneetches full version*" in the search box.

After sharing the story, ask the class:

- How were the Star-Belly Sneetches acting?
  (Better than everyone else, rude, mean, prejudiced.)

- Why? *(They had stars on their bellies, and thought this made them superior.)*

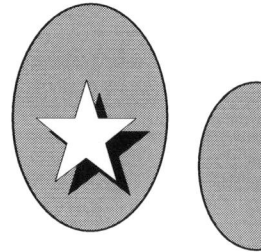

- Were they showing unity? *(No. They were showing prejudice. They didn't like the sneetches without stars, even before they got to know them. They also didn't treat them very nicely. Prejudice is a barrier to unity, and we should work to eliminate it.)*

5. SIMULATION: "The Sneetches" (25-30 min.)

As a follow-up activity, you can conduct the simulation exercise on the next page to help children understand the emotional impact of unfair treatment. This activity will also help students realize that the goal is to change discriminatory attitudes and practices and not the characteristics that make us different from one another.

For activity #5

Sneetches Simulation

Begin by explaining that we are going to play a game. Let's pretend we are all Sneetches—some with stars and some without stars. Then divide the class in half and put colored stickers or large paper stars on half of the children.

Tell the star-children to stand in the center of the room and brag about how smart, talented and good-looking they are—while the others watch. Explain to the class that the star-children are indeed special and will get extra privileges all year. They can choose their favorite games during recess, drink first at the water fountain, get higher grades, extra credit, etc. Then praise the star-children and give them some candy or other small treat.

After a few minutes (or allow more time if needed), switch roles and repeat the simulation, giving the stars and the candy to the other half of the class.

Stop the simulation and ask the children:

- What was the main difference between the two groups?
- Do you think it's fair that one group gets privileges just because they have a star?
- How did you feel when you had a star?
- When you did not have a star?
- When you did <u>not</u> have a star, how did you feel about those who <u>did</u>?
- When you <u>did</u> have a star, how did you feel about those who did <u>not</u>?
- What kinds of things do actual people have that are like stars?
- What kinds of things do we do to make people feel *special* or to feel *left out*?
- What did you learn from this activity?

Ask the children to find a partner, discuss the statement in the box below, then share their thoughts with the class.

> List some actions <u>you</u> can take to help everyone feel like they belong.

**End the lesson by providing a snack for all and enjoying it together.
Ask: How do we all feel now?**

(Simulation adapted from the Teaching Tolerance website:
< www.tolerance.org/activity/anti-racism-activity-sneetches >.

6. PUTDOWNS (20-30 min.)

Distribute scratch paper and pencils, then tell the class:

- Putdowns are another barrier to unity.
  Do you know what a putdown is?
  *(An insult or mean comment meant to hurt someone.
  Putdowns can also include rude gestures and sounds.)*

- Why do you think people use putdowns?
  *(To feel important, to gain attention or power,
  to blame others, to fit in with the crowd...)*

- Putdowns have hurt many people.
  Even if others laugh and think it's funny,
  the person who is the target still feels bad.

*You're an idiot.
Nobody likes you.
Fatso! Wimp! Sissy!
Nerd! Retard! Loser!
That's so gay.*

- We're going to write some of the common putdowns that we've heard.
  Print the words on your scratch paper (no swear words please).

***While the students are writing their putdowns, draw a large outline
of a child on chart paper. Then tape the paper to the wall.***

A. Give the child a name, for example, Alex. Explain that Alex is about their age, and he is feeling sad because the other kids are putting him down.

B. Ask 8-10 students to come to the front, one at a time, and read their words to Alex while tearing off a small piece of his picture. Have any remaining students stand and read their words.

(You can also use pre-prepared putdowns written on slips of paper which students can pull from a box to read one at a time.)

(Do not laugh as the words are read. This is a serious issue and the teacher's attitude is critical.)

C. When all of the students have had a turn, ask how they think Alex feels.

D. Then ask the students to think of words that might help Alex feel better, for example: *I'm sorry I said you were stupid*, or *Would you like to sit with us today?*—while taping the torn child back together.

E. After everyone has had a turn, ask how they think Alex feels now. *(Although he has been put back together, the scars remain. Even if you apologize, you can't erase all the pain caused by hateful words.)*

***Bring out a trash can and invite the students to tear up
their slips of paper and throw them away, to symbolically
show that we don't want to use putdowns any more.***

Teaching Unity, Unit 4: Overcoming Prejudice, p. 84

7. PERSONAL STORIES (30-40 min.)

Explain that we are going to share some personal stories about what it feels like when someone is prejudiced against you or isn't treating you nicely. Later we'll practice ways to respond.

Divide the class into groups of three to discuss the questions below. The questions should already be listed on a separate board or poster. They are also included at the end of this lesson (page 91). Make photocopies for any assistants who will be working with the small groups. Children might relate better to youth assistants rather than adults for this activity.

Ask the students:

A. How does it feel when someone is prejudiced against you or isn't treating you nicely?

B. Tell about a time when you were teased, put down, treated unfairly or left out. (3-5 min. each)
- What happened?
- How did you feel?
- What would have helped?

C. Do you know of anyone in your life right now who might feel put down or left out?

D. What can you do to make that person feel included?

Tell students not to share anything that should remain private.

Walk around the room to observe the group discussions and to make sure everyone has a chance to participate. Be prepared in case there are a few tears.

If there is time to report back, have each group share a summary of their thoughts.

8. PUT-UPS (20-25 min.)

Give each child a paper cup with his or her name on it, or write each name on a blank page and post these on the wall. Children will also need scratch paper or sticky notes. Then tell the class:

- If someone is feeling sad or left out, we can say something positive to encourage them. Let's call this a "put-up" since we're building people up rather than putting them down.

- Let's brainstorm a list of nice things we could say.
  (I like how you shared your game. You're very patient.)

  Write the children's suggestions on the board.

- Now let's write a "put-up" for each classmate. Think of their best qualities. Print legibly on a separate slip of paper for each person. Put the paper in their cup or stick it on the page with their name. Then silently read the ones you have received.

  Ask: How did this activity make you feel? What can we learn from this? (Discuss)

9. READING: "Dealing with Putdowns and Prejudice" (10-15 min.)

Ask the class:

- If someone says something hurtful or rude, what do you think will happen if you respond with another putdown?
  (Both may get upset. It could start a fight. It adds more insults to the situation and makes it harder to create unity.)

- Instead, we can learn to speak up in ways that are polite and clear.

- Speaking up takes courage. It helps to know which words to say and when it is better to say nothing. If the situation is unsafe, sometimes it's better to just walk away.

- Let's look at examples of some things we *can* say.

Have students locate "Dealing with Putdowns and Prejudice" (in their handout packet and at the end of this lesson on page 92). Call on volunteers to read each section aloud and encourage children to add their own ideas as well.

10. WORKSHEET AND SKITS: "Name It, Claim It" (30-45 min.)

"Name It, Claim It, Stop It" is another strategy for dealing with putdowns and prejudice. Have students locate the worksheet (in their handout packet and on page 93) and choose a partner. Read through the worksheet with the class, then have partners do the exercises together. Allow about ten minutes to work. Then ask for volunteers to act out the example they have created.

Next, to show the value of working together in unity, have one pair of students perform the *purple people* skit from the middle section of the handout.

Then have them act it out a second time, but instead of only one person standing up for justice, ask two people to stand up and say "Stop!" Repeat with five people arising, then again with the entire class.

After the demonstration, ask each actor how he or she felt when only one person stood up and how they felt when everyone did.

The more people who stand up for justice, the more power they will have. There is strength in unity.

11. ROLE PLAYS: "Creating Unity" (45-60 min.)

Have students turn to "Creating Unity" (in their handout packet and on page 94). These role plays can be modified to fit your own students.

   A. Explain that we have been talking about ways to create unity by building bridges and breaking down barriers between people. In order to be successful, we can't just <u>believe</u> in unity. We must <u>act</u> on our beliefs. These skits will give us an opportunity to practice.

   B. Divide the class into small groups of 3-4, and put an assistant in charge of each group.

   C. Assign one or more role plays to each group, or cut up the role play cards and allow each group to pick one from a bowl. The children will be performing these for the class. Give the groups 10-15 minutes to prepare.

   D. Have them act out each role play twice: first in a negative way and again in a way that creates unity. After each group's performance, the children can discuss the issues presented or act out alternative solutions if desired.

   E. After all of the performances, ask the class what they have learned.

   (Guide the children to understand that it is important to stand up for others—especially when they can't stand up for themselves. It takes courage to do what is right. You might be the only one standing at first, but you will have helped another human being, and as a result of your good example, others may join you too.)

12. THOUGHT FOR THE DAY: "Darkness cannot ..." (10-15 min.)

Write these words on the board with one phrase on each line. If the quote is too long for the children, just use the second part. ⟶

> **Darkness cannot drive out darkness; only light can do that.**
>
> **Hate cannot drive out hate; only love can do that.**

Read the quote aloud slowly, then ask students:

- What do you think these words mean?

   *(Darkness is not a force in itself.
   Rather, it is the absence of light.
   We can't get rid of darkness by adding more darkness.
   But we can turn on the light. It's the same with hate.)*

Continue with the memorization process outlined in Unit #1, page 27.

13. FELT LESSON: "Barriers into Bonds" (15-20 min.)

Present the felt lesson on "Barriers into Bonds" (see patterns and instructions on pages 96-102). Then ask if several children would like to try the presentation in front of the class.

14. WORKSHEET: "Barriers into Bonds" (15-20 min.)

With the completed felt lesson still on display, give students the worksheet on "Barriers into Bonds" (in the handout section and on page 103). Have them answer the questions (using the back side of the page if necessary) and color in the picture. When done, students can share their answers with the class.

15. CRAFT: "Barriers into Bonds" (45-60 min.)

Craft projects are designed to reinforce the material presented during class. Students will be making a cut-and-paste diagram to illustrate the concept of turning people-made barriers (skin color, language, nationality and other differences) into bonds of unity. Begin by showing students a sample of each craft. (See instructions on pages 104-108).

16. FINAL REVIEW: The Light of Unity (25-30 min.)

A. Divide the class into small groups and ask each group to develop a list of 10 or more key points relating to unity. They can include definitions, examples, concepts such as *unity in diversity*, information about skin color, ways to respond to biased remarks, and any other topic studied so far. Allow 10-15 minutes to work. Let them use their notes and handouts if desired.

B. Reconvene the class and have each group share one item. Write these on the board. Continue in this way until all ideas have been shared. Then praise the students for what they have learned.

C. End the review with a group recitation of all the memory quotes learned so far:

So powerful is the light of unity that it can illuminate the whole earth.

We are all the fruits of one tree, the flowers of one garden, the waves of one sea.

What should it matter that one bowl is dark and the other is pale, if each is of good design and serves it purpose well?

*Darkness cannot drive out darkness; only light can do that.
Hate cannot drive out hate; only love can do that.*

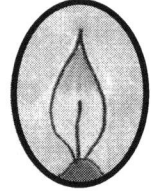

17. SONG: "What Mankind Has to Learn" (15 min.)

Have students locate their song sheets and teach them the song. See music section for teaching ideas and musical score.

18. VISUALIZATION: "The Circle of Unity" (15 min.)

This final activity can be used at the end of the unit or as part of a closing ceremony for a weekend retreat or summer camp. Take the children outside or into a large room and have them stand in a circle. Enlist the help of several assistants and space them around the circle next to children who might need extra help.

Tell the class you are going to imagine how it might feel if the world were truly unified and everyone treated people with kindness, justice and respect. When the children are quiet, give each one a short length of red yarn and read the "The Circle of Unity" (page 109). Modify the reading to fit the culture and life circumstances of your students. Play soft instrumental music in the background if desired.

* * * * *

Poem excerpt for activity #4

The Sneetches

From *The Sneetches and Other Stories* by Dr. Seuss.
TM & copyright © by Dr. Seuss Enterprises, L.P, 1953, 1954, 1961, renewed 1989.
Used by permission of Random House Children's Books, a division of Random House, Inc.

Now the Star-Belly Sneetches
Had bellies with stars.
The Plain-Belly Sneetches
Had none upon thars.

Those stars weren't so big
They were really so small.
You might think such a thing
Wouldn't matter at all.

But because they had stars
All the Star-Belly Sneetches
Would brag, "We're the best kind
Of Sneetches on beaches."

With their snoots in the air,
They would sniff and they'd snort
"We'll have nothing to do with
The Plain-Belly sort!"

And whenever they met some
When they were out walking,
They'd hike right on past them
Without even talking….

When the Star-Belly Sneetches
Had frankfurter roasts
Or picnics or parties
Or marshmallow toasts,

They never invited
The Plain-Belly Sneetches.
They left them out cold
In the dark on the beaches.

They kept them away.
Never let them come near.
And that's how they treated them
Year after year…

Personal Stories

Instructions for group leaders for activity #7

> Gather your small group and find a quiet place. You will have about 15 minutes to work. Your job is to ask the questions below and encourage the children to share their thoughts and experiences. Do not require them to speak but make sure everyone who wants to has an opportunity. Be prepared in case there are a few tears.
>
> Do not allow the children to laugh at or tease each other. Take notes below. If there is time to report back, prepare the group to share a brief summary of their thoughts.

Explain that we are going to share some personal stories about what it **feels** like when someone is prejudiced against you or isn't treating you nicely. When one person in our group is speaking, the others should listen respectfully and try to understand what happened even if we don't agree with it. Later we'll practice different ways to respond.

1. How does it feel when someone is prejudiced against you or isn't treating you nicely?

2. Tell about a time when you were teased, put down, treated unfairly or left out. (3-5 min. each)

   A. What happened?

   B. How did you feel?

   C. What would have helped?

3. Do you know of anyone in your life right now who might feel put down or left out?

4. What can you do to make that person feel included?

Teaching Unity, Unit 4: Overcoming Prejudice, p. 91

Reading for activity #9

Dealing With
PUTDOWNS AND PREJUDICE

If someone calls you a name:
- Stay calm.
- Say: That's mean and I don't like it.
- Say: That's not funny. Please stop.
- Walk away.
- Tell some friends.
- Tell an adult.

"That's not cool!"

Things to say to someone else who is called a name:
- It was wrong of her to say that about you. Are you okay?
- Can I help you report it to the teacher?
- Would you like to eat lunch with us from now on?

Ways to respond to prejudiced remarks:
- In our house, those words are not allowed.
- What makes you believe that about _____?
- You're too nice a person to hurt someone like that.
- That's not okay. It's disrespectful to say that about others.
- If someone said that about you, you wouldn't like it either.
- Do you really mean what you said? Here's what I understood…
- It makes me upset when you talk about _____ like that. Please stop.
- I don't like that kind of joke. It puts down my family—the human family.

Try some *put-ups*:
- I'm happy to see you!
- Come and join us.
- You can do it.
- Good job!
- You look nice today.
- I like the way you shared your game.
- You were very helpful just now.
- Would you like to be friends?

Teaching Unity, Unit 4: Overcoming Prejudice, p. 92

Worksheet for activity #10

NAME IT, CLAIM IT, STOP IT

Adapted from a workshop given by Peggy Federici, Camp Peace, Idaho

"Name It, Claim It, Stop It" is another strategy for dealing with putdowns and prejudice. It's not enough just to learn about these things. We also need to act. When you hear a biased remark, you can respond with three simple statements:

1. Name the behavior. *(Say what the person is doing wrong.)*
2. Claim it by stating how it makes <u>you</u> feel.
3. Tell the person to stop.

Here's an example:

> **Biased remark:** "How many green people does it take to change a light bulb?"
> **Name it:** "That's a mean joke."
> **Claim it:** "I don't like it when you put down green people like that."
> **Stop it:** "Please don't tell those jokes anymore."

See if you can label all three parts in the example below:

> **Biased remark:** "I don't like purple people. They're all stupid!"
> 1. "What you just said about purple people—that's prejudice." _____
> 2. "It makes me sad to hear you say things like that." _____
> 3. "Please don't talk that way around me." _____

Now try your own example:

> **Biased remark:** "_____"
> **Name it:** _____
> **Claim it:** _____
> **Stop it:** _____

Practice with your partner and be ready to act out your example for the class.

Handout with role plays for activity #11

CREATING UNITY

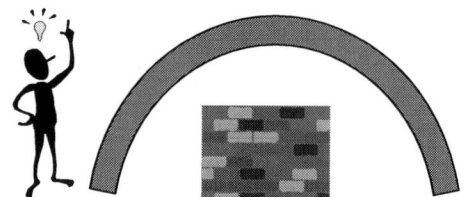

Your group will be assigned one or more of the situations below. For each one, read and discuss it with your group. Then act it out twice—first in a negative way and then in a more positive way that creates unity. Refer to the handouts on "Putdowns and Prejudice" and "Name It, Claim It, Stop It" for ideas. Be ready to perform your skits for the whole class.

1. There is a new student at school. She always eats lunch by herself and doesn't seem to have any friends. Today, you see her sitting alone again.

2. On the bus to school, some older kids are teasing a boy who is overweight. They call him a fat pig and say they are going to beat him up after school.

3. All of your friends want to stop at the snack shop on the way home from school, but one of them doesn't have enough money, so he pretends he isn't hungry.

4. While playing with friends at the park, a group of younger children walks by. They are making fun of people who speak with accents.

5. You sit with friends every day at lunch. There is an open space at your table, and a new girl sits down to eat. No one talks to her, but after she leaves, your friends make fun of her hair and clothing.

6. There is a student from Japan in your class. Before class begins, some of the other students tease him, making fun of the shape of his eyes. Everyone laughs.

7. During recess, the boys decide to play hide-and-seek. A girl wants to join them, but they say that girls aren't allowed to play.

8. Your teacher passes out feathers for an art project. Several classmates stick the feathers in their hair and dance around wildly, shouting "Me, Indian!"

9. A boy in your math class has trouble doing the homework and always makes a lot of mistakes. The other children laugh and call him "stupid" and "retard."

10. A girl at your school uses a wheelchair. She wants to be in the class play, but the teacher says she can't because there are no parts for someone in a wheelchair.

– Role play cards for activity #11 –

Creating Unity: *This page can be copied and the cards cut out and distributed, one to each group. If you plan to re-use the cards, laminate them for greater durability. Students can also be given the handout with the complete list of scenarios.*

---

(1) There is a new student at school. She always eats lunch by herself and doesn't seem to have any friends. Today, you see her sitting alone again.

(2) On the bus to school, some older kids are teasing a boy who is overweight. They call him a fat pig and say they are going to beat him up after school.

(3) All of your friends want to stop at the snack shop on the way home from school, but one of them doesn't have enough money, so he pretends he isn't hungry.

(4) While playing with friends at the park, a group of younger children walks by. They are making fun of people who speak with accents.

(5) You sit with friends every day at lunch. There is an open space at your table, and a new girl sits down to eat. No one talks to her, but after she leaves, your friends make fun of her hair and clothing.

(6) There is a student from Japan in your class. Before class begins, some of the other students tease him, making fun of the shape of his eyes. Everyone laughs.

(7) During recess, the boys decide to play hide-and-seek. A girl wants to join them, but they say that girls aren't allowed to play.

(8) Your teacher passes out feathers for an art project. Several classmates stick the feathers in their hair and dance around wildly, shouting "Me, Indian!"

(9) A boy in your math class has trouble doing the homework and always makes a lot of mistakes. The other children laugh and call him "stupid" and "retard."

(10) A girl at your school uses a wheelchair. She wants to be in the class play, but the teacher says she can't because there are no parts for someone in a wheelchair.

Teaching Unity, Unit 4: Overcoming Prejudice, p. 95

"Barriers into Bonds"

Teacher's Guide, Script, and Patterns for Felt Lesson

Adapted from the Star Study Program felt lesson
on "The Elimination of Prejudice" © 1975 US-NSA

TO THE TEACHER: This packet contains a script, instructions and patterns for making a felt lesson on "Barriers into Bonds." In order to present the lesson, you will need either a felt board or carpet board (see instructions on page 45). A carpet board is more durable and has a more finished look.

After preparing the board, cut out the pattern pieces and stack them in order of use. Read through the script and repeat the actions until you can present the lesson smoothly. Read slowly and clearly with brief pauses for placement of the felt pieces. The objectives of the lesson are listed below. The children will be able to:

(1) List some of the ways that people are different.

(2) Explain how prejudice has made differences into barriers.

(3) Show how these barriers can be turned into bonds.

Teaching Unity, Unit 4: Overcoming Prejudice, p. 96

– Script for felt lesson –

"Barriers into Bonds"

	NARRATION	ACTION
1	All around the world people are different in many ways.	Place globe in center of felt board and add the people around it in a circle.
2	We have different skin colors, speak different languages, come from different cultures, live in different countries, and practice different religions.	As each difference is mentioned, place it above one of the people.
3	Some people dislike others without even knowing them just because of these differences. This is called prejudice. Because of prejudice, our differences have become barriers between us.	Place the barriers between the people.
4	But we can overcome these prejudices through the power of unity.	Clasp your hands together.
5	When we realize that we all belong to the same human family, we will see our differences as a source of beauty and strength. Then these barriers will become bonds.	Flip the barriers over and turn them sideways to form bonds.
6	When the human family is united, the world will finally be at peace.	Add the dove above the earth.

Instructions for Making Felt Pieces

1. Photocopy the pattern pages, and laminate the copies for durability if desired.
2. Carefully cut out the patterns and labels.
3. Place each pattern on the correct color of felt and trace.
4. Carefully cut out each felt piece.
5. Glue labels to the felt pieces and add velcro as indicated on the next page.
6. Store script and felt pieces in a zip-lock plastic bag for ease of use.

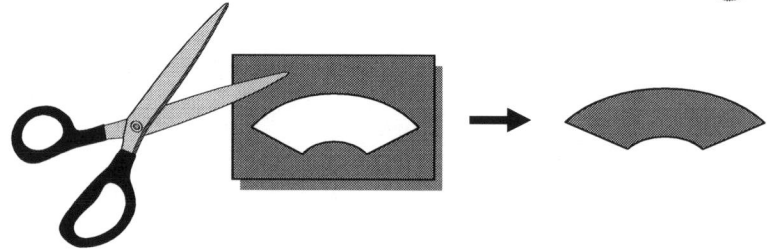

Materials

- ❑ Pattern pieces (on following pages)
- ❑ Pen for tracing patterns
- ❑ Sharp scissors
- ❑ Different colors of felt
- ❑ Stick-on velcro (plastic loop side)
- ❑ White paper to print labels
- ❑ White craft glue

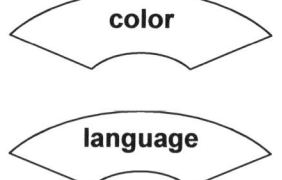

Pre-cut felt people can also be purchased through teacher supply stores, elementary classroom catalogs or online. For example:
- www.kidscraftsplus.com > felt people
- www.hyglossproducts.com > felt people
- www.multiculturalkids.com > felt figures

Patterns for Felt Lesson on "Barriers into Bonds"

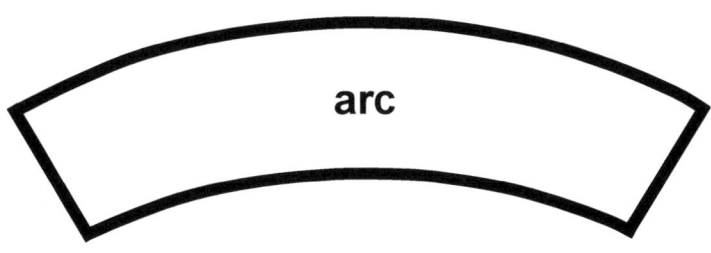

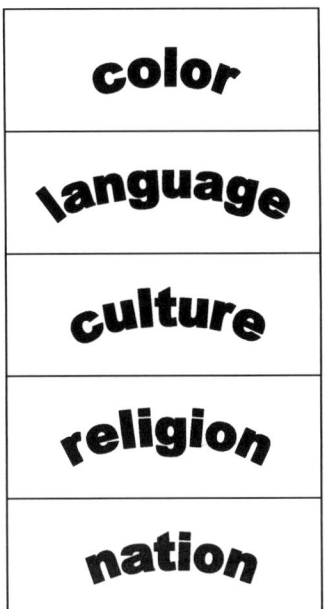

1. Photocopy this page, laminate if desired and cut out the arc pattern.

2. Using the **arc** pattern, cut out 5 identical pieces of white felt.

3. Using the same pattern, cut 5 more pieces of felt, each from a different color.

   Use bright colors that contrast with the felt board, for example, red, blue, dark yellow, light green and dark green.

4. Glue each white piece to a colored piece to make 5 felt sandwiches, and allow to dry.

5. Cut out the 5 labels and glue each one onto the white side of a different felt sandwich.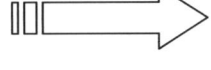

6. Add small pieces of velcro on both sides of each felt sandwich, as indicated below.

Tip: For easier cut-outs, if not laminating the patterns, copy them onto peel-and-stick adhesive paper.

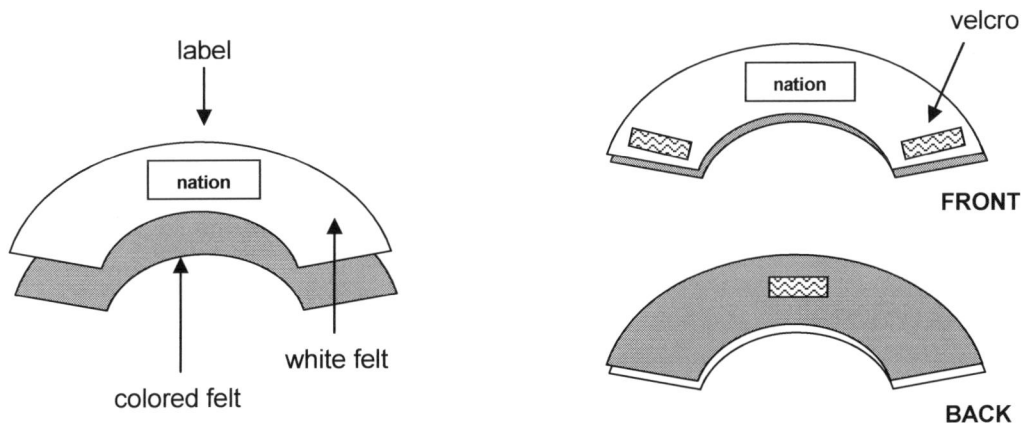

Tip: Use a generous amount of glue so it soaks into the felt for a stronger bond.

Teaching Unity, Unit 4: Overcoming Prejudice, p. 99

Patterns for felt lesson on "Barriers into Bonds"

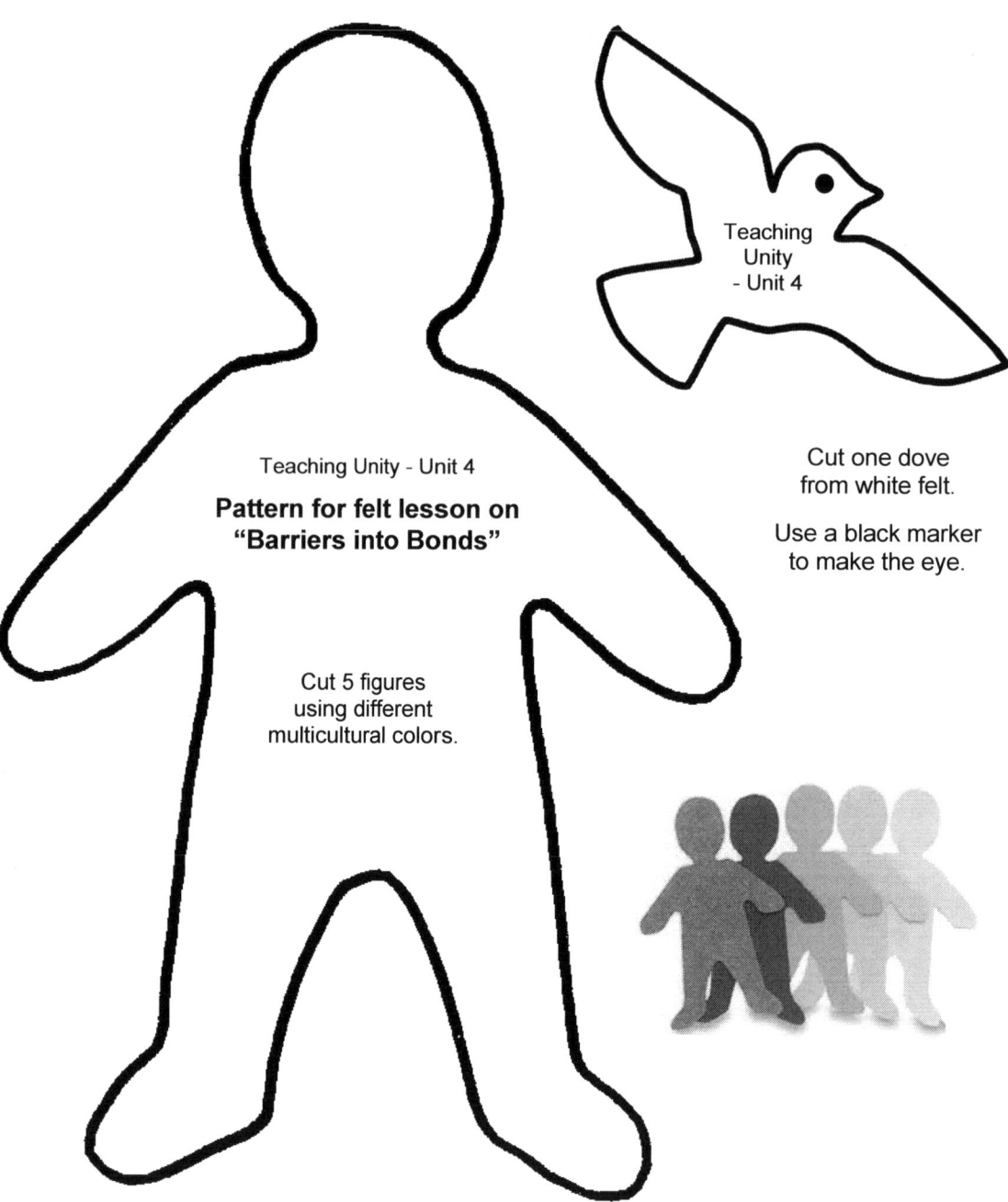

Teaching Unity - Unit 4

Pattern for felt lesson on "Barriers into Bonds"

Cut 5 figures using different multicultural colors.

Teaching Unity - Unit 4

Cut one dove from white felt.

Use a black marker to make the eye.

Photocopy this page. Using the people pattern as a guide, cut out five identical figures, each one from a different color of felt. Use multicultural colors, for example, light brown, dark brown, off-white, copper, pink or beige.

Teaching Unity, Unit 4: Overcoming Prejudice, p. 100

Patterns for felt lesson on "Barriers into Bonds"

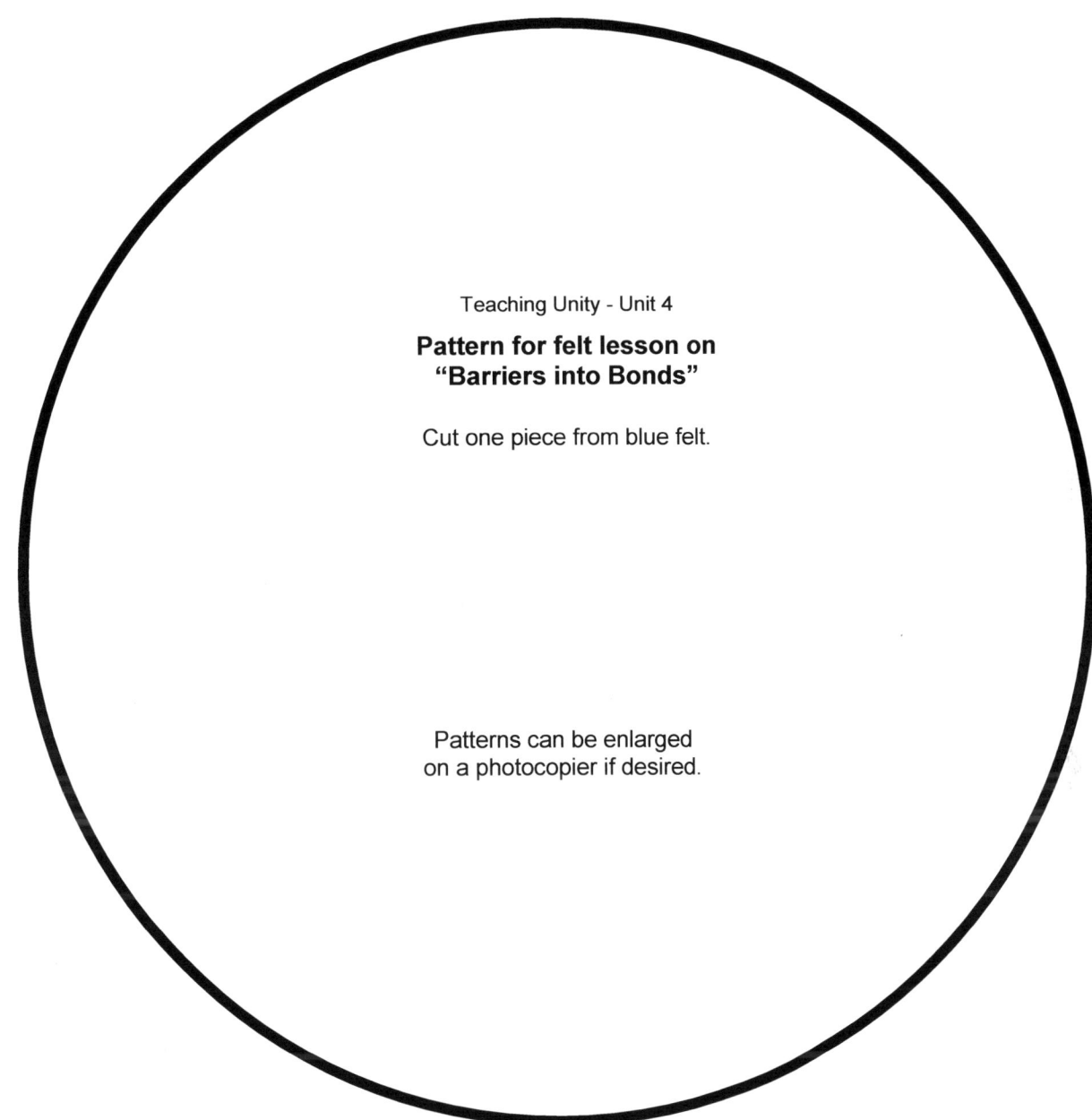

Teaching Unity - Unit 4

Pattern for felt lesson on "Barriers into Bonds"

Cut one piece from blue felt.

Patterns can be enlarged on a photocopier if desired.

Photocopy this page. Using the pattern as a guide, cut out one blue felt circle to make the earth.

Patterns for felt lesson on "Barriers into Bonds"

Teaching Unity - Unit 4

Cut from green felt.

Pattern for felt lesson on "Barriers into Bonds"

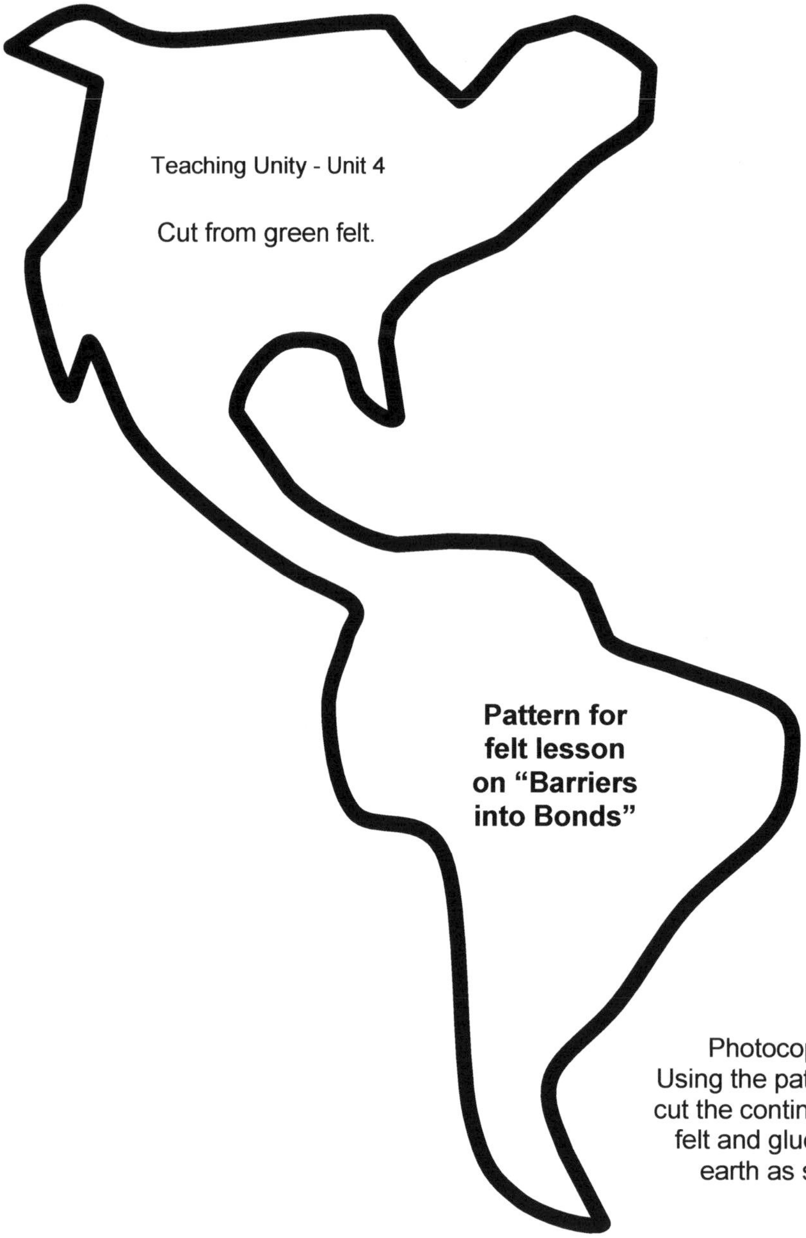

Photocopy this page. Using the patterns as a guide, cut the continents out of green felt and glue them onto the earth as shown below.

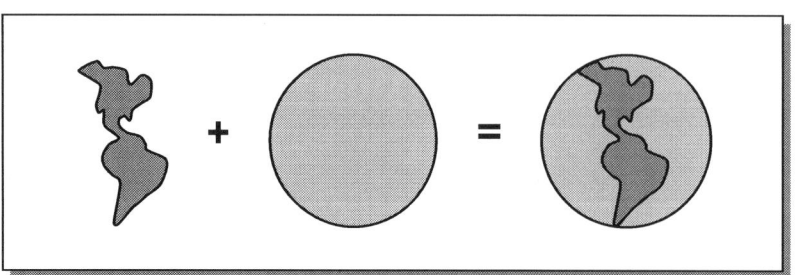

Teaching Unity, Unit 4: Overcoming Prejudice, p. 102

Worksheet for activity #14

BARRIERS INTO BONDS

Answer the questions below, then color in the picture.

1. List some ways that people are alike: _____
   _____

2. List some ways that people are different: _____
   _____

3. Explain how prejudice has made our differences into barriers between people: _____
   _____

4. What is prejudice? _____
   _____

5. How can we turn those barriers into bonds? _____
   _____

Teaching Unity, Unit 4: Overcoming Prejudice, p. 103

Craft for activity #15

BARRIERS INTO BONDS

Students will be making a diagram to illustrate the concept of turning people-made barriers (skin color, language, nationality and other differences) into bonds of unity. Younger students may wish to make the simpler cut-and-paste version using colored paper. Older students may prefer the more challenging moveable version using vinyl or craft foam.

The children will have about 45 minutes to work. When they have completed their project and cleaned up their work area, they may assist others who need help. Remind them to label all projects with their names. Quiet music can be played in the background if desired.

Materials

- ❏ Sharp scissors
- ❏ White glue or glue sticks
- ❏ Felt markers for printing title
- ❏ Pens or pencils for tracing patterns
- ❏ Pattern pieces (one set for every 4-5 students)
- ❏ Ruler or straightedge for aligning title (optional)

- ❏ Construction paper in a variety of colors
- ❏ White poster board (approx. 11 x 14 inches or 28 x 36 cm)

for the paper version

- ❏ Craft foam and thick vinyl in a variety of colors*
- ❏ Long metal brads (5 per student) and an awl (one for every 8-10 students)
- ❏ White foam core board (approx. 14 x 18 inches or 36 x 45 cm)
  (The foam board needs to be larger to allow room for the arcs to turn.)

for the moveable version

* The five moveable arcs can be cut from thick solid-color vinyl placemats, available at dollar and discount stores. The remaining pattern pieces can be cut from regular craft foam or from peel-and-stick craft foam which is easier for children to use.

Preparation

1. Photocopy the pattern page and laminate.

2. Carefully cut out the patterns which will be used for students to trace.
   (Make one set for every 4-5 children and store in labeled zip-lock plastic bags.)

3. Cut the construction paper into 1/4 sheets so children will have smaller pieces to work with—creating less waste. Save out a few whole sheets for making the titles.

Instructions for paper version

1. Select the paper needed for your design (see box below).

2. Trace around each pattern and cut out to make the following:

What	How Many	Color
earth	1	blue
continents	1	green
arcs	5	5 different colors (e.g. red, orange, yellow, purple, turquoise)
humans	5	5 different colors (e.g. light brown, dark brown, black, white, pink)

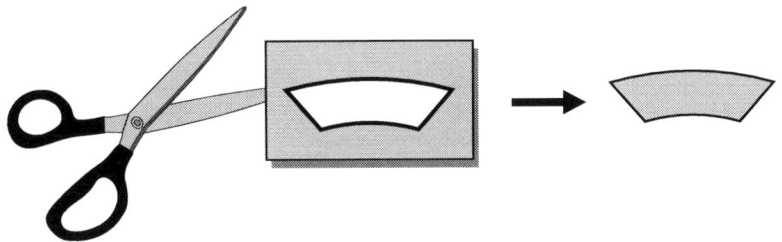

3. Arrange the pieces on the poster board with people's feet touching the earth and arcs at about shoulder height. Leave some room at the top for a title.

4. When you are satisfied with the arrangement, glue the pieces down, beginning with the earth.

5. Write a title on a separate strip of paper and glue near the top of the poster. (See example below.) Use a ruler or straightedge to help align the letters.

Turning Barriers into Bonds
through unity in diversity

6. Find someone else who has finished and take turns presenting your project to each other.

Tips:

You can cut out the humans and arcs one at a time or stack the colored paper and cut through several layers at once to save time.

When gluing, make sure any sides with ink are facing down. For the continents, if you don't want the ink to show, trace the pattern upside down.

Teaching Unity, Unit 4: Overcoming Prejudice, p. 105

Instructions for moveable version

1. Use foam core board as the backing for your design. As an alternative to foam core, cut a piece of cardboard to the desired size and cover with plain light-colored contact paper. Poster board will also work but is not as sturdy.

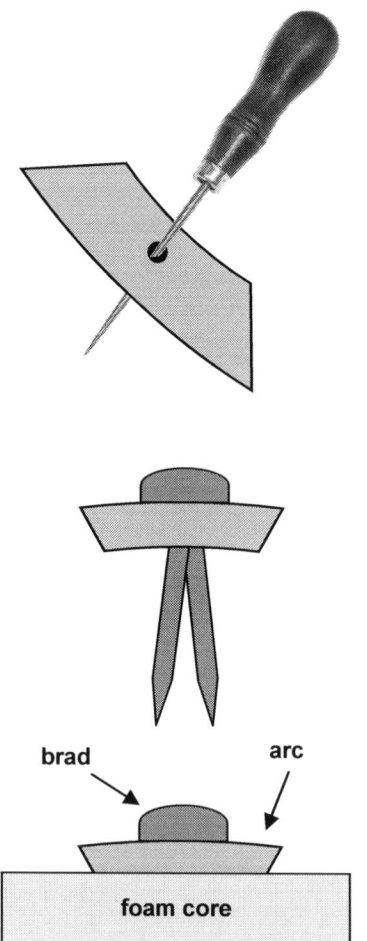

2. Follow the same basic directions for making the paper version but cut the arcs from thick vinyl instead of paper. Craft foam also works but is not as sturdy. The earth and people can be cut from construction paper or craft foam.

3. After arranging the pieces on the board, glue everything down except for the arcs.

4. Using a pen, make a dot in the center of each arc. An easy way to do this is to bend (not fold) the arc gently in half to find the center.

5. Using the awl, carefully poke a small hole through the center of each arc. (Adult supervision or assistance is needed for this step.)

6. Mark the spot on the foam board where you want to place each arc. An easy way to do this is to position the arc, then gently push the tip of the pen through the hole to mark the spot. Make the top of the arc even with the top of the heads, so there is room for it to turn.

7. Using the awl, carefully poke holes through the five spots you just marked on the foam board. Attach each arc to the board with a brad. This will allow the arcs to turn.

8. When presenting your project, start with all of the arcs perpendicular to the earth to form barriers between people. When talking about the importance of unity, turn the barriers sideways to form bonds.

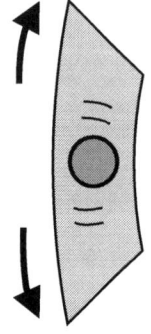

Teaching Unity, Unit 4: Overcoming Prejudice, p. 106

Craft patterns for "Barriers into Bonds" - activity #15

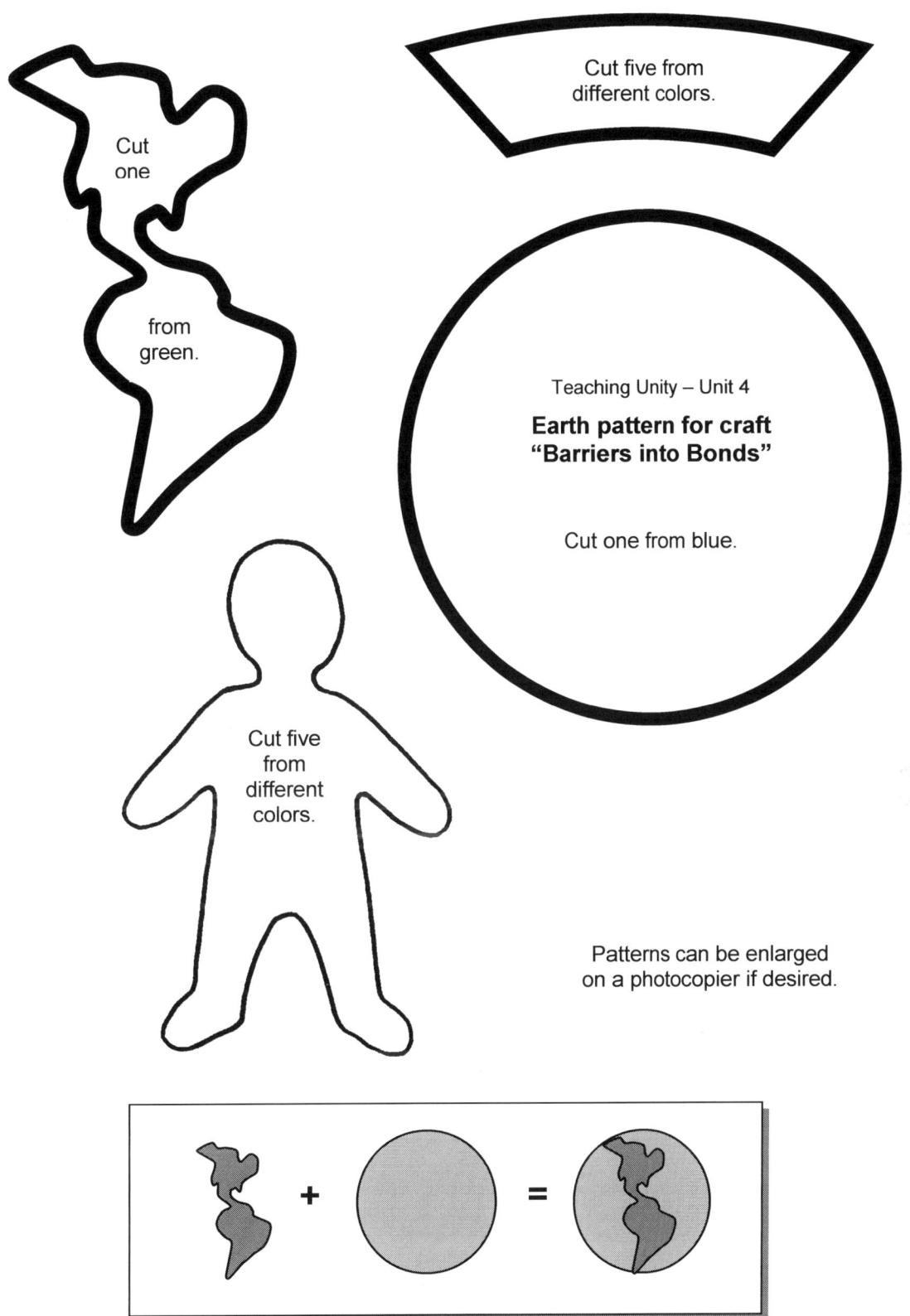

Cut one from green.

Cut five from different colors.

Teaching Unity – Unit 4

Earth pattern for craft "Barriers into Bonds"

Cut one from blue.

Cut five from different colors.

Patterns can be enlarged on a photocopier if desired.

Samples of the "Barriers into Bonds" craft

Paper version

Moveable version

To make a frame, glue your finished project onto a slightly larger poster board of a different color.

Reading for activity #18

The Circle of Unity

(Read slowly with feeling.)

We are going to make a unity circle using red yarn. Red is a symbol of the blood of all human beings. We are all part of the circle of life. Each thread represents your contribution—your special gift to the world.

As you stand in this circle, quietly tie the ends of your yarn together with your two neighbors, making one knot on the left and one on the right. This shows that we are all connected.

Now take a moment and just think quietly about our circle as we stand here together. We have been working and sharing and learning together all _____ *(weekend/week/semester/year)*. We are united, and that feels good.

Now, close your eyes and without moving, imagine your family and all of your friends joining us here in the circle.

Now, in your mind, widen the circle. Keep your eyes closed and picture all of your neighbors joining us here. Imagine your teachers coming too, your doctor, the bus driver, the mail carrier, people who work at the store, firefighters and police officers—all the people you know. Imagine everyone smiling. People are happy to see each other. They are happy to be together.

Now, in your mind, make the circle even larger. Invite all of _____ *(your town)* into the circle. Without moving, imagine the circle just keeps growing and growing. Everyone in _____ *(state or province)* is joining us. Now add everyone in the whole country and, finally, the entire world. Invite every human being to join our circle of unity. Our arms reach around the planet.

Now, with your eyes still closed, think of one person that you know. Think of something you can do to help that person feel like part of our circle. What can you do today, or next week, to make that person feel included and happy? Remember what you are thinking. Take it with you when you leave here today and then act on it.

Now, still keeping your eyes closed, let's end this class with our first memory quote about the light of unity. Are you ready? All together:

> *So powerful is the light of unity that it can illuminate the whole earth.*

Good! Now slowly open your eyes, look around you, and remember.

MATERIALS NEEDED – UNIT 4

> Note to Teachers: Most of the handouts are included with the lessons and are grouped in the handout section of this book for ease of photocopying. They are also available for download from our website (below). The remaining items, once obtained, can be re-used for many years. The wide variety of activities and materials allows for diverse learning styles. It also increases understanding and retention of the concepts, and it makes the lessons more memorable and enjoyable for the students.

Downloads available from: www.TeachingUnity.com

- ☐ **General Items**
  - White board, easel, markers, eraser
  - Folders and song sheets for each student
  - Paper and pens / pencils for all

- ☐ **Introduction** (activity #1, p. 78-79)
  - Candle, fruit, bowl

  The questions are also found in the PowerPoint review of Units 1-3, available as a free download from our website.

- ☐ **Bridges and Barriers** (activity #2, p. 80)
  - One red and one green 3x5 index card for each student (or two other colors)
  - Blank classroom wall or large bulletin board on which to attach the cards
  - Black markers (one for every two students)
  - Tape or pushpins

- ☐ **The Sneetches*** (activity #4, p. 82)
  - Handout with excerpt from *The Sneetches* by Dr. Seuss
  - *The Sneetches* book and/or online versions of the poem (optional)

- ☐ **Sneetches Simulation** (activity #5, p. 82-83)
  - Colored stickers or large paper stars with masking tape (one for each student)
  - Wrapped candy or other small treats (enough for all of the students)
  - Snacks for all

- ☐ **Putdowns** (activity #6, p. 84)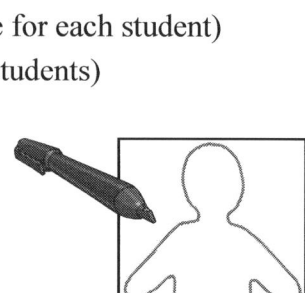
  - Sheet of chart paper and large marker for drawing the child
  - Scratch paper, tape, small trash can
  - Small box filled with common putdowns (ugly, weird, retarded…) written on individual slips of paper (optional)

- ❏ **Personal Stories** (activity #7, p. 85)
    - Handout for group leaders (if using assistants)
    - Poster with questions for small group discussion (if not using assistants)

- ❏ **Put-ups** (activity #8, p. 85)
    - A paper cup for each student or a blank page with their name taped to the wall
    - Scratch paper or post-it notes (enough so every student has one for each other student)

- ❏ **Putdowns and Prejudice** (activity #9, p. 86)
    - Handout on "Dealing with Putdowns and Prejudice"

- ❏ **Name It, Claim It** (activity #10, p. 86)
    - Handout on "Name It, Claim It, Stop It"

- ❏ **Creating Unity** (activity #11, p. 87)
    - Handout and/or role play cards on "Creating Unity"

- ❏ **Barriers into Bonds** (activity #13, p. 88)
    - Felt board and easel
    - Felt lesson (script and patterns included)

- ❏ **Barriers into Bonds** (activity #14, p. 88)
    - Worksheet for each student
    - Colored pencils, markers or crayons

- ❏ **Barriers into Bonds** (activity #15, p. 88)
    - Craft samples and instructions
    - Craft materials (see separate list)

- ❏ **The Circle of Unity** (activity #18, p. 89)
    - Reading on "The Circle of Unity" (included with lesson)
    - Red yarn cut into 18-inch (46 cm) lengths (one per student)

---

* The excerpt from *The Sneetches and Other Stories* is used here with permission. The illustrated book (ISBN: 0-394-80089-3) can be ordered from the publisher, Random House Books for Young Readers: **www.randomhouse.com**, or from **www.Amazon.com**. Pictures can be found online at: **www.Google.com/images**. Type *"sneetches"* in the search box. If pictures are not available, you can cut out a green five-pointed star to show the children while you read the poem.

★ ★ ★ ★ ★

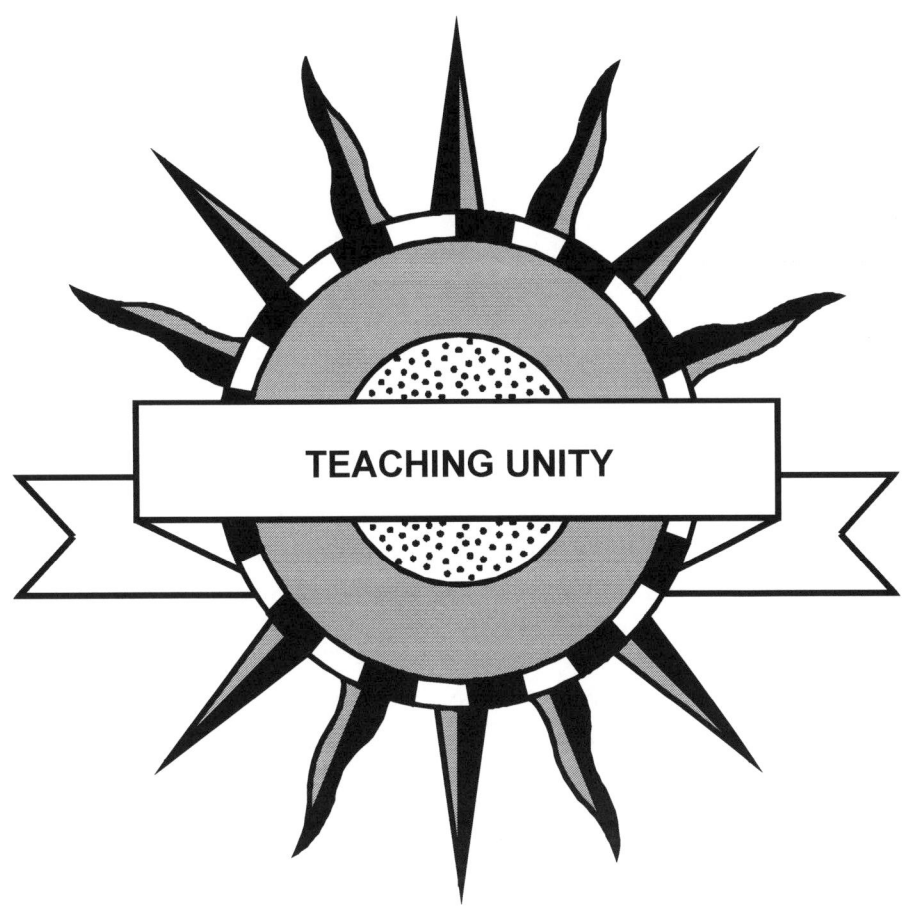

Music

Music Program

To the Music Coordinator

Singing brings people together for an enjoyable activity. It uplifts the spirit and connects the hearts. It is also an excellent tool for memorizing information and for teaching and reinforcing new ideas.

The songs included in this teacher's guide have been selected to help children learn about unity. The students should have song sheets in their handout packets. As the music coordinator, your job is to help them learn some of these songs.

If classes are held during an intensive format such as a summer camp or weekend retreat, a morning sing-a-long can be scheduled each day for this purpose. There may also be opportunities for singing after lunch and in the evenings. Classroom teachers might need your assistance with leading songs that are part of their lesson. In addition, the music coordinator may be asked to help with a children's performance and rehearsal. Check with the organizers for a schedule with the exact times.

As the song leader, you should be enthusiastic, confident and encouraging. Be patient with children who are shy or who don't catch on right away. When teaching a song for the first time, you will need to sing slowly with a lot of repetition. If you play an instrument, you can bring it with you to accompany the singing and to keep the beat.

Be sure to learn the songs and the correct meaning and pronunciation of all the words beforehand. Arrive early so your session starts on time. Bring a music stand if available.

A song sheet and musical scores are included on the following pages. Some of the selections have been simplified and shortened for group singing with children. If you know a different melody for a particular song, feel free to use your version.

You may be familiar with additional songs related to the theme of unity and these can be included as well. Examples can be found at: **www.raffinews.com** and **www.rembakids.com**.

To start a sing-a-long session:

- Ask the children to take out their song sheets and find the first song.
- Ask them what they think the song is about and explain if necessary.
- Pronounce and define any difficult words.
- Play the song through once, encouraging those who know it to sing with you.
- If necessary, have children repeat each line in a speaking voice before trying to sing.
- Give the starting note and play or clap out the rhythm while everyone sings.
- Practice several times before going on to the next song.

Transposing a Song

> Idea from Dick Grover

If the notes of a song are too high or too low to sing comfortably, you can easily change the song to a new key—called *transposing*. On a guitar, the easiest way to change the key is by using a capo. You can also follow the steps below.

1. Start by determining the original key (usually the first chord on the sheet music). Play that chord and sing a few lines of the song. If it is too high or too low, you will need to find a more comfortable key.

2. Play a different chord and try singing the song in that key. If it feels comfortable, you have found the right key. If not, play another chord and sing a few lines until you have found a comfortable key for you. You will transpose the song to that key. For example, if the song is too low in the original key of D but feels just right in the key of G, you will transpose the entire song to the key of G.

3. Using the chart on the right and moving clockwise, count the number of steps from the original chord to the transposed chord. For example, there are five steps from D to G.

4. Then go through the entire song, changing all the chords by the same number of steps. Based on our example, you would raise all the D chords to G. All the E chords would change to A. An A7 would become a D7, etc. Write the new chord directly over the syllable you will be singing with that chord, or you will be out of rhythm when you play the song.

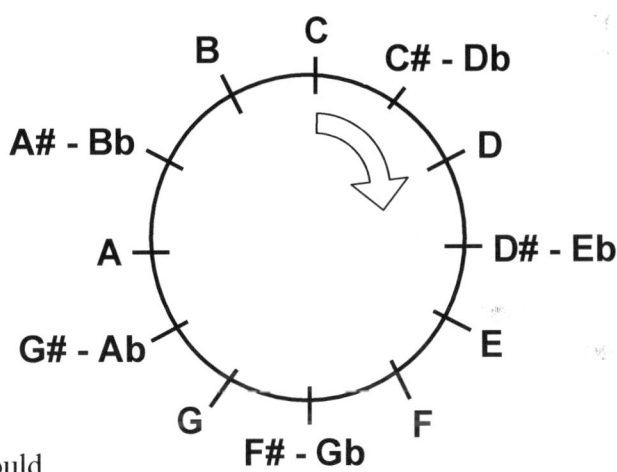

means "sharp" (It raises that note by a half step.)

b means "flat" (It lowers that note by a half step.)

C# and Db are the same note and count together as one step. This is also true for D#/Eb, F#/Gb, G#/Ab, and A#/Bb.

SONG SHEET

Most of these songs are copyrighted and are used with permission.

One Planet, One People

(Echo song by Sandee English)

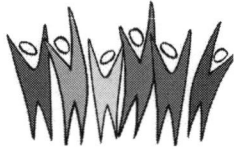

**One planet, one people,
We all live together.
One planet, one people, please.**

All the world is full of people,
And our hearts all beat as one.
Though we're different from each other,
We're illumined by the rays of just one sun.

(chorus)

We are flowers of one garden,
We are leaves of just one tree.
Though we're different from each other,
We're illumined by the light of unity.

(chorus)

What Mankind Has to Learn

(by Creadell Haley)

There's only one race
of people on the earth,
But man did divide it and so...
There's a Black race, a White race,
What mankind has to learn,
Is that there's only one race to know.

Earth was one country
back when it all began,
But man did divide it and so...
There's a China, a Turkey,
What mankind has to learn,
Is that Earth is one country to know.

There's only oneness
throughout the universe,
But man won't believe it and so...
He divides and multiplies it,
Oh won't he ever learn,
That there's only oneness to know.

Good Neighbors

(by Dick Grover)

**Good neighbors come in all colors,
Black, red, yellow and tan.
Our outsides may look different,
But we're the family of Woman and Man.**

When my doorbell starts to ring,
I can't see the ringer's skin.
Even if he had bright blue skin,
I'd welcome him right in. (chorus)

When my neighbor starts to cry,
That hurts him and that hurts I.
Even if he had orange eyes,
It hurts him when he cries. (chorus)

When my neighbor starts to share,
Joy and happiness everywhere,
Even if she had purple hair,
I wouldn't even care. (chorus)

Hawaiian Unity Song

(Echo song; composer unknown)

We are drops of one ocean,
We are waves of one sea...

**Come and join us...
In our quest for unity,
It's a way of life for you and me.**

We are flowers of one garden.
We are leaves of one tree... (chorus)

Black and white, red and yellow,
Lovely colors of humanity... (chorus)

All the earth is one country,
We are one family... (chorus)

We are drops of one ocean,
We are waves of one sea... (chorus)

Rapp Song*
(by Red and Kathy Grammer)

Now all across this big, wide world
There are lots of boys and lots of girls
With different eyes and different noses
Different hair and different clothes
It's a magical thing, it's a wonderful game
We all look different but we're all the same
Now the differences are great
and the differences are small
But that's just part of the beauty of it all
We're all like notes that make up a song
We need everybody so come on sing along.

**Hello (hello) Hola (hola) Jambo, Jambo
Gan lowee lay mun ho ma**

Now some folks think that they are the best
They don't know how to get along
They say the heck with the rest
So they go their own way
and they do their own thing
But the song sounds weak
when its time for them to sing
But if you gather up folks
from all kinds of places
With different ways of talking
and different color faces
There's something special
each one brings along
And when they all sing together,
now you really got a song.

(chorus)

So open up your eyes and take a look around
There's all kinds of kids that live in your town
Maybe black, maybe white,
maybe rich, maybe poor
You've got to get to know them all
That's what friends are for
'Cause the differences are great
and the differences are small
But that's just part of the beauty of it all
We're all like notes that make up a song
We need everybody so come on sing along.

(chorus)

Listen*
(by Red and Kathy Grammer)

Listen...can you hear the sound
Of hearts beating all the world around
Down in the valley, out on the plain
Everywhere around the world
a heartbeat sounds the same.

**Black or white, red or tan
It's the heart of the family of man
Whoa beating away (3x)**

Listen...can you hear the sound
Of laughter all the world around
High in the mountains, down by the sea
Everywhere around the world
laughter sounds the same to me.

**Black or white, red or tan
It's the heart of the family of man
Whoa laughing away (3x)**

Oo la la la la la... (8x)

Listen...can you hear the sound
Of singing all the world around
Walking through the jungle
or on a busy city street
Everywhere around the world
singing always sounds so sweet.

**Black or white, red or tan
It's the heart of the family of man
Whoa singing away (3x)**

> * "Listen" and "Rapp Song" are from the recording *Teaching Peace* © 1986 Smilin' Atcha Music. Written by Red and Kathy Grammer, distributed through Red Note Records, < www.redgrammer.com >.

SONGS ABOUT UNITY

1. Good Neighbors 119

2. Hawaiian Unity Song 120

3. One Planet, One People 121

4. What Mankind Has to Learn 122

5. Listen ....(see below)

6. Rapp Song ....(see below)

7. We Can Build a Beautiful World 123

Notes and Acknowledgements

Our gratitude goes to Jonathan Gottlieb for transcribing the music for several of these songs. Appreciation to Tony Lee for permission to use the "Hawaiian Unity Song" that first appeared in the *Building Bridges* songbook published by Kalimát Press: Los Angeles, 1984.

"Listen" and "Rapp Song" are from *Teaching Peace*, Red Grammer's award-winning children's recording. The CD is available on his website: **www.redgrammer.com**, or the songs can be purchased individually from: **www.apple.com/itunes.** The children may also enjoy singing along with Red's other inspiring songs about unity, including "Teaching Peace," "I Think You're Wonderful," "With Two Wings" and "Places in the World." The lyrics for these songs can be found on his website. Red is also available for school concerts, teacher workshops and keynote presentations.

For an informal rendition of "Good Neighbors Come in All Colors" by Dick Grover, visit: **www.youtube.com** and enter "good neighbors Bangalore" in the search box.

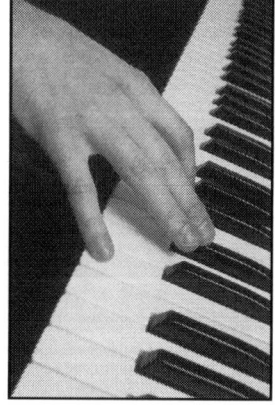

Russ Garcia's wonderful children's opera, "We Can Build a Beautiful World," is part of the children's performance. Both the music and script are included here.

Some of these songs have been simplified and shortened for group singing with children.

Good Neighbors

Dick Grover
Used with permission

Good neighbors - come in all co-lors: Black, red, yel-low and tan; Our
out-sides may look dif-ferent, but we're the fami-ly of Wo-man and Man.

1. When my door-bell starts to ring,___ I can't see the ring-er's skin;___
2. When my neigh-bor starts to cry,___ that hurts him and that hurts I;___
3. When my neigh-bor starts to share,___ joy and happi-ness ev'-ry where,___

Ev-en if he had bright blue skin, I'd wel-come him right in. 'Cause
Ev-en if he had or-ange eyes, it hurts him when he cries. 'Cause
Ev-en if she had pur-ple hair, I would-n't ev-en care. 'Cause

Hawaiian Unity Song
(Echo Song)

Composer unknown
From Building Bridges songbook
Used with permission

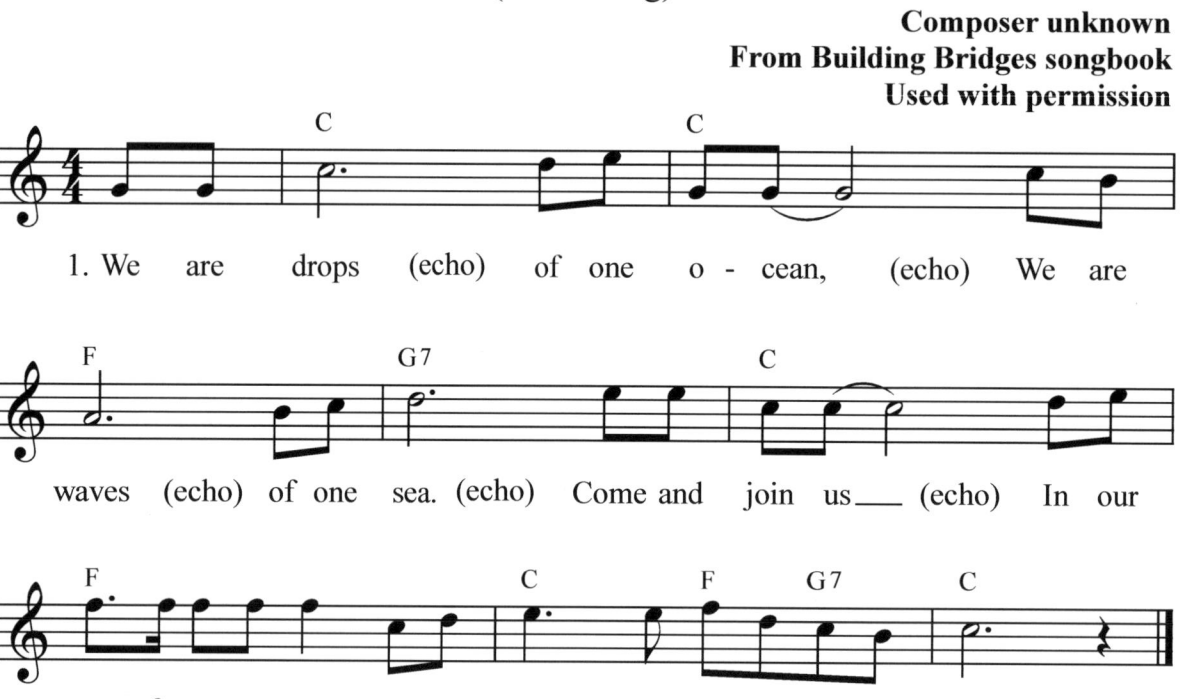

CHORUS (together):
In our quest for unity.
It's a way of life for you and me.

2. We are flowers of one garden,
   We are leaves of one tree.
     Come and join us... (chorus)

3. Black and white, red and yellow,
   Lovely colors of humanity.
     Come and join us... (chorus)

4. All the earth is one country,
   We are one family.
     Come and join us... (chorus)

5. We are drops of one ocean,
   We are waves of one sea.
     Come and join us... (chorus)

One Planet, One People, Please

Sandee English
Used with permission

[Note: The chorus is sung in unison. The verses begin with
the leader singing a phrase which is echoed by the group,
until the last line of each verse which is sung in unison.]

Teaching Unity, Music, p. 121

What Mankind Has to Learn

Creadell Haley
Modified for use with school children

1. There's only one race, of people on the earth, But man did divide it, and so... There's a Black race, a White race, What mankind has to learn, is that there's only one race to know.
2. Earth was one country, back when it all began, But man did divide it, and so... There's a China, a Turkey, What mankind has to learn, is that Earth is one country to know.
3. There's only oneness throughout the universe, But man won't believe it, and so... He divides and multiplies it, Oh, won't he ever learn, that there's only oneness to know.

We Can Build a Beautiful World

(c) Russ Garcia
Used with permission
Excerpted and simplified

(A) Green peo-ple are the best. Far bet-ter than the rest. We hate you be-
(B) Purple peo-ple are the best. Far bet-ter than the rest. We hate you be-

cause you're dif-ferent! We are su-pe-ri-or. You are in-fe-ri-or.
cause you're dif-ferent! We are su-pe-ri-or. You are in-fe-ri-or.

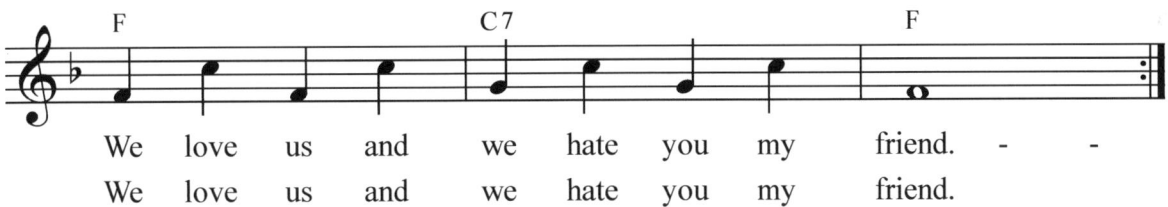
We love us and we hate you my friend. - -
We love us and we hate you my friend.

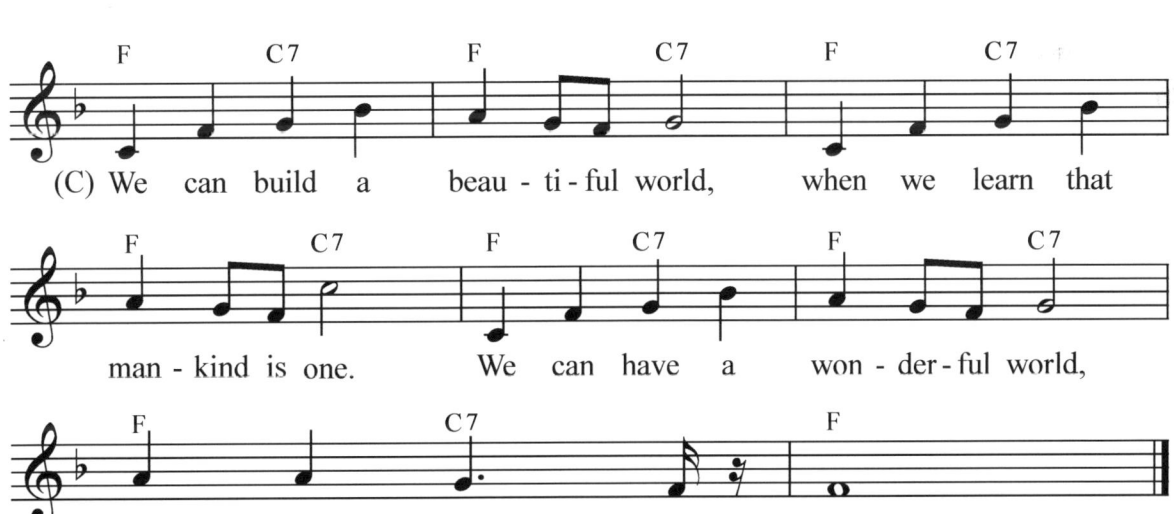
(C) We can build a beau-ti-ful world, when we learn that
man-kind is one. We can have a won-der-ful world,
when we learn to love!

Group A sings the first verse. Group B sings the second verse. Then Group A repeats the first verse.
When they sing, "We hate you...," Group B starts again to create a round.
When Group A sings "friend" for the second time, Group C begins. Later, all join in.
(See next page for script and additional verses.)

Teaching Unity, Music, p. 123

We Can Build a Beautiful World

© Russ Garcia. Music excerpted and simplified. Used with permission.

Divide children into three groups with costumes as indicated below. Include choreographed gestures if desired. The audience can also be divided into three groups, given the words, and asked to join in.

Group A: Green people are the best. Far better than the rest.
We hate you because you're different!
We are superior, you are inferior.
We love us and we hate you, my friend.

Group B: Purple people are the best. Far better than the rest.
We hate you because you're different!
We are superior, you are inferior.
We love us and we hate you, my friend.

(Sung in a round)

A: Green people are the best. Far better than the rest.
B: (silent)

A: We hate you because you're different!
B: Purple people are the best. Far better than the rest.

A: We are superior, you are inferior.
B: We hate you because you're different!

A: We love us and we hate you, my...
B: We are superior, you are inferior.

A: ...friend.
B: We love us and we hate you, my...
C: We can build a ...

A: We love us and we hate you.
B: ...friend.
C: ...beautiful world...

A: (silent)
B: We love us and we hate you.
C: ...when we learn that...

A: (silent)
B: (silent)
C: ...mankind is one.

Costumes
Group A: Green T-shirts
Group B: Purple T-shirts
Group C: Red or multi-colored T-shirts

Sample Gestures
For Us: Thumbs up, pat heart, thumbs in lapels

For Them: Thumbs down, press palm out, hold nose

Unifiers: Help all join hands.

All: We can have a wonderful world, when we learn to love.

We can build a beautiful world,
When we learn the earth is one land.
We can have a wonderful world,
When we learn to love.

We can build a beautiful world,
When we learn to love all mankind.
We can have a wonderful world,
**WHEN WE LEARN TO LOVE!
LOVE!! LOVE!!! LOVE!!!! LOVE!!!!!**

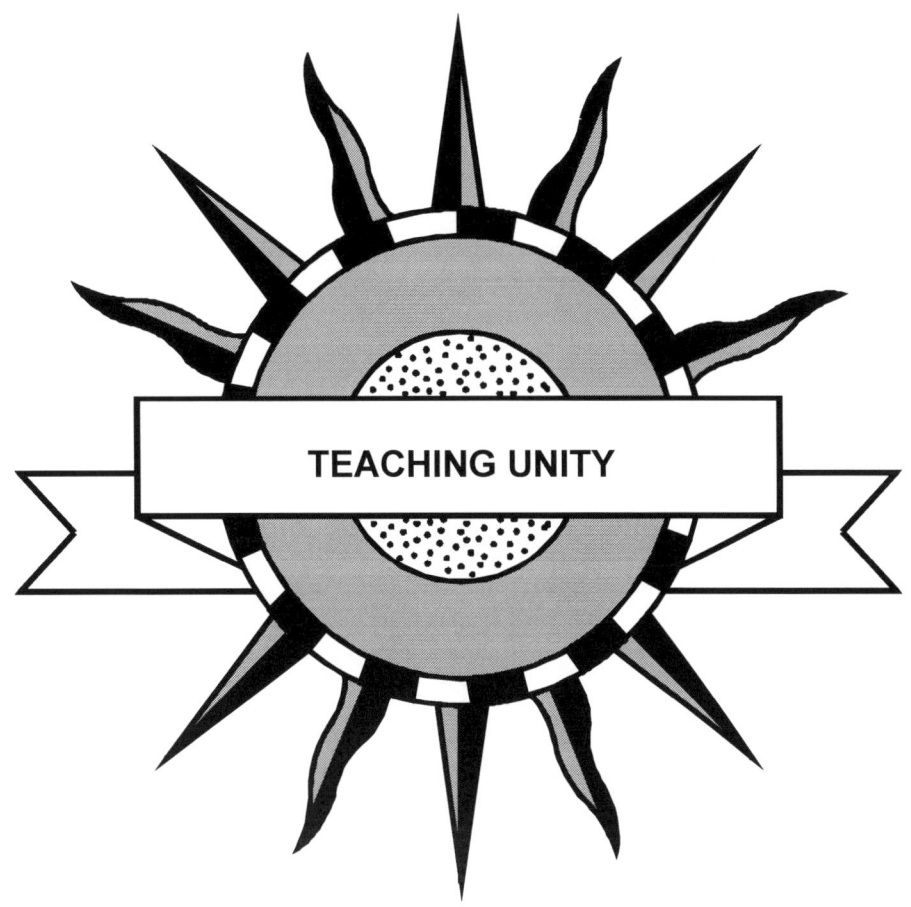

Handouts

HANDOUTS

Student handouts from all of the lessons are included in this section for ease of photocopying. These handouts, along with full-page color illustrations designed to accompany the lessons, can also be downloaded from: **www.TeachingUnity.com**. Illustrations can be posted on the wall during classes as an aid for visual learners and to help bring the readings to life.

For All Lessons

The Light of Unity (packet of readings)	127
Thought for the Day	141
Song Sheet	142

UNIT 1: The Light of Unity

Unity Is / Disunity Is	129
Word Puzzles	130
Unity (reading)	131

UNIT 2: Unity in Diversity

Unity in Diversity (reading)	133
Machines in Motion (group discussion questions)	48
Unity in Diversity (instructions for group leaders)	49

UNIT 3: The Colors We Are

Class Features Activity (instructions for group leaders)	66
Class Features Chart	67
Hooray for Skin (poem)	135
Personal Poster (blank form for craft project)	72

UNIT 4: Overcoming Prejudice

The Sneetches (poem excerpt)	136
Personal Stories (instructions for group leaders)	91
Dealing with Putdowns and Prejudice	137
Name It, Claim It, Stop It	138
Creating Unity (role plays)	139
Barriers into Bonds (worksheet)	140

THE LIGHT OF UNITY

Name: _____

THE FLOWER GARDEN OF HUMANITY

Teaching Unity, Handouts, p. 128

Unity Is:

- Knowing that we are part of one human family
- Treating all people with respect
- Valuing diversity
- Serving others
- Consulting together
- Making sure everyone is included
- Listening and trying to understand
- Working to make things better for all
- Solving conflicts peacefully
- Being kind to others even when they aren't perfect
- Showing cooperation and teamwork
- Forgiving people
- Making friends

Disunity Is:

- Being selfish
- Insisting on your own way
- Not getting along with others
- Thinking you are better than everyone else
- Showing prejudice and hatred
- Shouting at people
- Telling lies about others
- Leaving people out
- Name calling and putdowns
- Laughing when someone makes a mistake
- Arguing or fighting
- Hurting other people
- Not caring about others
- Backbiting

WORD PUZZLES
How many can you solve on your own?

1	2	3	4
[SAND]	MAN / BOARD	STAND / I	DICE DICE

5	6	7	8
WEAR / LONG	R / O / ROADS / D / S	RIGHT TIME	CYCLE CYCLE CYCLE

Teaching Unity, Handouts, p. 130

UNITY

One Human Family: There is only one race of people in the world. Do you know what it is called? That's right! It's the human race, and we all belong to it. We come in different shapes, sizes and colors, but we are one human family.

We may be young or old, tall or short, male or female, rich or poor. We may have dark skin, light skin or a color in-between. Some of us were born in China, South Africa, Canada, India or Brazil. We may speak English, Spanish, Arabic or Japanese. Some of us are good at sports, others at math, music or art. Some are Christians or Jews. Others are Hindus or Buddhists, agnostics, Muslims or Bahá'ís. We are alike and different in many ways. But we all share one planet—our common home.

Aloha
Bonjour
Hello
Hola
Jambo
Shalom

The Importance of Unity: Our world will be a better place when people learn to live and work together in unity. How can the human race make progress if we are each thinking only of ourselves? Without unity, how can we solve the world's most difficult problems like war, poverty, hunger, pollution and disease? Wouldn't it be better if we stopped fighting and worked together for peace, if we treated each other with justice and love, if we were united with our brothers and sisters from all around the world?

Like a Human Body: The human race is like a human body. The body has many different parts (eyes, ears, heart, lungs), and each part plays an important role. They all work together, so the person can be healthy and function well. What would happen if the different parts of the body refused to cooperate—if the mouth decided not to eat, the heart decided not to beat, or the left and right hands were always fighting with each other? In the same way, human beings (whether we are part of a family, a classroom, a neighborhood or village, a nation or the entire world) must learn to get along.

We Are Connected: People who understand unity know that everything in the whole universe is connected. Everything depends on something else to live. Animals must eat other animals or plants in order to survive. Plants need sunshine and rain to grow. Human beings are also connected to each other like links in a chain. Everything we do affects our planet and the other people on it. Every link is important. You are one of the links in that chain.

The Power of Unity: Unity is a powerful force that can connect us all. It can connect families, communities and countries. Unity gives us strength. We are more powerful working together than alone. Unity is like medicine for the world's sickness. Unity can bring peace, progress and light to the world.

UNITY IN DIVERSITY

The Flowers of One Garden: Imagine the flowers in a garden. Each flower has a different shape, its own special color and sweet-smelling perfume. But they all grow from the same earth, the same sun shines upon them, and the same clouds give them rain. Each flower is pleasing by itself, but when the different flowers are all together, the garden is even more beautiful.

It is the same with people. We are like beautiful flowers growing in a garden. We each have a different shape and our own special color. We speak different languages, wear different clothing, enjoy different music and eat different foods. Our diversity adds beauty to the garden of humanity.

The Value of Diversity

- Think of all the colors in nature. Can you name some of them?
- Can you imagine if the entire world were all <u>one</u> color?
- Which color should it be?
- Would a rainbow be as beautiful if all the bands were the same shade?
- Could you bake a cake with only one ingredient?
- What if all the musical instruments in an orchestra made the same sound?

Just think how dull it would be if all people everywhere looked and acted and thought and talked and dressed exactly the same! What if you had to eat the same food every day, wear the same clothes, read the same books and think the same thoughts for the rest of your life? What if you never, <u>ever</u> got to try anything new?

And what if all your friends were exactly like you?

Diversity is important because it gives us beauty, variety, choices and new ideas. Fresh ideas and different points of view are valuable as they can help us find creative solutions to the problems that confront us.

Unity Is Not Sameness: Unity does not mean sameness. Unity means respecting our differences and working together in harmony. It means knowing that each part has something valuable to contribute to the whole. Each member of the human family has something special to offer to the human race.

When we have **unity in diversity**, there is harmony, like the sound of different notes joined together in a perfect chord. We are showing unity in diversity when we all work and play and live together in peace.

HOORAY FOR SKIN
by Susan Engle

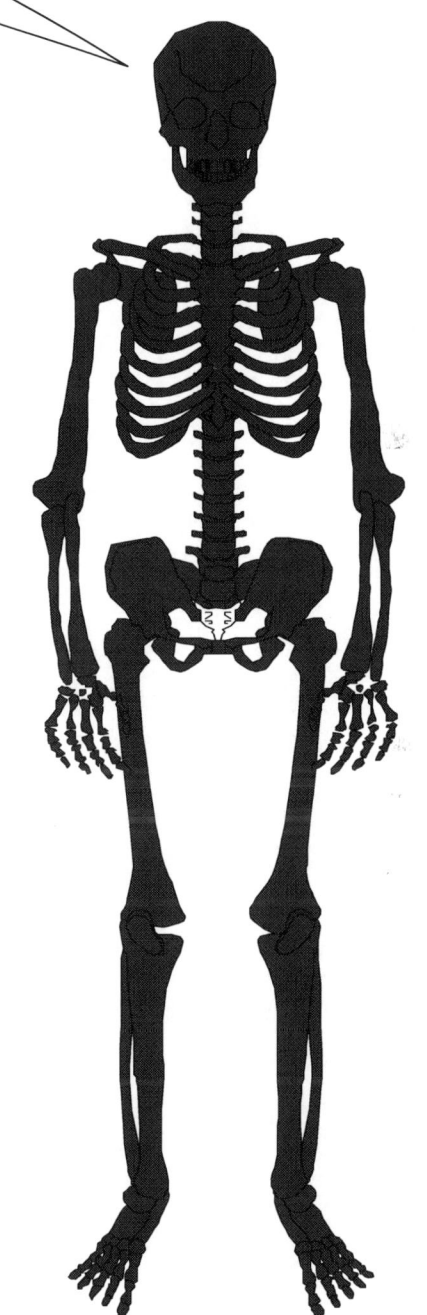

Rejoice and celebrate the skin
That keeps the veins and muscles in,
That keeps the cold and germies out.
That is what skin is all about.

Suppose that when you got your skin,
You found the skin side outside-in.
So when you talk to Mrs. Jones,
Your eyes meet over fat and bones,
And tissues, blue and white and red,
That stretch from toe to hand to head.
It makes me glad to have a skin
To keep the outside boneside-in.

Now there are folks who would be mad
If our insides were all they had
To tell all kinds of folks apart.
Maybe they'd learn to read the heart
Instead of judging from a hue
If one man's false and one man's true.

Let's all join hands and feast our eyes
On skins of every shape and size,
Of every tone of gold or white,
Of luscious black, of dark or light,
Of every shade that folks come in.
Rejoice and celebrate the skin.

© 1986, Susan Engle. Used with permission.

The Sneetches

From *The Sneetches and Other Stories* by Dr. Seuss.

TM & copyright © by Dr. Seuss Enterprises, L.P, 1953, 1954, 1961, renewed 1989.
Used by permission of Random House Children's Books, a division of Random House, Inc.

Now the Star-Belly Sneetches
Had bellies with stars.
The Plain-Belly Sneetches
Had none upon thars.

Those stars weren't so big
They were really so small.
You might think such a thing
Wouldn't matter at all.

But because they had stars
All the Star-Belly Sneetches
Would brag, "We're the best kind
Of Sneetches on beaches."

With their snoots in the air,
They would sniff and they'd snort
"We'll have nothing to do with
The Plain-Belly sort!"

And whenever they met some
When they were out walking,
They'd hike right on past them
Without even talking….

When the Star-Belly Sneetches
Had frankfurter roasts
Or picnics or parties
Or marshmallow toasts,

They never invited
The Plain-Belly Sneetches.
They left them out cold
In the dark on the beaches.

They kept them away.
Never let them come near.
And that's how they treated them
Year after year…

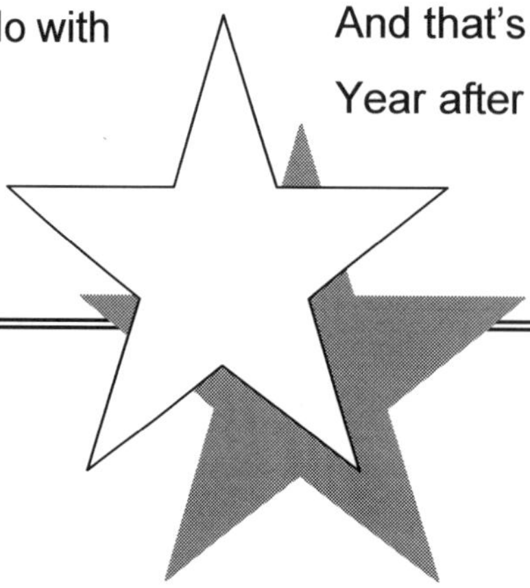

Dealing With
PUTDOWNS AND PREJUDICE

If someone calls you a name:
- Stay calm.
- Say: That's mean and I don't like it.
- Say: That's not funny. Please stop.
- Walk away.
- Tell some friends.
- Tell an adult.

"That's not cool!"

Things to say to someone else who is called a name:
- It was wrong of her to say that about you. Are you okay?
- Can I help you report it to the teacher?
- Would you like to eat lunch with us from now on?

Ways to respond to prejudiced remarks:
- In our house, those words are not allowed.
- What makes you believe that about _____?
- You're too nice a person to hurt someone like that.
- That's not okay. It's disrespectful to say that about others.
- If someone said that about you, you wouldn't like it either.
- Do you really mean what you said? Here's what I understood…
- It makes me upset when you talk about _____ like that. Please stop.
- I don't like that kind of joke. It puts down my family—the human family.

Try some *put-ups*:
- I'm happy to see you!
- Come and join us.
- You can do it.
- Good job!
- You look nice today.
- I like the way you shared your game.
- You were very helpful just now.
- Would you like to be friends?

NAME IT, CLAIM IT, STOP IT

Adapted from a workshop given by Peggy Federici, Camp Peace, Idaho

"Name It, Claim It, Stop It" is another strategy for dealing with putdowns and prejudice. It's not enough just to learn about these things. We also need to act. When you hear a biased remark, you can respond with three simple statements:

1. Name the behavior. *(Say what the person is doing wrong.)*
2. Claim it by stating how it makes <u>you</u> feel.
3. Tell the person to stop.

Here's an example:

Biased remark: "How many green people does it take to change a light bulb?"
Name it: "That's a racist joke."
Claim it: "I don't like it when you put down green people like that."
Stop it: "Please don't tell those jokes at our school."

See if you can label all three parts in the example below:

Biased remark: "I don't like purple people. They're all stupid!"

1. "What you just said about purple people—that's prejudice." _____
2. "It makes me sad to hear you say things like that." _____
3. "Please don't talk that way around me." _____

Now try your own example:

Biased remark: "_____"
Name it: _____
Claim it: _____
Stop it: _____

Practice with your partner and be ready to act out your example for the class.

CREATING UNITY

 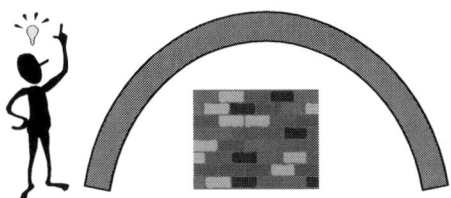

Your group will be assigned one or more of the situations below. For each one, read and discuss it with your group. Then act it out twice—first in a negative way and then in a more positive way that creates unity. Refer to the handouts on "Putdowns and Prejudice" and "Name It, Claim It, Stop It" for ideas. Be ready to perform your skits for the whole class.

1. There is a new student at school. She always eats lunch by herself and doesn't seem to have any friends. Today, you see her sitting alone again.

2. On the bus to school, some older kids are teasing a boy who is overweight. They call him a fat pig and say they are going to beat him up after school.

3. All of your friends want to stop at the snack shop on the way home from school, but one of them doesn't have enough money, so he pretends he isn't hungry.

4. While playing with friends at the park, a group of younger children walks by. They are making fun of people who speak with accents.

5. You sit with friends every day at lunch. There is an open space at your table, and a new girl sits down to eat. No one talks to her, but after she leaves, your friends make fun of her hair and clothing.

6. There is a student from Japan in your class. Before class begins, some of the other students tease him, making fun of the shape of his eyes. Everyone laughs.

7. During recess, the boys decide to play hide-and-seek. A girl wants to join them, but they say that girls aren't allowed to play.

8. Your teacher passes out feathers for an art project. Several classmates stick the feathers in their hair and dance around wildly, shouting "Me, Indian!"

9. A boy in your math class has trouble doing the homework and always makes a lot of mistakes. The other children laugh and call him "stupid" and "retard."

10. A girl at your school uses a wheelchair. She wants to be in the class play, but the teacher says she can't because there are no parts for someone in a wheelchair.

BARRIERS INTO BONDS

Answer the questions below, then color in the picture.

1. List some ways that people are alike: _____
   _____

2. List some ways that people are different: _____
   _____

3. Explain how prejudice has made our differences into barriers between people: _____
   _____

4. What is prejudice? _____
   _____

5. How can we turn those barriers into bonds? _____
   _____

THOUGHT FOR THE DAY

(1)

*So powerful
is the light of unity
that it can illuminate
the whole earth.*

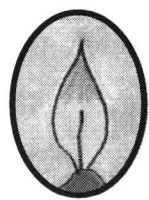

(2)

*We are all
the fruits of one tree,
the flowers of one garden,
the waves of one sea.*

(3)

*What should it matter
that one bowl is dark
and the other is pale,
if each is of good design
and serves its purpose well?*

(4)

*Darkness cannot
drive out darkness;
only light can do that.*

*Hate cannot drive out hate;
only love can do that.*

Name _____

SONG SHEET

Most of these songs are copyrighted and are used with permission. See music section for details.

One Planet, One People

(Echo song by Sandee English)

**One planet, one people,
We all live together.
One planet, one people, please.**

All the world is full of people,
And our hearts all beat as one.
Though we're different from each other,
We're illumined by the rays of just one sun.

(chorus)

We are flowers of one garden,
We are leaves of just one tree.
Though we're different from each other,
We're illumined by the light of unity.

(chorus)

What Mankind Has to Learn

(by Creadell Haley)

There's only one race
of people on the earth,
But man did divide it and so…
There's a Black race, a White race,
What mankind has to learn,
Is that there's only one race to know.

Earth was one country
back when it all began,
But man did divide it and so…
There's a China, a Turkey,
What mankind has to learn,
Is that Earth is one country to know.

There's only oneness
throughout the universe,
But man won't believe it and so…
He divides and multiplies it,
Oh won't he ever learn,
That there's only oneness to know.

Good Neighbors

(by Dick Grover)

**Good neighbors come in all colors,
Black, red, yellow and tan.
Our outsides may look different,
But we're the family of Woman and Man.**

When my doorbell starts to ring,
I can't see the ringer's skin.
Even if he had bright blue skin,
I'd welcome him right in. (chorus)

When my neighbor starts to cry,
That hurts him and that hurts I.
Even if he had orange eyes,
It hurts him when he cries. (chorus)

When my neighbor starts to share,
Joy and happiness everywhere,
Even if she had purple hair,
I wouldn't even care. (chorus)

Hawaiian Unity Song

(Echo song; composer unknown)

We are drops of one ocean,
We are waves of one sea…

**Come and join us…
In our quest for unity,
It's a way of life for you and me.**

We are flowers of one garden.
We are leaves of one tree… (chorus)

Black and white, red and yellow,
Lovely colors of humanity… (chorus)

All the earth is one country,
We are one family… (chorus)

We are drops of one ocean,
We are waves of one sea… (chorus)

Rapp Song*
(by Red and Kathy Grammer)

Now all across this big, wide world
There are lots of boys and lots of girls
With different eyes and different noses
Different hair and different clothes
It's a magical thing, it's a wonderful game
We all look different but we're all the same
Now the differences are great
and the differences are small
But that's just part of the beauty of it all
We're all like notes that make up a song
We need everybody so come on sing along.

**Hello (hello) Hola (hola) Jambo, Jambo
Gan lowee lay mun ho ma**

Now some folks think that they are the best
They don't know how to get along
They say the heck with the rest
So they go their own way
and they do their own thing
But the song sounds weak
when its time for them to sing
But if you gather up folks
from all kinds of places
With different ways of talking
and different color faces
There's something special
each one brings along
And when they all sing together,
now you really got a song.

(chorus)

So open up your eyes and take a look around
There's all kinds of kids that live in your town
Maybe black, maybe white,
maybe rich, maybe poor
You've got to get to know them all
That's what friends are for
'Cause the differences are great
and the differences are small
But that's just part of the beauty of it all
We're all like notes that make up a song
We need everybody so come on sing along.

(chorus)

Listen*
(by Red and Kathy Grammer)

Listen...can you hear the sound
Of hearts beating all the world around
Down in the valley, out on the plain
Everywhere around the world
a heartbeat sounds the same.

**Black or white, red or tan
It's the heart of the family of man
Whoa beating away (3x)**

Listen...can you hear the sound
Of laughter all the world around
High in the mountains, down by the sea
Everywhere around the world
laughter sounds the same to me.

**Black or white, red or tan
It's the heart of the family of man
Whoa laughing away (3x)**

Oo la la la la la... (8x)

Listen...can you hear the sound
Of singing all the world around
Walking through the jungle
or on a busy city street
Everywhere around the world
singing always sounds so sweet.

**Black or white, red or tan
It's the heart of the family of man
Whoa singing away (3x)**

* "Listen" and "Rapp Song" are from the recording *Teaching Peace* © 1986 Smilin' Atcha Music. Written by Red and Kathy Grammer, distributed through Red Note Records, < www.redgrammer.com >.

PART III
Additional Activities

Additional Activities

Warm-ups

1. Birthday line-up 149
2. Link-ups 149
3. Human knot 149

Craft Projects

1. Rainbow chain 150
2. Paper people 150
3. Ribbon of hearts 150
4. Chalk mural 151
5. Leaves of one tree 151
6. Leaves of one tree poster 153
7. Pigment posters 154
8. Paper carnations 155
9. Friendship bracelets 156
10. Colorful clay light switch covers 157
11. Mosaic art 158
12. Hands of humanity cookies 160
13. Patchwork quilt 162

Outdoor Games

1. Tug of peace 168
2. Cooperative musical chairs 168
3. Freeze dance 169
4. Beach ball volley 169
5. Hoop game 170
6. Lava island 170
7. All aboard 170
8. Fingertip touchdown 171
9. Trust walk 171

10. Electric fence 172
11. Centipede 172
12. Parachute games 173
13. Maypole dances 173

Skits, Demonstrations and Puzzles

1. Colors of the heart 177
2. Felt lesson design 177
3. Flower garden skit 178
4. Cooperation skit 179
5. Apple turnovers 181
6. Tangrams 181
7. The human body 186

Speaking, Reading, Writing and Research

1. International pen pals 193
2. Quotation recitation 193
3. Famous figures monologues 194
4. Letters from history 194
5. Public presentations 194
6. What's in a name? 195
7. The Cold Within poem 195
8. Personal interview 196
9. World citizen passport 197

Further Reading and Research 200

Warm-up Activities

No materials needed

1. BIRTHDAY LINE-UP (5-10 min.)

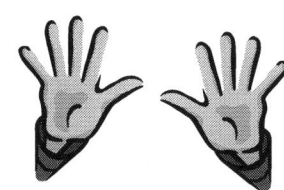

This is a fun activity that requires cooperation in order to succeed.

Tell the children to silently line up in order by age. Youth and adults can play too. There should be no talking or mouthing the words. They can only communicate using gestures. Ask what they would do if several people are the same age. Once the line has been formed, have them check for accuracy by stating their birthdates aloud in turn.

2. LINK-UPS (5-10 min.)

This activity requires group cooperation, helps the children get to know each other better, and highlights some of the things we have in common.

Have the children form a line at the front, beginning with one student (let's call her Keisha) standing alone. She should say her name and one thing about herself, for example: *"My name is Keisha and I like to ride bikes."*

Another student who also likes to ride bikes, can then link arms with Keisha and say, *"This is Keisha. She likes to ride bikes. My name is Nabil. I also like to ride bikes, and I'm wearing blue shorts."*

If another child is wearing blue shorts, he can link arms with Nabil and say, *"This is Nabil. He's wearing blue shorts. My name is Marcus. I'm also wearing blue shorts, and I have two sisters."*

If no one else has two sisters, Marcus has to think of something else. In the same way, the remaining students link to the chain, one at a time. The last person must find something in common with the first person in the chain, then link arms to form a complete circle.

3. HUMAN KNOT (5-10 min.)

This activity requires cooperation, group problem solving and leadership.

- Have all the children stand in a tight circle, shoulder to shoulder.
- Each person grabs the hands of two different people across the circle.
- The goal is for the whole group to untangle itself to form one large circle with everyone still holding hands. People can be facing in or out, but they cannot let go. Sometimes the knot unwinds into two or more smaller circles. You can start with smaller groups of 5-10 for an easier experience.

Teaching Unity, Additional Activities, p. 149

Craft Projects

Display samples of each craft and allow children to work at their own pace. Completed projects can be used to decorate the facility.

1. RAINBOW CHAIN

Materials: Construction paper, ruler, pencils, scissors, glue

Instructions

1. Mark construction paper into strips.
2. Cut out strips from different colors of paper.
3. Glue ends of one strip together to form a ring.
4. Repeat with each strip, looping through previous ring before gluing.

2. PAPER PEOPLE

Materials: Construction paper, pencils, scissors, glue

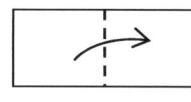 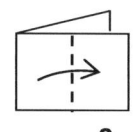 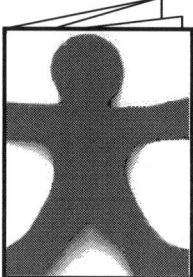

Instructions

1. Fold long strip of paper in half.
2. Fold in half again.
3. Draw a person with the hands and feet touching both sides.
4. Cut along outline being careful not to cut through folds at the hands and feet.
5. Unfold the paper and glue to other people chains.

3. RIBBON OF HEARTS

Materials: Construction paper, pencils, scissors, glue, ribbon

Tip: For younger children, the teacher may wish to use heart stencils or make a few heart patterns for tracing.

Instructions

1. Draw hearts on construction paper.
2. Cut out hearts and glue to ribbon.

4. CHALK MURAL

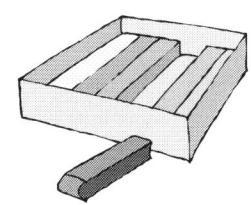

Materials: Large colored chalk sticks

Instructions: Provide chalk and a driveway, sidewalk or other large cement surface. Invite the children to choose a theme such as "We Are One Family" or "Flowers of One Garden," and to draw a cooperative mural. They can work alone or in groups.

5. LEAVES OF ONE TREE

Materials: Construction paper, pencils, leaf patterns, scissors, black marker, masking tape, bare tree branch

Instructions:

1. Trace leaf pattern onto construction paper and cut out.
2. Print your name on leaf with black marker.
3. Tape leaf onto tree.

Preparation

1. Obtain a branch from a real tree and strip off all the leaves. (Find one with lots of smaller branches.)
2. Set the branch upright in a large bucket or planter and weight it down with rocks or sand.
3. If desired, spray the branch with gold paint and cover the bucket with colorful fabric.
4. Set out a tray with ¼-sheets of construction paper in a variety of bright colors.
5. Pre-cut several leaf patterns out of cardboard or stiff vinyl for children to trace (next page).
6. Post the sign about the leaves of one tree.
7. These materials can also be set out during the children's performance, and audience members can be invited to add their own leaves to the tree.

We are all the leaves of one tree.

Add your name to the tree of humankind.

Copy onto cardstock. Cut on dotted line and post sign next to tree. ⤴

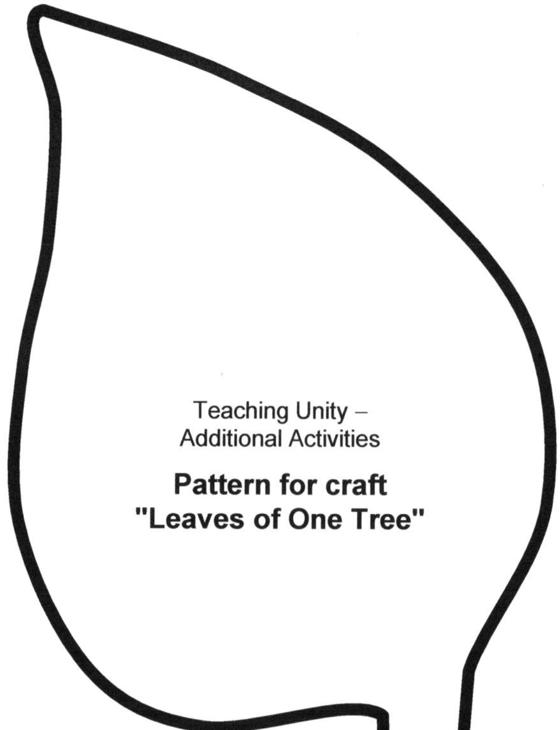

Teaching Unity – Additional Activities

Pattern for craft "Leaves of One Tree"

Teaching Unity – Additional Activities

Pattern for craft "Leaves of One Tree"

Make several copes of each leaf pattern out of cardboard or stiff vinyl for children to trace.

6. LEAVES OF ONE TREE POSTER

Materials: Wrapping paper, scrapbooking paper or wallpaper; pencils, scissors, glue sticks, markers, poster board for each child (approx. 11 x 14 inches or 28 x 36 cm)

Instructions

1. Choose a piece of colorful paper for your design.

2. Turn the paper upside down and using a pencil, trace your hand and forearm (up to the elbow). Make sure your fingers are spread wide, and you hold the pencil straight up and down. This becomes the tree.

3. Cut out the "tree" and glue onto the poster board.

4. Using paper of different colors, cut out some leaves and glue them onto the branches of the tree.

5. If desired, you can also add fruit shapes, flowers, birds or other designs.

6. Write a title at the top or bottom of the poster and remember to add your name.

We are all the leaves of one tree.

7. PIGMENT POSTERS

<u>Materials</u>: Poster board, pencils, rulers, scissors, glue sticks, construction paper or paint sample strips in multicultural colors

Multicultural construction paper can be found at craft and teacher-supply stores. It can also be ordered online, for example: *www.dickblick.com* > enter "multicultural construction paper" in the search box. Paint samples can be found at paint and hardware stores.

<u>Instructions</u>

1. Cut the construction paper or paint color strips into a variety of shapes.
2. Glue the shapes onto the poster board to form an abstract design.
3. If desired, include one of the memory quotes about skin color or add your own thoughts about the beauty of our diverse skin tones.
4. Write your name on the back of the poster.

"*If we say we do not see color… we fool ourselves. We are all different… But that's what makes us beautiful as a human race.*" -C. JoyBell C.

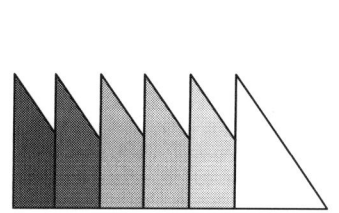

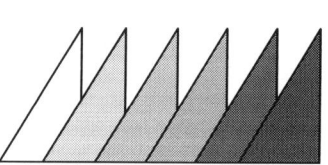

8. PAPER CARNATIONS

Colorful tissue paper flowers are a traditional craft of Mexico. These carnations symbolize the flower garden of humanity and can be used as decorations for the children's performance.

Materials

- ❑ Large sheets of tissue paper (approx. 20 x 20 inches or 50 x 50 cm) in a variety of colors
- ❑ Small plate or circular lid to trace around (4-5 inches or 10-12 cm in diameter)
- ❑ Awl or large needle for poking holes in the paper
- ❑ Green pipe cleaners (one per flower)
- ❑ Artificial leaves with stems (optional)
- ❑ Floral tape (optional)
- ❑ Scissors
- ❑ Pencils

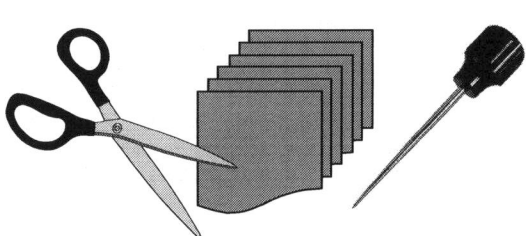

Instructions

1. Fold the tissue paper in half 4 times to make a square 16 layers thick.
2. Draw freehand or trace a circle onto the tissue paper. (Larger circles make larger flowers.)
3. Using the awl, carefully poke two holes through the paper near the center.
4. Bend the pipe cleaner in half and insert each end through a different hole.
5. Gently pull tight and twist the ends together under the flower to make a stem.
6. Cut out the circle.
7. Gently separate each piece of tissue paper starting with the top one, and crinkle upwards to form the petals.
8. If desired, use floral tape to wrap a few leaves onto the carnation stem.

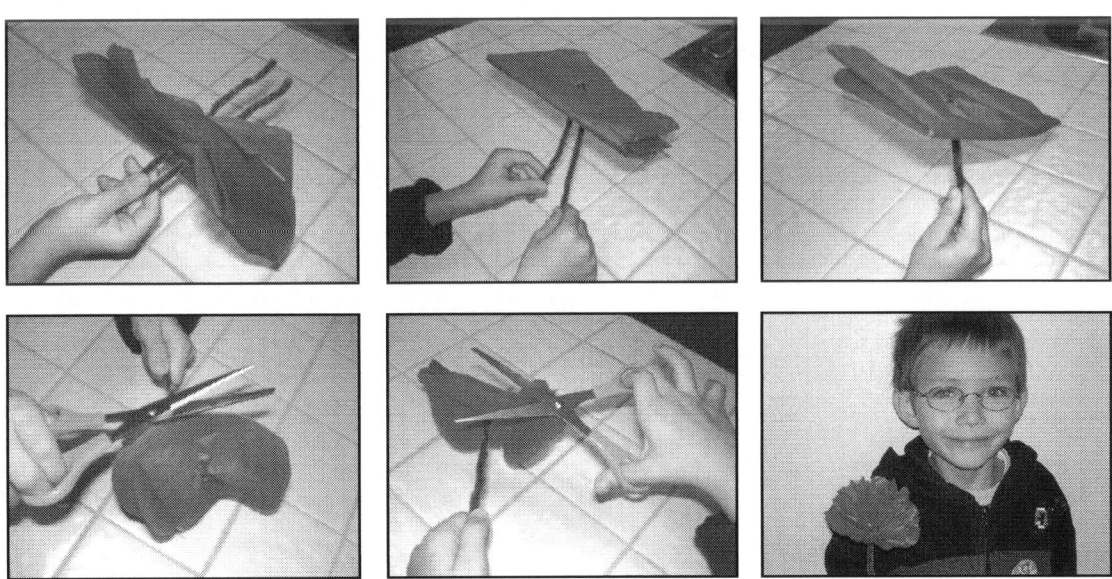

For more detailed instructions with clear photo illustrations:
http://foldingtrees.com/2008/08/flower-week-tissue-paper-carnations

9. FRIENDSHIP BRACELETS

A friendship bracelet is a handmade woven bracelet given by one person to another as a token of friendship. These colorful bracelets can also serve as a symbol of unity in diversity. They make a great craft for boys and girls and are popular throughout the world.

The bracelets are commonly made of embroidery floss. Thicker yarn is easier for small fingers to control. There are a great variety of styles and patterns to choose from. To see some online examples visit: **www.Google.com**, click on "images" and type "friendship bracelets" in the search box. Wikipedia also has a good description of this craft (see references at the bottom of this page).

Step-by-step diagram of basic knot by Tosk Albanian [1]

For additional ideas, patterns and instructions, visit the following websites:

- www.planetpals.com/IKC/peacebracelet.html
- www.how-to-make-jewelry.com/friendship-bracelet-instructions1.html
- http://friendship-bracelets.net

Designs and photo by de:Benutzer:Ra'ike [2]

Used with permission under the Creative Commons license
1. http://en.wikipedia.org/wiki/Friendship_bracelets
2. http://en.wikipedia.org/wiki/File:Friendship_Bracelet_special_forms.jpg

10. COLORFUL CLAY LIGHT SWITCH COVERS

This craft will remind the children about the light of unity and the first and last quotes they memorized.

Idea from Mrs. Pasha Mohajerjasbi

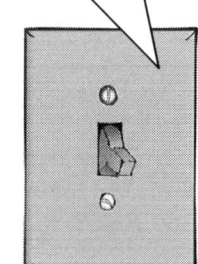

Preparation: Before class, spray one coat of plastic primer on the switch covers and let dry. This will prepare the surface so the clay will stick.

Materials

- Light switch covers (one per child)
- Spray can of plastic primer
- Tarp to protect work table
- Fimo or Sculpey clay in a variety of colors*
- Cookie sheet covered with waxed paper or baking parchment
- Clay modeling tools (rolling pins, plastic knives, toothpicks, etc.)
- Polyurethane spray (optional; use only with adequate ventilation)

Instructions

1. Start with clean hands.
2. Preheat oven to 250 degrees F (120 °C). (Do not microwave.)
3. Use pre-softened clay (e.g., Fimo or Sculpey) or knead firm clay until soft.
4. Press different colors of clay onto the light switch cover to form a design. (Press firmly or clay pieces may pop off after baking.)
5. Bake on cookie sheet for 30 minutes to harden clay.
6. Let cool gradually in oven to prevent tiny cracks.
7. Spray with polyurethane for a hard gloss finish if desired.

---

* Fimo or Sculpey pre-softened modeling clay is ideal for children. It is soft and easy to knead, comes in an assortment of bright colors, won't dry out when exposed to the air, and hardens in the oven. Additional shades can be created by mixing colors. The clay can be found at craft supply stores and online:

- **www.reuels.com > enter "fimo" or "sculpey" in the search box**
- **www.artsuppliesonline.com > fimo or sculpey**
- **www.sculpey.com/products/clays/original-sculpey**
- **www.fimo.com**

     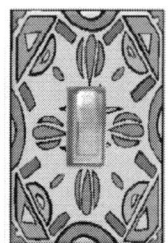

11. MOSAIC ART

A mosaic is made by using small pieces of colored material to create a design or picture. The earliest mosaics were created over 4,000 years ago by the ancient Sumerians and later the Greeks and Romans. Tiled mosaics were also used in early Christian and Islamic art—often to decorate the floors, walls and ceilings of churches, mosques and palaces.

Dome of the Rock, Jerusalem.
Photo by Steven E. Gottlieb.

Classically, mosaics were created with clay tiles or colored glass, but today a great variety of materials are used—pebbles, dry beans, sunflower seeds, torn bits of paper from old magazines, rice, popcorn kernels, macaroni, wrapping paper, aluminum foil, pottery fragments, plastic gemstones, buttons, flat marbles, crushed eggshells, colored pumpkin seeds, craft foam, coffee beans, small sea shells, etc.

The pieces can be glued onto a flat surface like construction paper or illustration board, or they can be fixed to a solid base such as an old picture frame, dinner plate, clay flower pot, vase, coaster, wooden box, cement stepping stone, bottle or tin can.

Mosaic art offers children a chance to express their creativity while improving concentration and fine motor skills. It also serves as a reminder of the "multicultural mosaic" of humanity.

Materials

- ❑ Pencil and paper to sketch the design
- ❑ Mosaic surface or base (see list above)
- ❑ Mosaic pieces (see list above)
- ❑ Small containers to hold the colored pieces (one for each color)
- ❑ Glue and/or grout*
- ❑ Scissors (to cut up old magazines)
- ❑ Spoon (to pick up small seeds or beans)
- ❑ Hatpin or large needle (to pick up tiny pieces of paper)

* **Regular white glue** or **glue sticks** can be used for attaching mosaic pieces made from paper. **Craft glue** works better for seeds or beans. **Tile grout** or **special mosaic adhesive** (available from home improvement stores) can be used for attaching glass, ceramic tiles or other heavier pieces. Follow directions on the package for mixing and applying grout.

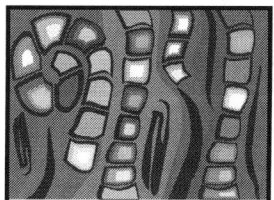

Preparation

1. Plan your design and sketch it on some drawing paper. The design can also be made up as you go along.

2. Decide which colors you want for each part of the design.

3. Determine what materials you will use to make your mosaic, then prepare the pieces. For example, if you will be using bits of colored paper from old catalogs or magazines, first tear out pages that have the colors you need. Then cut or tear the pages into strips and the strips into smaller bits of paper.

4. Sort each color into a separate container.

5. Prepare the surface. For example, if you are using a piece of wood, sand the surface to make it smooth. Next wipe with a soft cloth to remove any dust.

Instructions

1. Draw or trace your design onto the surface.

2. Beginning with the background, place the mosaic pieces inside your design. There are several ways to do this.

   A. <u>If using flat items</u> like bits of paper, spread a thin coating of glue over one section of the design and set the pieces in place on top of the glue. A straight pin can be used to pick up the pieces. Glue one area at a time until your design is finished, then let dry.

   B. <u>If using small objects</u> like rice, beans or seeds, a thicker coating of craft glue should be applied. The pieces can easily be transferred with a spoon. After gluing, allow to dry completely. Then gently tap off any loose pieces before starting the next color.

   C. <u>If using larger or heavier objects</u> like ceramic tiles or cut glass, coat the back of each piece with a thick layer of grout or mosaic adhesive and set in place, leaving a narrow gap between each piece. As an alternative, the grout can be applied directly to the surface (for example a clay flower pot) and the pieces gently pressed into the grout.

   When dry, spread another layer of grout over the top of your project to fill in the gaps and secure the tiles in place. Immediately wipe off the excess grout with a damp sponge. When dry, use a grout sealer if your project will be used near water or outside.

Some references

- google.com/images > search for "mosaic art for kids"
- http://familycrafts.about.com > search for "mosaics kids"
- www.firstpalette.com > search for "mosaic" ⟶
- www.ehow.com/list_6305353_mosaic-ideas-kids.html
- www.ehow.com/list > search for "mosaic tile crafts for kids" (and skip over the ads)

Photo courtesy of
www.FirstPalette.com

12. HANDS OF HUMANITY

Using this basic cookie recipe, or a sugar-cookie recipe of your own, the children will be making different colors of hands to represent our human family. Allow about three hours to make the dough, chill it and bake it. Begin by assembling all of the ingredients and tools. You will need two cups of flour for each cookie color.

Common Ingredients

- 1½ cups softened butter
- 2 cups sugar
- 5 eggs
- 2/3 cup milk
- 1 tablespoon baking soda
- 1/2 teaspoon salt
- 2 teaspoons vanilla

Tools

- Measuring cup
- Measuring spoons
- Five mixing bowls
- Mixing spoons
- Rolling pin and board
- Cookie sheet
- Dull knife

This wonderful edible craft comes from Meg Andersen and is used here with permission.

Instructions

1. Have children wash and dry their hands.

2. Mix the common ingredients in one large bowl, as follows:
    a. Cream butter and sugar together until smooth.
    b. Beat in the eggs.
    c. Dissolve soda and salt in milk, then add to mixture.
    d. Add vanilla.

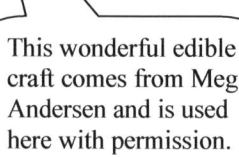

3. Divide the mixture equally into five bowls.

4. Make each bowl a different flavor by adding the special ingredients on the following page, in the order listed.

5. If necessary, cover the dough and refrigerate for 30 minutes to make it firm enough for cutouts.

6. Preheat the oven to 350 degrees F (175°C).

7. Using a floured board and rolling pin, roll out each flavor of dough to 1/4-in. (6 mm) thick.

8. Flour the palm of a child's hand and place gently on the dough. Cut around the hand with a dull knife, pulling away excess dough to make additional cookies.

9. Use a spatula to transfer the cookies to a greased cookie sheet. Arrange the hands separately on the sheet or intertwined to show unity.

10. Bake for 8 minutes in preheated oven. Watch closely and remove from oven when edges just begin to brown.

11. After baking, remove cookies from the tray and cool before eating.

> Note: If desired, cookies can be iced after baking, or before baking they can be sprinkled with decorator's sugar (also called sparkling sugar, sanding sugar and pearl sugar). It adds a sparkle to the finished cookies, won't melt in the oven, and comes in a variety of colors. You can also color your own by adding a few drops of food coloring to a jar with 5 tablespoons of the decorator's sugar. Then seal the jar and shake.

Spice
1/4-cup dark molasses
1/4-teaspoon cinnamon
1/8-teaspoon cloves
2 cups flour

Chocolate
1/3-cup cocoa powder
2 tablespoons sugar
2 tablespoons chocolate syrup
2 cups flour

Peanut Butter
1/3-cup peanut butter
2 teaspoons dark molasses
2 cups flour

Vanilla
2 cups flour

Berry
1/2-teaspoon red jello powder
or 2 tablespoons red fruit jam
2 cups flour

Other Flavors
Orange
Apple butter
Maple
Honey
Pumpkin

13. PATCHWORK QUILT

A patchwork quilt is a type of bed cover composed of three layers: a decorative cloth top assembled from smaller squares, a cloth back, and a layer of soft filler in the middle for insulation—all stitched together to form a fabric sandwich.

A quilt composed of student-made squares is an example of unity in diversity. It provides opportunities for group collaboration as well as individual expression. Quilts can be used as a metaphor to help children see one another as individuals with many similarities and differences—yet all are members of the same classroom and the same larger community.

Preparing the Class

1. Have the class read the story *The Patchwork Quilt* by Valerie Flournoy and Jerry Pinkney, Dial Publishers, 1985 (available on **www.Amazon.com**). This award-winning story portrays the warm bonds that create the fabric of family life.

2. Tell the class that each student will be making a patch to represent him or herself, and we will bind these together to make a quilt that represents our classroom community.

3. Explain the metaphor of many individual pieces combining to create a beautiful, stronger whole, and how this can apply to human beings.

4. Set the tone for the project by sharing with the students some quilting history and traditions. (See following page.)

5. If possible, bring in several quilts so students can see and touch some examples.

6. Ask which students have quilts of their own, what they like about them, who made them and how they are used.

7. Consult together to determine what will be done with the finished quilt. For example, it might be displayed in the classroom or the school library. It could be auctioned to raise money for something needed by the school. It might be donated to a local charity—such as a women's shelter or children's hospital.

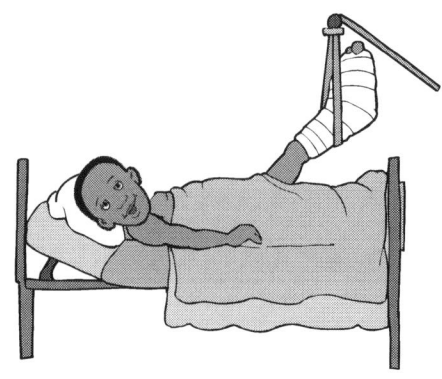

Teaching Unity, Additional Activities, p. 162

Quilting History and Traditions

In addition to serving as a warm bed cover, quilts are sometimes given to mark important life events such as a marriage, birth or graduation. They can also be used for clothing, wall hangings and other decorative items.

Quilts have a long tradition in Europe, Asia and Africa. The first known quilted object is a linen carpet found in a Mongolian tomb, dating from around the first century A.D., although a carved ivory figure found in the Temple of Osiris shows an Egyptian pharaoh from 3400 B.C. wearing a quilted robe. Quilted fabrics were also used as gowns for both men and women in ancient China, as padding for Crusader armor, and as fashionable tunics for men during the European Middle Ages. The Ottoman Empire has a rich tradition of quilted bedcovers and magnificent ceremonial kaftans which were worn by the nobility. In Africa, local history and culture were preserved in the patterns and colors of patchwork textiles, including the well-known *Kente* cloth woven by the Akan people of Ghana. *Kente* cloth was considered sacred, and was originally worn only by kings.

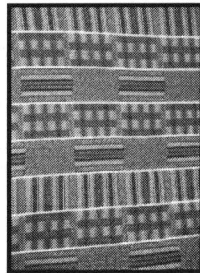

Quilting traditions are particularly strong in the United States. In colonial times, many families economized by saving small scraps of worn out clothing which were joined together to make quilts for the cold winter months. A patchwork quilt thus became the record of a family's history, incorporating bits of garments and household textiles. These heirlooms were often passed from generation to generation.

During the U.S. Civil War, quilts were used as coded maps of the Underground Railroad. When the United States entered World War I in 1917, the government urged citizens to make quilts in order to "save the blankets for our boys over there." During World War II, quilts were sold to raise money for the Red Cross. In small towns, quilting was often a communal activity, and the "quilting bee" was an important social event. These group quilts were often auctioned to raise money for other community projects.

References
- www.quilthistory.com/quilting.htm
- www.quilting-in-america.com/History-of-Quilts.html
- http://en.wikipedia.org/wiki/Kente_cloth
- www.black-collegian.com/african/quilts999.shtml
- www.turkishculture.org/fabrics-and-patterns/fabrics-and-textiles/textiles-and-ceremonies-802.htm
- http://history.cultural-china.com/en/183History5923.html
- *The Quilt: A History and Celebration of an American Art Form,* by Elise Schebler Roberts, Voyageur Press, 2007

Materials

- ❑ *A Patchwork Quilt* by Valerie Flournoy and Jerry Pinkney
- ❑ Fabric squares, one or more per child (see *squares* below)
- ❑ Large rectangle of fabric or a bed sheet (see *backing* below)
- ❑ Soft cotton batting (see *filling* below)
- ❑ Fabric for sashing, borders and binding (optional)
- ❑ Measuring tape, yard or meter stick
- ❑ Sharp scissors (one per child)
- ❑ Pencils, paper, construction paper
- ❑ Glue sticks or tacky craft glue
- ❑ Permanent markers
- ❑ Large safety pins
- ❑ Sewing needles and thread
- ❑ Yarn needles and yarn
- ❑ Sewing machine (optional)
- ❑ Iron (if needed; to be used by adults only)
- ❑ Colorful fabric scraps in various textures and other materials for making the designs, for example: felt, corduroy, canvas, burlap, silk, suede, velveteen, fleece, knits, craft foam, fabric crayons, glitter pens

Preparing the Fabric

Squares: Cut a number of squares from 100% cotton fabric. Use plain white fabric or a variety of solid colors for children to choose from.

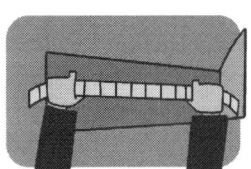

The squares can be any size you want depending on the number of children in your class and the desired dimensions of your finished quilt. You can determine this yourself or include it as part of your math lesson and help the students do the calculations and measurements. If you will be adding sashing and quilt borders, be sure to take this into account. Common sizes for the squares are 6 x 6 inches (15 cm), 8 x 8 (20 cm), and 12 x 12 (30 cm).

By way of example, 24 squares will make a quilt 4 blocks wide by 6 blocks long; 48 squares will make a quilt 6 blocks wide by 8 blocks long; 30 squares will make a 5 x 6-block quilt.

Cut the squares slightly larger than desired to allow for the seams. For example, if you want a 12-inch finished block, make the pieces 12.5 inches square. You can use a bed sheet (twin, full, double, queen or king) to help determine the size of the finished quilt.

Backing: Like the squares, the backing can be made from 100% cotton fabric. It should be slightly larger than the finished quilt to allow for the seams. The easiest method is to use an actual bed sheet with the desired dimensions. Choose a solid color that complements your quilt design.

Filling: For the quilt filling, use soft cotton batting (also called wadding). It should be the same size as the quilt backing. It comes in a roll from the fabric store and is available in several thicknesses. Thicker batting will create a warmer quilt; thinner batting is easier to sew. (Many quilters recommend the "Warm and Natural" brand.)

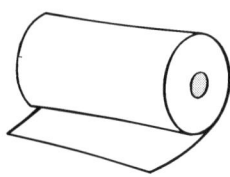

Making the Squares

1. Tell students that they will be creating a picture to represent themselves. Each child's square might contain a self portrait, a handprint, an important event in their life, a drawing of their home, their family, a special cultural object, a musical instrument, an abstract design, or a favorite pet, sport or hobby.

2. Have children plan their artwork. They can make a sketch or play with small pieces of construction paper to map out the design. They should leave a minimum 1-inch (2.5 cm) border on all four sides to allow for seams. Encourage creativity and preview their ideas before transferring them to the squares.

3. Give each student a square. Have them draw or trace their designs onto the fabric scraps, cut out the designs, then glue the pieces onto the square.

4. Student names and fine details can be added with permanent markers or fabric pens.

Joining the Squares

If you are an experienced quilter or can recruit a parent or community volunteer to assist, you may wish to finish the quilt yourself, adding plain fabric strips *(sashing)* between the finished squares, a decorative border, and a fabric binding to seal the edges. You could also help the children join the squares either with a sewing machine or by hand following the instructions on the next page.

1. Place two squares together face-to-face and anchor them with safety pins. Using a needle and double thread with a knot at the end, stitch the squares together along one edge. Use a running stitch (in and out) leaving a margin of about ½ inch (12 mm). Finish with another knot to hold the stitches in place.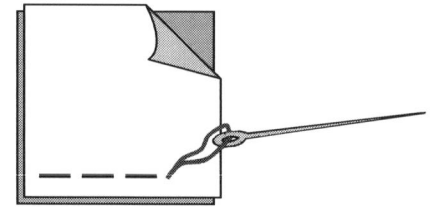

2. Add additional squares to make a row of six—or whatever number of blocks are in each row.

3. Form equal rows with the remaining squares. Then stitch all the rows together to form the front of the quilt.

4. When the front of the quilt is finished, cut another piece of fabric for the back—making it the same size as the front. (You can use a bed sheet if it has the desired dimensions.)

5. Next, cut a layer of cotton batting for the filling. Make it the same size as well.

6. Place the three quilt layers together on a flat surface such as a large table or clean floor. Start by spreading out the quilt top, right side up. Next, add the quilt back, right side down. Then roll out the filling on top. Smooth all three layers to remove any wrinkles before the quilt is stitched and bound.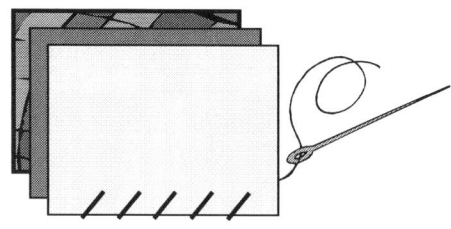

7. Pin the layers together with large safety pins beginning in the center of the quilt and working out toward the edges. Smooth and straighten as you go.

8. Sew the layers together along three edges using an overcast stitch (diagonal stitches that loop around the edge of the fabric). Leave the fourth side open. Remove the pins.

9. Turn the quilt right side out, fold the loose edges inside and stitch the fourth side closed.

10. Starting in the center of the quilt, make a yarn knot in the corner of each square. Using the yarn needle, sew in and out once, remove the needle and tie the ends of the yarn in a knot. Clip the yarn about 1 inch (2.5 cm) from the quilt. The knots will serve as decoration while at the same time holding the filling in place.

Teaching Unity, Additional Activities, p. 166

Stitching Practice

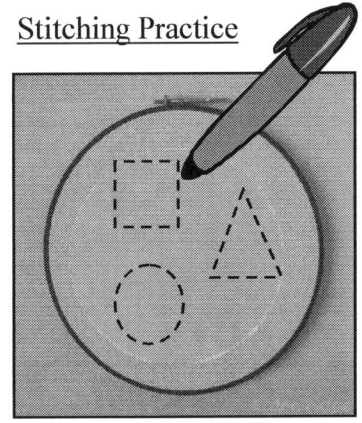

Some children may not have had an opportunity to sew by hand before. You can show them how and encourage them to practice before they begin stitching the quilt together. You will need a piece of burlap in a large embroidery hoop and a large dull needle threaded with yarn. Using a permanent marker, draw a line, triangle, circle and square on the burlap. Tie a knot in one end of the yarn and start stitching. When the yarn is used up, remove and start again.

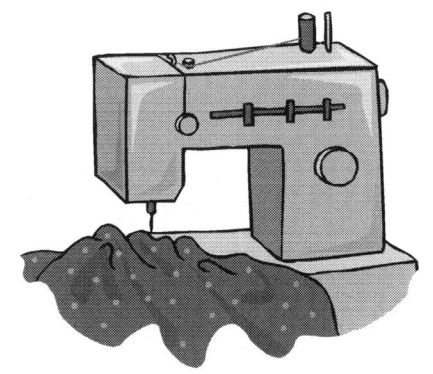

If using a sewing machine, make sure that it is in good working order and that you know how to fix common problems quickly. Bring all the necessary tools, bobbins and spools of thread. It is also helpful to have an extension cord, fabric scissors and extra needles in case one breaks. Children can learn to use the machine with practice and careful adult supervision.

Culminating Activity

When the quilt has been completed, you can invite other classes, parents and administrators to a presentation of the project. The students can explain their designs and share thoughts about the process. How are the squares (and the students) alike and different? How did each person contribute? What did they learn about working together? How does the quilt relate to the concept of unity in diversity? They can also share some quilting history and traditions. End by taking a class photo with the quilt and giving each child a copy to bring home.

Additional Ideas and References

- http://thecraftstudio.com/qwc/resources/pictureblocks.htm
- www.ehow.com/how_6737683_make-quilt-kids.html
- www.goosetracks.com/TshirtQuilt.html
- www.sabine.k12.la.us/zes/quilts/default.htm

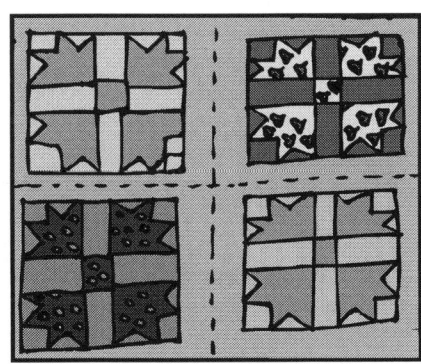

Outdoor Games

The following activities are fun, easy to organize, require few materials, and relate to the theme of unity. Prizes can be provided after the games. Allow 20-30 minutes for each activity.*

1. TUG OF PEACE

Materials: Sturdy rope, 10–20 feet long (3–6 meters)

Form a circle with a length of sturdy rope that has been tied in a knot. Have the children stand equally-spaced around the circle. Then have them squat down while holding onto the rope with both hands. At the count of three, the children should lean back while pulling on the rope and slowly stand up together. When everyone is up, you can count to three again and have them carefully lean back and squat down. A shorter rope makes this easier.

This game contrasts with the typical tug-of-war in which players pit their strength against one another and beat their opponents by dragging them through the mud. Tug of Peace serves as a graphic demonstration of cooperation and mutual support and makes it obvious to the children that they are able to achieve something together that they could not do alone.

2. COOPERATIVE MUSICAL CHAIRS

Materials: Sturdy chairs, lively music

Consider the following scenario. An adult is leading a group of children in a typical game of musical chairs. They are instructed to walk around the chairs to music. When the music stops, they sit in the closest chair. There is one less chair than the number of children, so the child without a chair is out of the game. Before the music starts again, another chair is removed.

The children do as they are told, circling around the chairs and eyeing each other with nervous suspicion. When the music stops, they scramble for a seat, knocking each other over and shoving others out of the way. If two children try to sit on the same chair, the stronger one pushes the weaker one to the floor.

The child who is eliminated goes over to the corner to cry. A well-meaning adult approaches and says, "It's just a game. You're not being a very good sport." The chairs are removed one by one, and when the game is over a single child is victorious—the last one left with a chair. Aggressive behavior has been rewarded and the teacher asks, "Now wasn't that fun?"

What do students learn from playing this game? They learn that there are not enough chairs to go around, that pushing and shoving are rewarded, that weaker children should be taken advantage of, and that winning is the most important thing. This kind of competition is destructive to community.

* The first two games were adapted from *Because We Can Change the World* by Mara Sapon-Shevin. Games 6-10 adapted from: < www.usscouts.org/usscouts/games > and < www.group-games.com >.

Instead, we could play *cooperative* musical chairs. In this version of the game, children walk around the chairs to the music, and although there are fewer chairs than children, the goal is that everyone must be on a chair for the group to win. (You can use carpet squares or small towels if chairs are not available.) Remove one chair before the music starts each time and have the children work together to make sure everyone is included. They can squeeze together, sit on laps or drape across each other. The challenge increases as the number of chairs is reduced, and the children must engage in problem solving and negotiation to achieve the goal. Use chairs that are sturdy enough to hold the weight of several children. Adult safety monitors are recommended. Be prepared for laughter. The game ends when there is one chair left for every 4-5 children.

3. FREEZE DANCE

Materials: A small object for each child, lively music

This activity is designed to teach cooperation and helpfulness. Unlike most games where the object is to eliminate others, the goal of Freeze Dance is to make sure everyone is included. It can be played by any size group of various ages and levels of mobility.

The participants each place a small object on their heads (e.g., a knotted sock, toy animal, paper plate or bean bag), and begin to dance while lively music is played in the background.

If someone's bean bag falls off, that person must freeze until another player notices and replaces the bean bag without losing his or her own. If the helper's bean bag falls off, the helper is also frozen until someone else comes to the rescue. Keep playing as long as everyone is having fun or until the music runs out!

4. BEACH BALL VOLLEY

Materials: Inflated beach ball or large balloon

Have children stand in a circle an arm's length apart. Give them the ball to volley and have them practice gently popping it from person to person. Then challenge them to keep it in the air for 10 hits, then 20, etc. Encourage them to develop strategies such as passing the ball around the circle or putting someone in the middle.

5. HOOP GAME

Materials: 2-3 hula hoops or bike inner tubes

Tell the children to stand in a circle and join hands. Start with a hula hoop hanging over one pair of joined hands. Each person in the circle must pass the hoop over him/herself and on to the next person without letting go of hands. For an added challenge, try this with two or three hoops of different sizes going in different directions at the same time.

6. LAVA ISLAND

Materials: Rope, small object for each child

In a relatively clean flat area, form the rope into a circle on the ground. The circle should be large enough to hold all the children comfortably. Each child should have a small object (e.g., a paper cup, pencil or water bottle).

Have the children sit evenly-spaced around the outside of the circle, feet straight out touching the rope. Have them place their objects behind them on the ground and then go stand inside the circle. This is the island.

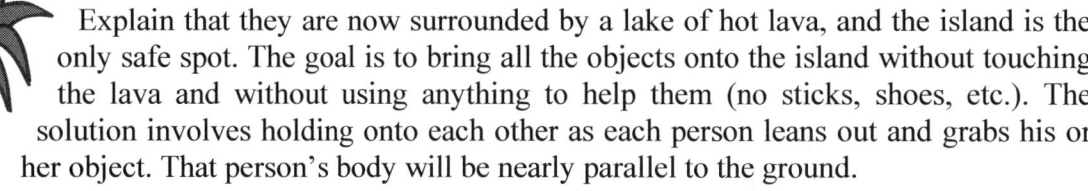

Explain that they are now surrounded by a lake of hot lava, and the island is the only safe spot. The goal is to bring all the objects onto the island without touching the lava and without using anything to help them (no sticks, shoes, etc.). The solution involves holding onto each other as each person leans out and grabs his or her object. That person's body will be nearly parallel to the ground.

This is a great team-building game. It can be played by several groups at once or by the class as a whole.

7. ALL ABOARD!

Materials: Tarp or old sheet

This game is similar to Cooperative Musical Chairs. Start with something foldable and not too slippery (e.g., a tarp) to represent a train. Spread the tarp on the ground and explain that when "All aboard!" is called, everyone must stand on the train without touching the ground. Try it once to be sure everyone understands the directions. Then say, "Now, everyone <u>off</u> the train!"

Next, fold the tarp in half. Lay it back on the ground and call "All aboard!" once again. The children must cooperate in order for everyone to ride the train. Strategies include standing on one leg or riding piggyback. Keep folding the tarp in half until it's too small to continue.

With a large group, break into smaller teams of 5 to 10. Teams should be roughly equal in the number and size of the children. Safety monitors are recommended.

8. FINGERTIP TOUCHDOWN

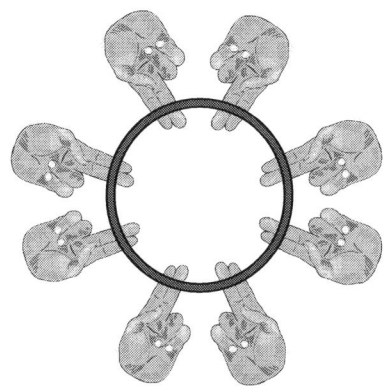

Materials: One hula hoop for every four children

This activity requires concentration and teamwork. Divide the class into groups of four and give each group a hula hoop. The children should stand in a circle around the hoop, holding it from underneath with two fingertips from each hand. On the count of three, have them lower the hoop to the ground and raise it back up again without anyone's fingertips losing contact. It's harder than it looks!

For an additional challenge, have them try it again without talking, or do it with their eyes closed, or add more people, or see how many touchdowns each team can make in one minute.

9. TRUST WALK

Materials: Blindfolds for half the children, obstacles, flags or cones to mark start and finish lines

This activity teaches trust, cooperation and communication. It requires a large safe open space and a variety of large and small objects to serve as obstacles (hay bales, cardboard boxes, water balloons, rolled up socks, Frisbees, plastic wading pools, rubber snakes, ropes, pillows, etc.), but nothing sharp or dangerous.

Mark start and finish lines for the game area and set out the obstacles. More obstacles make for a more challenging course. Station assistants around the field for safety.

Begin the game by having everyone form pairs at the starting line. Spread them out to avoid collisions on the field. One partner will be blindfolded, and the other will be the guide. Explain that the guides are responsible for their partner's safety. When everyone is ready, have the guides slowly spin their blindfolded partners around a few times so they lose their bearings.

From this point on, the guides should not touch their partners at all. They can use verbal cues to talk them through the obstacle course without touching anything, e.g., "In three more steps, there will be a water balloon. Step over it slowly." (As a variation, have partners place a hand on their guide's shoulder as they navigate the course silently.)

Anyone who touches an obstacle must return to the starting line. (Guides can hold their partner's hands when bringing them back, or blindfolds can be removed to allow for a speedier return.) When all have reached the finish line, have the partners switch roles so everyone has a turn.

Reflection: After the activity, you can ask the children what they learned from the experience. Some sample questions:

- What do you think was the purpose of this activity?
- What was it like to be blindfolded?
- What was it like to be the guide?
- How did it feel when you trusted each other and worked together to accomplish something challenging?

10. ELECTRIC FENCE

Materials: Rope, two posts

Tie a rope between two trees or two chairs, or select two people to hold the rope—which should be about waist level—just high enough so no one can step over it. Have the children gather on one side. Tell the group that this is an electric fence—the fence of prejudice—and anyone touching it will get a nasty shock.

The goal is to pass everyone safely over the fence, one by one. If someone touches the fence, the entire group must start over. Set a few ground rules (e.g., no crawling under the fence or diving over it, and you can take off your shoes). Then ask the children to consult together to figure out how to reach the other side. They should make a plan before they begin.

11. CENTIPEDE

Materials: Scarf, old necktie or rope for each child; flags or cones to mark start and finish lines

In the traditional version of this game, the three-legged race, two partners tie their inside legs together and compete against other teams in a short running race. They must cooperate in order to run together without falling.

In this new version of the game, all the children stand shoulder to shoulder along the starting line. Assistants can help them tie their legs to the person next to them on either side. Make bows (for easy removal) rather than knots. Be sure nothing is dangling that could trip the team.

Rather than competing against each other, the goal is for everyone to make it safely to the finish line together. It will take teamwork to make this centipede walk! For an added challenge, you can time them or have them walk backwards. Safety monitors are recommended.

12. PARACHUTE GAMES

Materials: A large round heavy-duty nylon sport parachute with optional handles

Parachute games offer an entertaining outdoor activity suitable for large groups of 25-30 children. The games teach cooperation and team-building skills. Parachutes are available online (Amazon.com sells several sizes of play parachutes) and from military surplus stores (be sure to remove cords before use).

Begin by explaining that a parachute game requires cooperation to make it work. Practice a few basic parachute movements such as lifting it together on the count of three, shaking it, holding it still, etc. (Children can hold onto an edge if there are not enough handles for everyone.) Then go over the rules for the first game. If there is an accompanying rhyme or song, practice that together before you play.

For examples of parachute games, visit:

- www.youthwork-practice.com/games/parachute-games.html
- www.ultimatecampresource.com > click on "camp games" then click on "parachute games"
- www.squidoo.com/parachute-games
- www.youtube.com > parachute games botswana 2010

13. MAYPOLE DANCES

Materials: A maypole, live or recorded music, dance instructions, optional costumes or different colored T-shirts to match the maypole ribbons

A maypole is a tall decorated pole that was used throughout Europe in various medieval folk festivals. Most of these celebrations occurred around the first day of May. The pole was hung with long brightly-colored ribbons that were woven into patterns in a ceremonial folk dance. Similar ribbon dances were performed in India and in pre-Columbian Latin America.

The origins of the maypole have been debated for centuries and still remain unknown. Some suggest that the dance was part of village festivities marking the return of summer and that the maypole symbolized the tree of life. Maypoles have recently experienced a revival in many parts of the world with new dances and styles being invented all the time.

Maypole dance music was played on bagpipes, fiddles, accordions or other instruments that could be easily heard in the open air. Today people often dance to recorded music including traditional European dance tunes, contra dance music and popular songs. The dances require energy, coordination and teamwork, and provide an enjoyable activity for both boys and girls.

For examples of maypole dancing:

www.youtube.com > enter "maypole dancing" in the search box **+** the following terms:

- **+** "Greenfields"
- **+** "Ladner"
- **+** "Unicycles"
- **+** "Eatonville Daniel"
- **+** "Eatonville Community"
- **+** "Wheatley"
- **+** "CWS 4th Grade"

For maypole history, music, costumes, workshops and more:

- www.tradamis.org > module information > maypole
- www.edaids.com > maypole

How to construct a maypole:

1. <u>Pole</u>: Find a pole about 10 feet (3 meters) tall. This could be a sturdy tree trunk, a tetherball pole, PVC pipe about 2 inches (5 cm) wide, a wooden closet bar or thick dowel.

2. <u>Base</u>: Choose a large open space and anchor the pole securely so it won't tip over. If you are outside, the pole can be set in the ground like a fence post, inserted in a tetherball stand, or placed in a large bucket or tire filled with cement. Indoors, you can use a patio umbrella stand or other sturdy foundation. Reinforce with concrete blocks if necessary.

3. <u>Top piece</u>: If desired, you can add a circular top piece or crown. This could be a bicycle wheel, wooden plate, grapevine wreath or something similar. Fasten the crown to the top of the pole and decorate with real or artificial flowers.

4. <u>Ribbon</u>: You will need an even number of ribbons in various colors—one per dancer. Use wide fabric ribbon or flat webbing with the ends sealed. Cut into lengths that are 1½ times the length of the pole. If the pole is 3 meters tall, each ribbon will be 4½ meters long.

5. <u>Attach the ribbons</u>: Arrange the ribbons equidistantly in a circle around the crown or top of the pole, so they spread out in a symmetrical pattern. Tie the ribbons on securely or attach them with a staple gun, nails, hot glue or duct tape as appropriate.

For additional construction tips and photos:

- www.tradamis.org/Maypole%20crown%20construction.htm →
- www.google/images > maypole ribbons
- www.ask.com > enter "construct maypole" in the search box
- www.ehow.com enter "build maypole" in the search box
- www.hipstersteaparty.com/2012/06/how-to-make-maypole.html

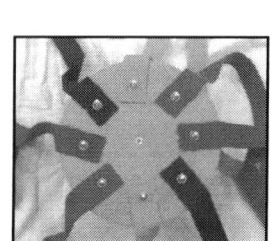

Photo courtesy of Tradamis.org

For maypole dance instructions and music:

- www.audiosparx.com > maypole music
- www.amazon.com > maypole music
- www.slowfamilyonline.com/tag/may-pole
- www.ehow.com > maypole dance steps
- www.wikihow.com/Do-a-Maypole-Dance
- www.rodstradling.co.uk/maypoledance
- www.thriftyfun.com/tf38128743.tip.html

Ribbon Dance, courtesy of The Barwick-in-Elmet Maypole Trust, used with permission.

The basic dance:

Dancers skip around the pole in opposite directions, weaving in and out to form a pattern until the ribbon is completely wrapped around the pole.

1. Participants stand in a circle around the pole, each holding a ribbon.

2. The children should alternate facing left or right. With younger children, it may be helpful to have them count off (1-2, 1-2) to determine which way to face.

3. When the music starts, the dancers will alternate—first going in towards the pole and under the ribbon of the person coming towards them, then going out away from the pole, raising their ribbon over the person coming towards them. (To start, tell the #1s that they will go *in and under* and the #2s that they will go *out and over*.)

4. There is a chant to go with the movements:

   > *In and out, in and out,*
   > *Weave the ribbons tight;*
   > *'Round the Maypole we will dance*
   > *To the left and right.*

5. The dance is over when the pole is completely wrapped with ribbons.

6. After the dance, tell the children that the maypole can serve as yet another example of unity in diversity. Each one of us holds a separate ribbon, but all of the ribbons are attached to one pole which connects us no matter which way we move or turn. Every person is like one of these ribbons as we weave together in the dance of life.

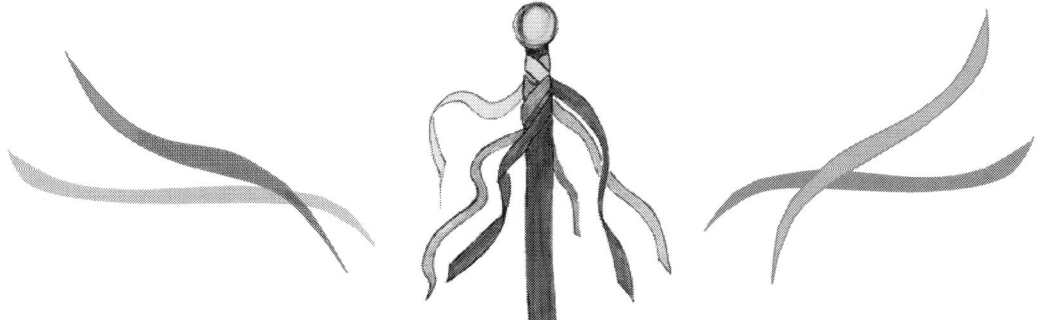

Image courtesy of www.warrinerprimaries.com

Our children's class enjoys some outdoor games

Teaching Unity, Additional Activities, p. 176

Skits, Demonstrations and Puzzles

These short skits and demonstrations are intended to reinforce the concepts presented during class. They can be included as part of the children's final performance and/or filmed if desired.

1. COLORS OF THE HEART

Materials

- ❏ M&M candies
- ❏ One bowl for each color of M&M
- ❏ Several blindfolds

Instructions

Begin by having students wash their hands. Explain that we are going to do a role play. One person will play the role of the teacher and 3-4 will be the students. Assign parts and have the children act out the following situation:

1. The teacher has students sort the M&Ms into different bowls by color.
2. The students are then blindfolded and are given one candy of each color.
3. The teacher asks them which color tastes best.
4. After eating them, the students say that they all taste the same.
5. The teacher asks them to repeat the taste test—with the same results.
6. The teacher then asks students to remove their blindfolds, and explains that while M&Ms *look* different on the outside, inside they're all chocolate!
7. People are like that too. We're different on the outside, but inside we're all human. What's important is not the color of the skin but what's in our hearts.
8. End with one or more students reciting quote #8 on page 262 (by MLK).

2. FELT LESSON DESIGN

Students can create their own felt lessons on any topic related to unity. These lessons can then be presented to another children's class or other interested group.

Materials: Sample felt lessons, pencils, paper, felt pieces, scissors for each student, white glue, felt boards. If desired, provide pre-cut felt pieces (people, animals, geometric shapes, etc.) available online and at teacher supply and craft stores.

Instructions: Have students work alone or in pairs. Begin by demonstrating several felt lessons from this book. Next have students demonstrate those same lessons. Then ask them to select their own topics, research the topics and write down key points they wish to teach. These can be worked into a simple script with a sketch to accompany each point.

3. FLOWER GARDEN SKIT

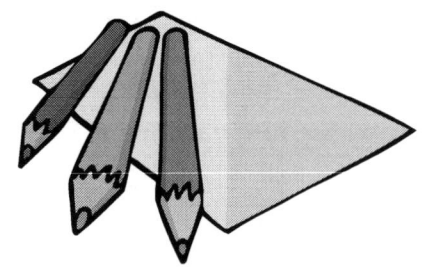

Materials

- ❏ Prepared drawings
- ❏ Crayons, colored pencils or markers

Instructions

Assign parts (one teacher, several students) and have the children act out the following scene using their own words. The skit takes less time and retains audience interest better when students prepare their drawings in advance and only pretend to color during the performance.

	Teacher	Students
1	Children, I'd like you each to choose a pencil or crayon of your favorite color.	My favorite is blue! I like green! (Etc.)
2	Good! Now draw a picture of a flower garden using only your favorite color.	Students work on their drawings.*
3	Hold up your work and let's see what you've done.	Students hold up their drawings.
4	Nice job! Now draw a second picture of the flower garden, this time using lots of different colors.	Students work on their second drawing.
5	Hold up both of your pictures side by side. Which one was more fun to draw? Which one do you like best? Why?	Students hold up both pictures and share their thoughts.
6	Yes, diversity adds beauty and makes the flower garden more interesting. It's the same with people!	Have one or more students recite the words below.

> If we meet those who are different from ourselves, we can think of them as beautiful flowers growing in the garden of humanity and be glad to be with them.

4. COOPERATION SKIT

Materials

- ☐ White board with marker
- ☐ Eleven students
- ☐ Poster board to make eleven large cards that spell out the word "cooperation"
  (A note to each student should be taped on the back of the cards—see next page.)

Instructions

1. Tell students that we will do a short skit to demonstrate the importance of working together in unity. In fact, we're going to spell the word "cooperation."

2. Write "COOPERATION" on the board.

3. Give each student one of the letters and tell them to line up in order—quickly and quietly.

4. Say: Excellent! Now, let's try it again but differently this time.

5. Return to your seats and read the instructions on the back of your card, but don't share this with anyone else.

6. When I say start, let's try to spell "cooperation" again. This time, follow the directions on your card.
   (If they follow the directions, they will not be able to spell the word.)

7. Give the signal to start, allow time for the role play, then call "Stop!"

8. Have children return to their seats and discuss what happened.

9. End the activity by repeating the role play with true cooperation.

Note: If children are performing this skit for an audience, they should do it the wrong way first then repeat it with cooperation the second time. If necessary, choreograph their movements and speech so that everyone can be seen and heard.

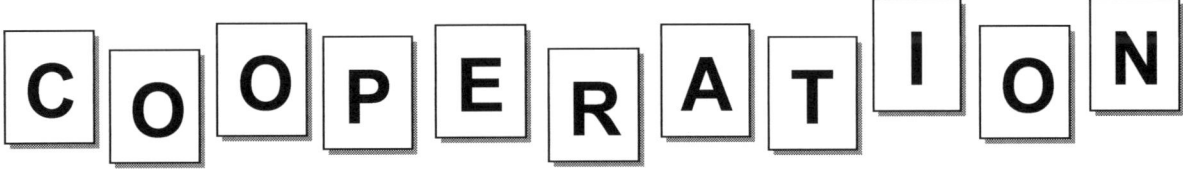

Tip: For a smaller class, you can do a similar skit with only five students. Have them spell the word "U-N-I-T-Y." (See next page for sample notes to tape on each card.) On the second try, students should be able to spell the word with no trouble. Close by having one student explain that we can reach UNITY by putting "U" before "I" ("you" before "I").

Teaching Unity, Additional Activities, p. 179

Instructions for "Cooperation Skit" role players

Photocopy this page, cut into rows and tape to the back of the appropriate card for skit #4.

C	Complain about everyone else.
O	Fight with the other O's over who should be the first O.
O	Fight with the other O's over who should be the first O.
P	Push people out of your way.
E	Line up at the end. Refuse to be in the middle.
R	Repeat the same thing over and over.
A	Insist that "A" is the first letter of the alphabet and should go first.
T	Tell everyone else how to line up.
I	Insist that "I" is the most important letter and should go first.
O	Fight with the other O's over who should be the first O.
N	Take a nap.

U	Push others out of your way since "you" are first.
N	Take a nap.
I	Insist that "I" is the most important letter and should go first.
T	Tell everyone else how to line up.
Y	Complain about everyone else. Yak, yak, yak!

5. APPLE TURNOVERS

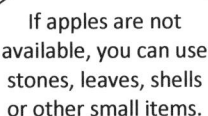

If apples are not available, you can use stones, leaves, shells or other small items.

Materials

- ❏ An apple for each student
- ❏ A basket to hold all of the apples

Instructions

1. Give each student an apple.

2. Explain that we are going to do a demonstration about similarities and differences.

3. All of these apples look pretty much the same, but each one is really unique.

4. What are some of their similarities? *(Basic shape, color, seeds, stem...)*

5. Are they the <u>exact</u> same size, shape and color? *(No)*

6. Study your apple carefully for a minute then replace it in the basket.
   (The teacher should then place the apples on a table one by one, turning them over so a new side is facing up.)

7. Now let's see if you can find your apple again. *(Allow students time to search. It might take a minute, but they are usually able to find their own.)*

8. What can this exercise teach us about people? *(We're all human, and we have many similarities, but each person is unique. There is no one exactly like us. Sometimes we have to look carefully to see the special characteristics that each person brings.)*

6. TANGRAMS

The tangram is an ancient Chinese puzzle consisting of seven flat pieces called *tans* which can be re-arranged to form a variety of shapes. A tangram set has 5 triangles, 1 square and 1 parallelogram—all cut from a single square.

The objective of the puzzle is to form a given shape using all seven tans—which must lie flat and touch each other without overlapping. Thousands of tangram designs have been created over the years including geometric patterns, animals and common objects. Solving each puzzle requires logic and spatial reasoning skills.

Teaching Unity, Additional Activities, p. 181

Making a tangram set

A tangram set can be made of sturdy cardboard, craft foam, felt, magnetic sheets, thick vinyl, paper or wood. You will need a square (approx. 6 x 6 inches or 15 x 15 cm) of whatever material you choose. The pattern on the following page can be photocopied onto cardstock and cut out to make the pieces. The cut-outs can also be used as patterns and traced onto another material. Any colors can be used. Students can also make their own tangram sets by following the instructions below:

1. Cut a large square from paper, construction paper or cardstock.
   (*www.wikihow.com/Make-a-Square-from-Rectangular-Paper*)

2. Draw thin lines on the square to form a 4 x 4 array of smaller squares as shown below.

3. Draw the bold lines as shown.

4. Carefully cut along the bold lines to form the seven pieces of your tangram set.

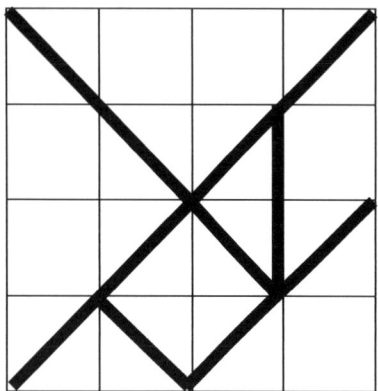

Tangram set by Nevit Dilmen
Used with permission under
the Creative Commons license

Teaching tangrams

1. Make sure each student has a set of tangram pieces.

2. Give them a copy of the large square with lines (next page) and have each student re-create the square using their own pieces. *(Students can work "freehand" or place their pieces directly on top of the pattern. Allow them to help each other as needed.)*

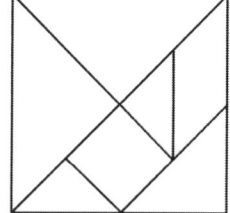

3. Show them other simple shapes with lines (a rectangle or triangle for example) and allow them time to work.

4. Once they understand how to do the puzzles, give them the worksheet of tangram designs <u>without</u> lines and encourage them to solve the puzzles by working alone or in pairs.

   (<u>Note:</u> Younger children may need to use the sheet with lines to construct their tangrams. More capable children can make up their own designs and challenge each other.)

Tangram pattern and puzzles for activity #6
This page can be photocopied for students, or the figures can be drawn on the board.

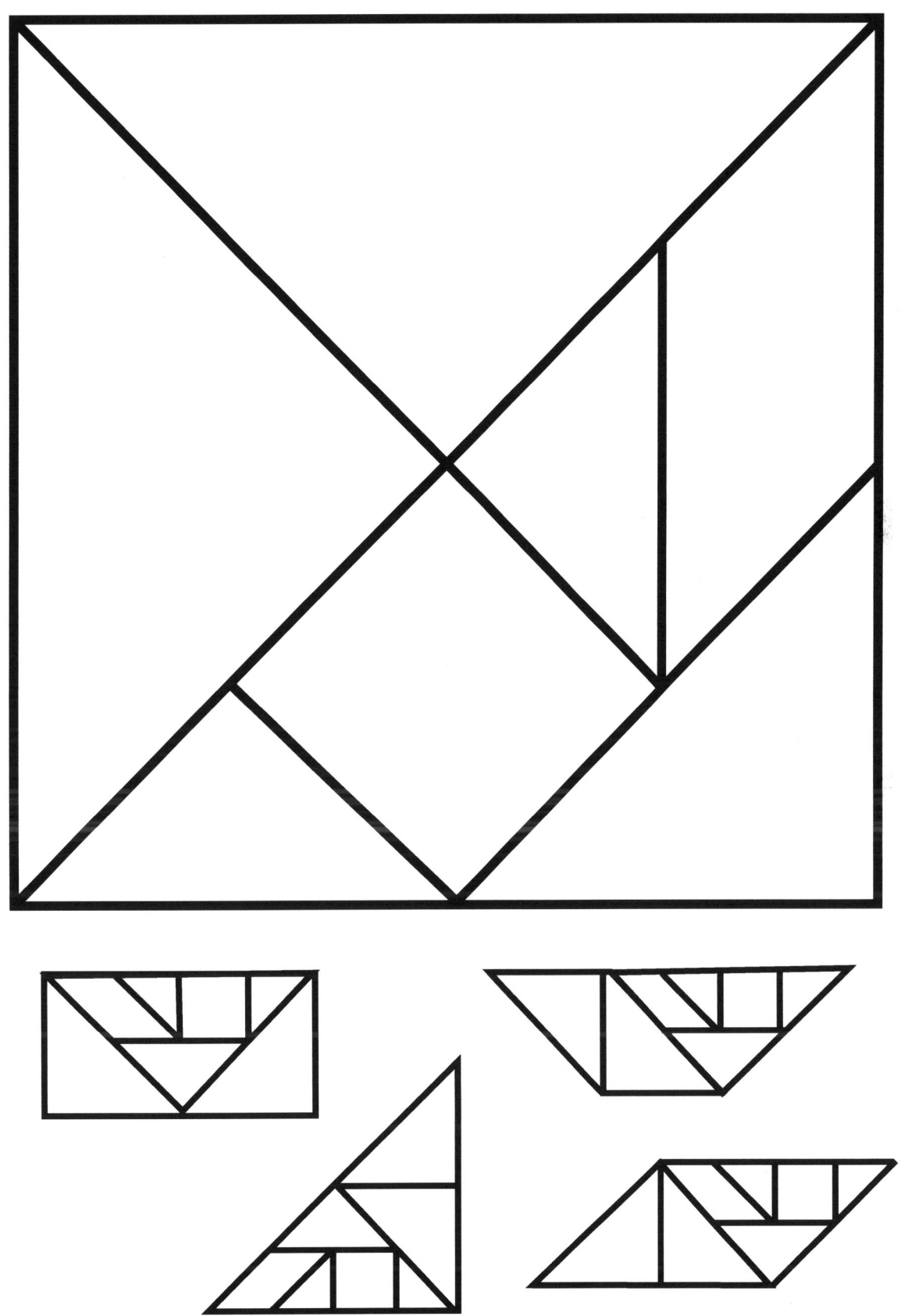

Teaching Unity, Additional Activities, p. 183

Tangram Worksheet

Teaching Unity, Additional Activities, p. 184

Tangram Solutions

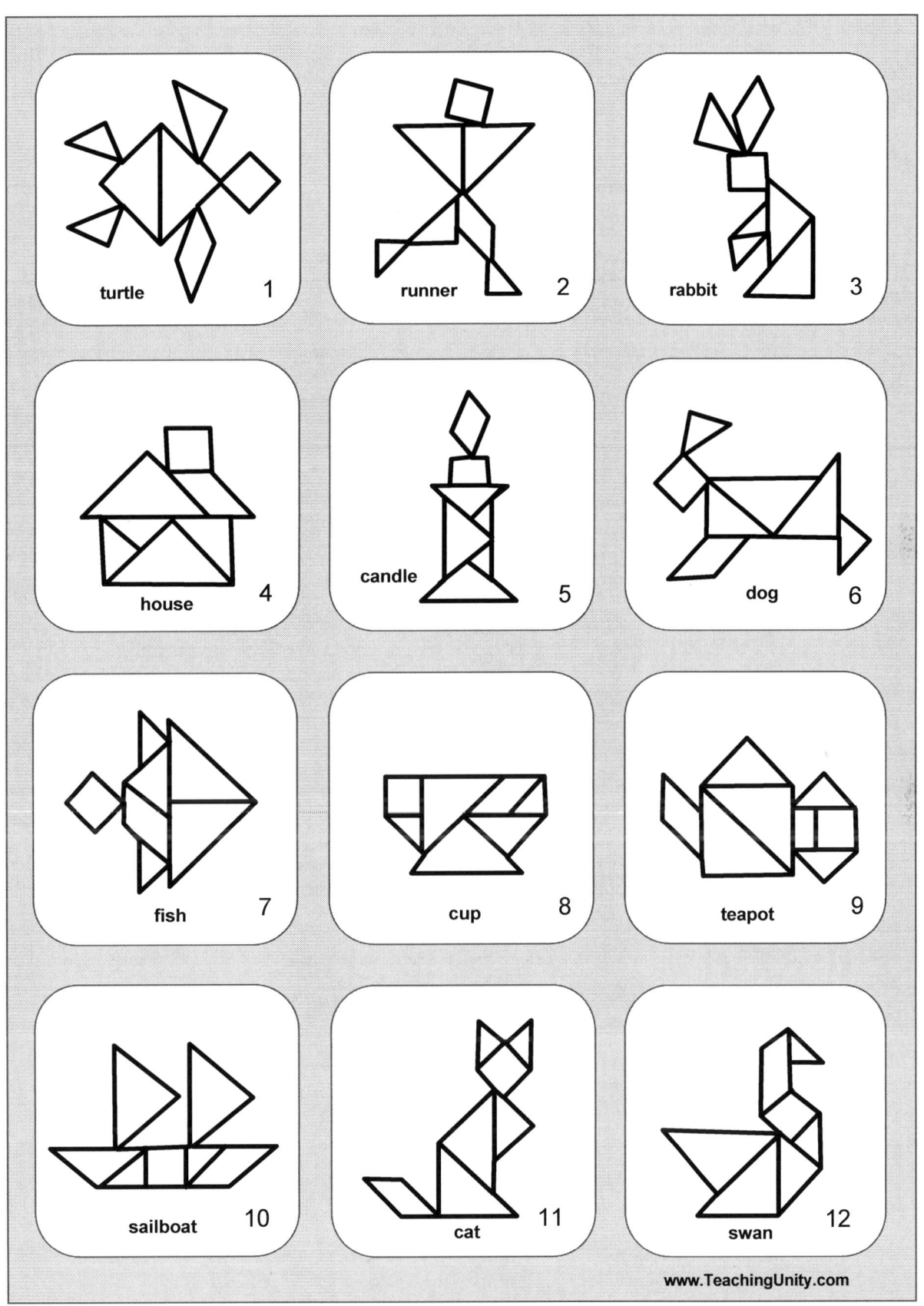

Tangram resources

Teachers will find a wealth of classroom materials for tangrams on www.Google.com/images. Enter "tangrams lessons," "tangrams printable," or "tangrams worksheets" in the search box.

Durable classroom sets made from hard plastic or wood can be found at teacher supply stores or online. Visit www.Amazon.com and search for "tangrams." Classroom sets are also available from: www.learningresources.com > tangrams.

For tangram history, templates, games, books, free online puzzles and more:
< www.fun-stuff-to-do.com/tangrams.html >.

Play tangrams online

- http://games.ztor.com/tang
- www.mathplayground.com/tangrams.html
- www.logicville.com/tangram.htm

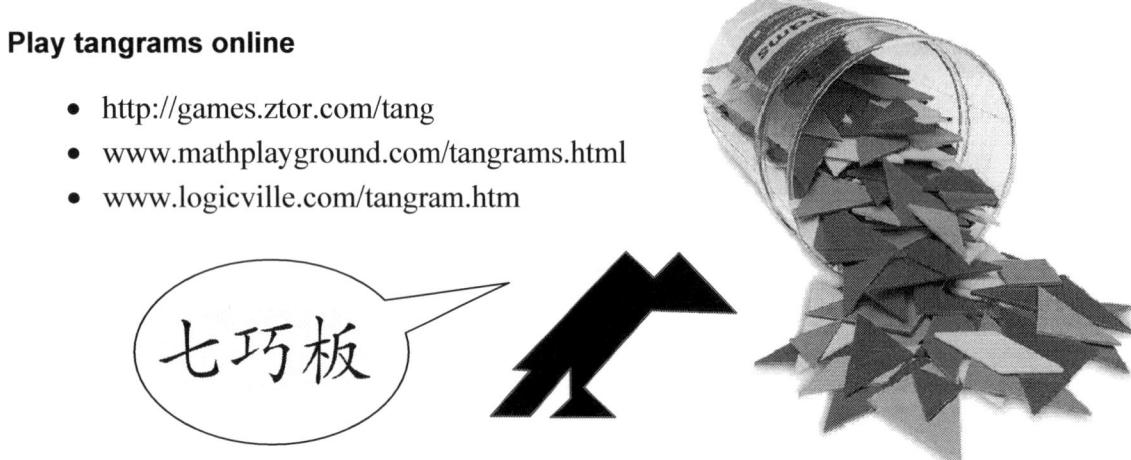

> Thousands of different designs can be made from the same seven *tans*. In like manner, the same basic human parts (2 arms, 2 legs, a body and a head) can be combined to make billions of different people—each one unique. Tangrams can serve as a reminder of our great diversity and, at the same time, our common humanity.

7. THE HUMAN BODY (felt lesson)

Present the felt lesson on "The Human Body" (see patterns and instructions on the following pages). Then invite several students to present it to the class.

"The Human Body"

Teacher's Guide, Script, and Patterns for Felt Lesson

TO THE TEACHER: This packet contains a script, instructions and patterns for making a felt lesson on "The Human Body." The lesson demonstrates the importance of unity in diversity, and the debilitating effects of prejudice. It builds on a previous felt lesson about "The Eye" from Unit 2.

You will need a felt board or carpet board and an easel. After cutting out the pattern pieces, read through the script and repeat the actions until you can present the lesson smoothly. The objectives of the lesson are listed below. The children will be able to:

(1) Depict the human body as a concrete example of unity in diversity.

(2) Describe the negative effects of prejudice and discrimination.

(3) Explain the value of diversity and the need for unity.

Script for Felt Lesson

"The Human Body"

	NARRATION	ACTION
1	**Consider the human body.** It begins as a single cell which grows and develops into the various tissues, organs and limbs.	Place cell on board. Cover cell with body.
2	Each part has an important role: • The heart pumps our blood… • The lungs enable us to breathe… • And the eyes allow us to see.	• Add heart. • Breathe in and out. • Add eyes.
3	If all the parts are strong, the body functions well.	Add smile.
4	Any single part (a heart, a lung, an eye) is useless by itself. It only has value when it works together with the rest of the body.	Hold up the heart. Put heart back on body.
5	• If one part is weak or missing, • the entire body is affected. • Or dead!	• Remove one leg. • Change smile to a frown. • Remove heart.
6	**The human race is like the human body.** Like the body's parts, people have different abilities and come in different shapes and colors. But together we are one human race.	Add leg and heart. Change frown to a smile.
7	Our diversity is our strength. No one group or person can make it alone. We need the contributions of each and all…	Hold up one eye, then replace it.
8	Including women and girls. Without their contributions, half of the body of humanity wouldn't function. We need all the parts of our human family to be healthy and strong.	Cover half of the body with your hand or a piece of paper, then uncover it.
9	**Prejudice is like a cancer** eating away at the heart of humanity. Discrimination against even one of us hurts us all.	Replace good heart with bad one, and change smile to frown.
10	If we meet those who are different from ourselves, we can think of them as beautiful flowers growing in the garden of humanity and be glad to be with them.	End with the good heart and a smile.

Felt lesson on "The Human Body"

Materials

- Different colors of felt (see chart below)
- Pattern pieces (on following pages)
- Sharp scissors
- Double-stick tape or large paper clips
- Stick-on velcro (plastic loop side)
- White craft glue

ITEM	COLOR
Cell body	Light orange
Cell nucleus	Black
Human body	Light brown
Heart	Red
Eyes	Dark blue
Mouth	Black

Instructions for Making Felt Pieces

1. Photocopy the pattern pages.
2. Using the copies, cut around each shape outside the line.
3. Attach each pattern to the appropriate color of felt using the tape or large paper clips.
4. Carefully cut out each piece, using the pattern as a guide.
5. Glue cell nucleus to cell body and allow to dry.
6. Add velcro as indicated (see instructions on pattern pages).
7. Store script and felt pieces in a zip-lock plastic bag for ease of use.

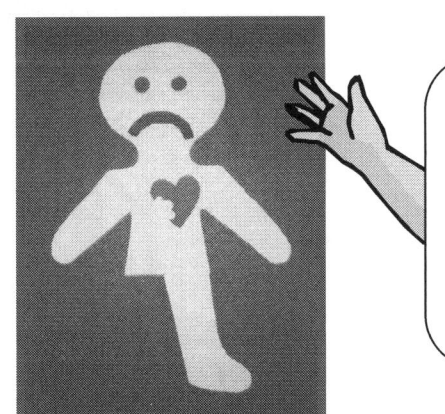

Tip: If making more than one set of felt pieces, you can make a more durable pattern by first laminating the paper copy. Then cut out the pattern along the lines, and trace it onto the felt.

Tip: For easier cut-outs if not laminating patterns, copy them on peel-and-stick paper. Then peel off backing, place sticky paper on felt, and cut through both at once–skipping steps #2-3.

Teaching Unity, Additional Activities, p. 189

Patterns for felt lesson on "The Human Body"

Cut one heart from red felt.

Teaching Unity – Additional Activities

Pattern for felt lesson on "The Human Body"

Join pattern to bottom half of body on next page, then cut figure from light brown felt.

Cut one heart from red felt.

Patterns can be enlarged on photocopier if desired.

Teaching Unity, Additional Activities, p. 190

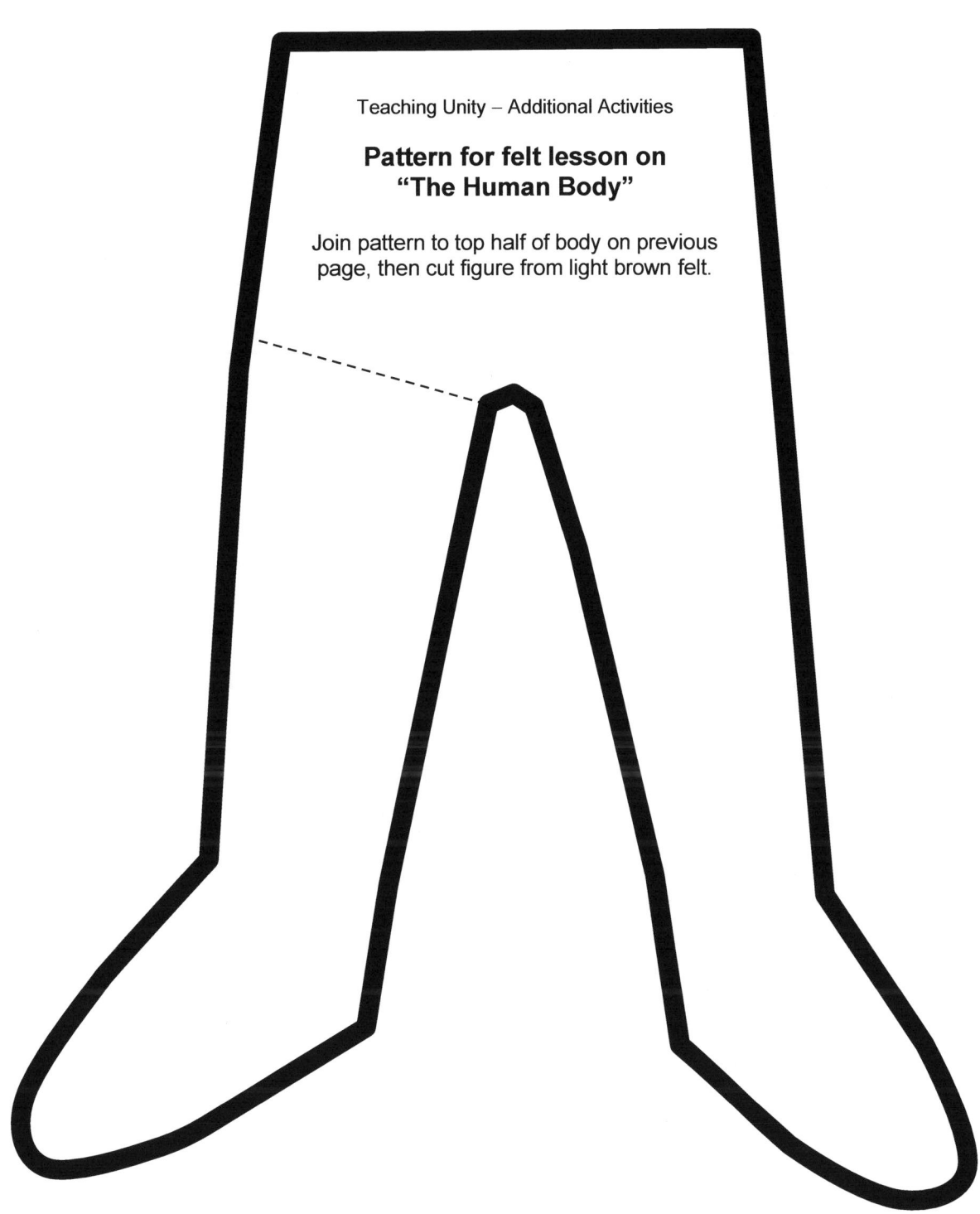

Patterns for felt lesson on "The Human Body"

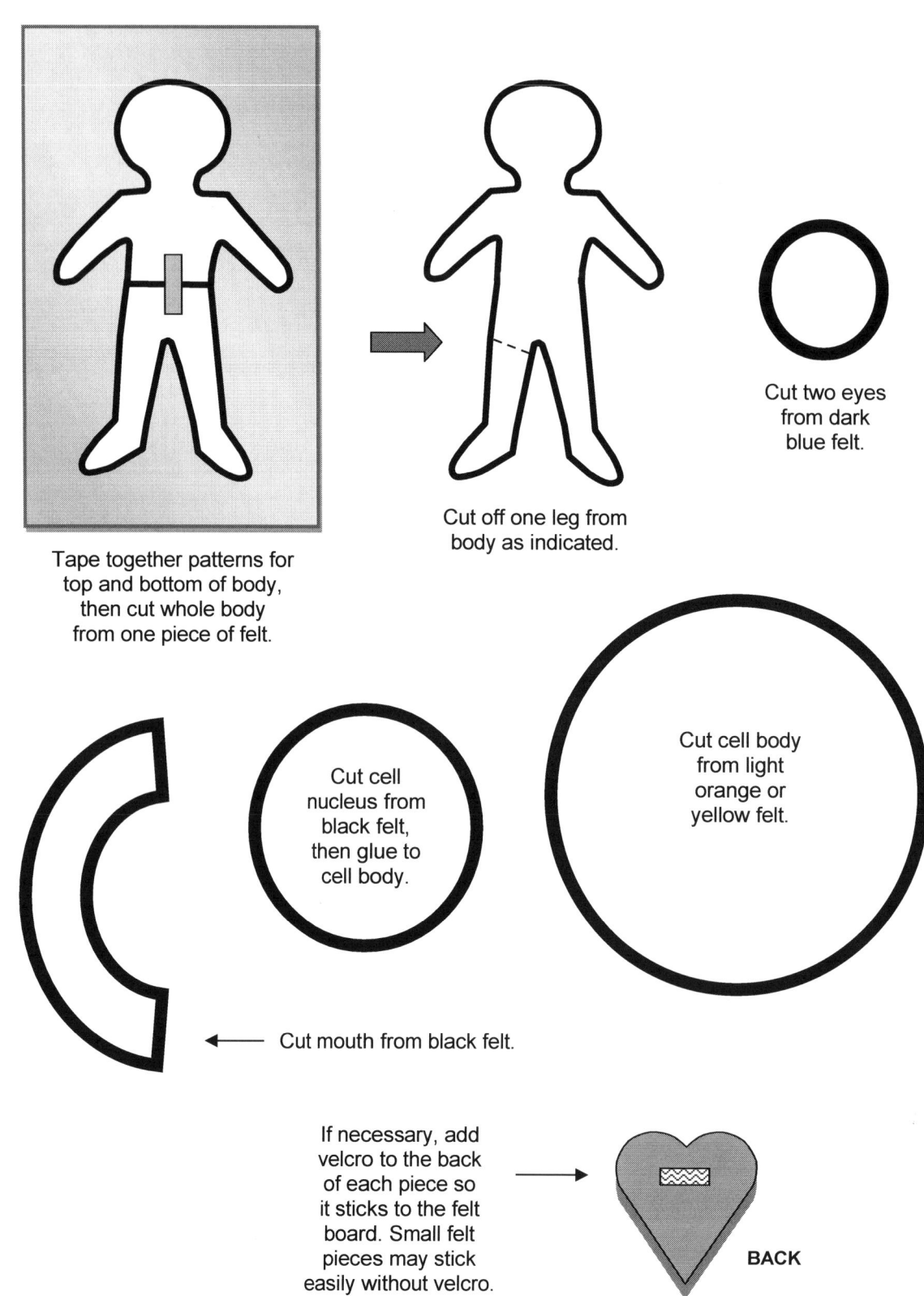

Tape together patterns for top and bottom of body, then cut whole body from one piece of felt.

Cut off one leg from body as indicated.

Cut two eyes from dark blue felt.

Cut cell nucleus from black felt, then glue to cell body.

Cut cell body from light orange or yellow felt.

← Cut mouth from black felt.

If necessary, add velcro to the back of each piece so it sticks to the felt board. Small felt pieces may stick easily without velcro.

BACK

Teaching Unity, Additional Activities, p. 192

Speaking, Reading, Writing and Research

Students may enjoy some of the following activities which relate to the theme of unity. The activities encourage speaking, reading, writing and research and may take place over several weeks, a semester or a full school year.

1. INTERNATIONAL PEN PALS

This is a great way to connect with other children from around the world. It also provides an opportunity to practice writing and speaking skills while learning about other countries and cultures. There are many websites that allow you to select individuals or classroom groups based on language, country, age, gender, etc. A few examples are listed below:

- www.ePals.com
- www.studentsoftheworld.info
- www.globalpenfriends.com
- http://kidworldcitizen.org
  (enter *pen pals* in the search box)

2. QUOTATION RECITATION

Children can recite the quotations they have memorized from each unit, as part of a larger performance for other students, family and friends. Additional quotations can be included (see Appendix A for quotations and program ideas). Begin with a self-introduction by each child, for example:

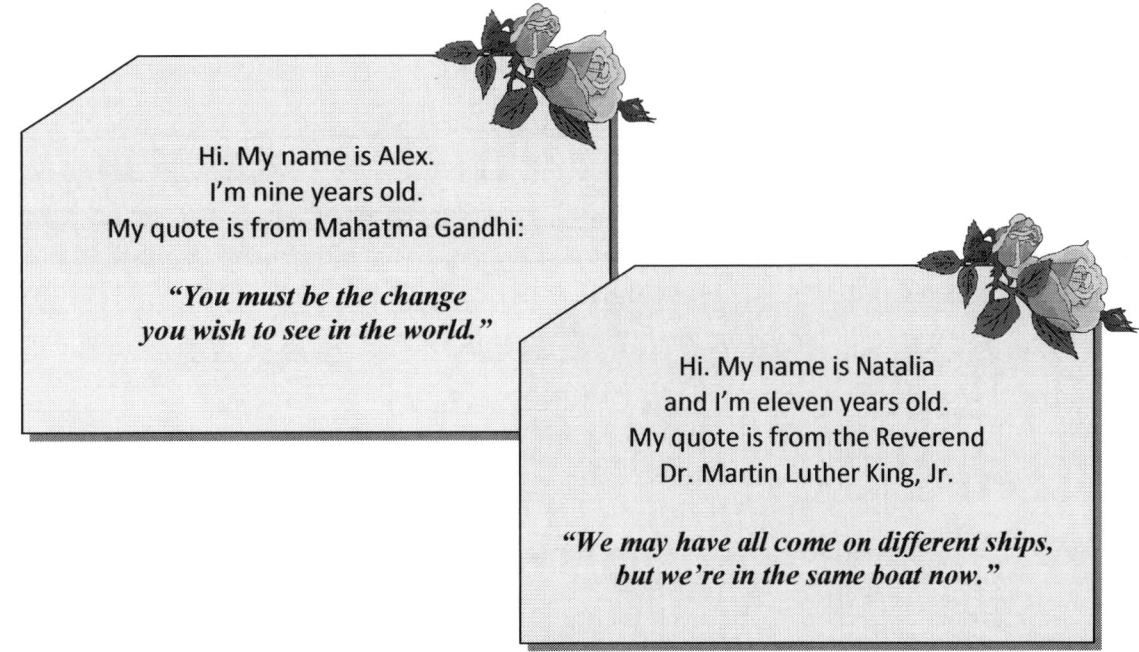

Hi. My name is Alex.
I'm nine years old.
My quote is from Mahatma Gandhi:

"You must be the change you wish to see in the world."

Hi. My name is Natalia
and I'm eleven years old.
My quote is from the Reverend
Dr. Martin Luther King, Jr.

"We may have all come on different ships, but we're in the same boat now."

3. FAMOUS FIGURES MONOLOGUES

Have each student select a different historical figure* who has worked for unity and justice, research that person, and prepare a monologue with highlights from their life. To assist their research, students can be given reference materials and asked to brainstorm a list of questions such as: Who was Mother Teresa? Why is she important? What was her childhood like? What inspired her work? What were some of the obstacles she faced? How did she overcome them?

Performances should be in the first person, for example: "My name is Mother Teresa. When I was only a little girl…" Dressing up to represent the figure, and employing props and background music can make the presentations more vivid. Allow plenty of time for practice before the performance. (Note: In some cultures, it would be considered disrespectful to portray certain religious figures.)

> * Jane Addams, W.E.B. Du Bois, Susan B. Anthony, Abraham Lincoln, Mahatma Gandhi, Eleanor Roosevelt, Martin Luther King, Jr., Jackie Robinson, Mother Teresa, Sojourner Truth, Albert Schweitzer, Nelson Mandela and others.

4. LETTERS FROM HISTORY

Have students write a letter to their family from an important time and place in history relevant to the topics under study. They might imagine, for example, that they are inside a Birmingham jail cell with Martin Luther King, Jr. in 1963, or among the crowd at the First Women's Rights convention in Seneca Falls, New York, in 1848. What did they see? Hear? Touch? Taste? Smell? How did they feel? Each student can choose a different event. Letters can then be edited, read aloud and/or compiled in a class book.

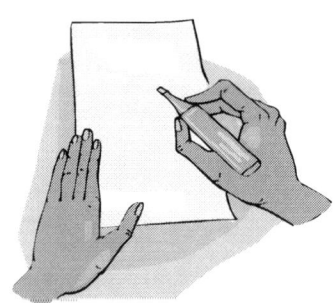

5. PUBLIC PRESENTATIONS

Small groups of students may wish to prepare a formal talk on one of the themes studied. Presentations can be given at school assemblies, neighborhood gatherings, Rotary Club meetings, special observances (e.g., Martin Luther King Day) or holiday celebrations. Arrange a time for students to consult on the following questions:

1. Who is the audience?
2. Purpose of the presentation?
3. Event date, time and place?
4. Topic or title of the talk?
5. Possible activities?
6. Agenda and who will do what?
7. Materials needed and who will bring them?

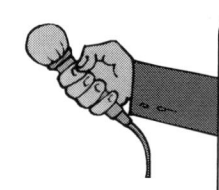

Sample agenda

- Welcome, introductions, music
- Memorized quotes
- Talk on "Unity in Diversity"
- Skit, felt lesson or demonstration
- Questions and answers
- More music, refreshments

6. WHAT'S IN A NAME?

This activity takes some thought and makes a good homework assignment. Tell students to use the letters of their first name to create a statement relating to one of the topics they have studied in class (see examples below). They can recite their statements for the children's performance.

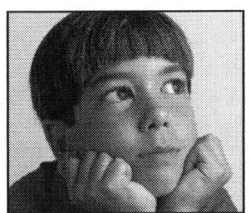

R = Racial
A = Amity
N = Not
D = Division
I = In
E = Every heart

D = Diversity
I = Is
A = Always
N = Nice
E = Everywhere

M = Mankind
A = Actually
N = Needs
U = Unity &
E = Extra
L = Love

7. THE COLD WITHIN

This poem by James Patrick Kinney (1923-1974) can be read aloud or memorized. It can be recited by an individual or by a group as a choral reading. For a description of choral reading techniques, visit: http://myweb.stedwards.edu/mikekb/ReadStrong/choralreading.html. For examples of a choral reading performance, visit: www.youtube.com and enter "choral reading examples" in the search box, and also "jazz chant lemery." The poem is in the public domain.

The Cold Within

Six humans trapped by happenstance
In bleak and bitter cold.
Each one possessed a stick of wood
Or so the story's told.

Their dying fire in need of logs
The first man held his back
For of the faces round the fire
He noticed one was black.

The next man looking 'cross the way
Saw one not of his church
And couldn't bring himself to give
The fire his stick of birch.

The third one sat in tattered clothes.
He gave his coat a hitch.
Why should his log be put to use
To warm the idle rich.

The rich man just sat back and thought
Of the wealth he had in store
And how to keep what he had earned
From the lazy shiftless poor.

The black man's face bespoke revenge
As the fire passed from his sight.
For all he saw in his stick of wood
Was a chance to spite the white.

The last man of this forlorn group
Did nought except for gain.
Giving only to those who gave
Was how he played the game.

Their logs held tight in death's still hands
Was proof of human sin.
They didn't die from the cold without
They died from the cold within.

8. PERSONAL INTERVIEW

The personal interview gives children an opportunity to reach outside their immediate circle, to learn firsthand about people from other backgrounds and, hopefully, to make a new friend.

Interview instructions:

1. Interview another person who is about your same age.

2. Choose someone from a different racial or cultural background than yourself or someone with a different religion, native language or skin color—preferably someone who you don't know very well. For example, an African–American could interview a Native American; an English speaker could interview a Spanish speaker (an interpreter might be needed); a Christian could interview someone of the Muslim or Jewish faith.

3. Find out about their life, for example:
   - Name, age, school and grade level or occupation?
   - Who is in their family and where do they live?
   - Where were they born and where did they grow up?
   - What was their early childhood like?
   - What are some of their cultural traditions or holidays?
   - What are their favorite activities or subjects in school?
   - Do they have any hobbies, pets, sports, etc?
   - What are some of the challenges they have faced?
   - What are their hopes and dreams for the future?

4. The interview should take about 30 minutes or more. You will need a pen and paper to record your questions and their answers. Write a summary of the answers rather than putting down every word.

5. When the interview is over, your partner may wish to interview you for the same assignment or they might choose someone else to interview.

6. Prepare a 1-2 page written report of your interview. Check for spelling, punctuation and neatness before turning it in to the teacher. Be sure to include your name.

7. You will also share with the class a short (3-4 min.) oral report of your interview highlights.

> **To the teacher**: If the class is small, the oral reports can be presented to the entire class. To save time, a large class can be divided into groups of 3-4 for sharing. Then ask each group to select one of the interviews to share with the entire class.
>
> Before listening to these oral reports, ask the students to pay attention to any similarities and differences in the stories. Then discuss these afterward as a class. Close by asking: What did we learn about others from this activity? What did we learn about ourselves?

9. WORLD CITIZEN PASSPORT

Explain to students what a passport is for and show them an example if you have one.

Materials
- ❑ Sample official passport (optional)
- ❑ Passport cover and insides for each student (on following pages)
- ❑ Paper cutter or scissors
- ❑ Glue sticks or white glue
- ❑ Pens and colored pencils, markers or crayons
- ❑ Small colorful stickers or rubber stamps, stamp pads with ink

Instructions
1. Photocopy the following page onto heavy paper.
2. Cut out the cover and fold it in half along the dotted line.
3. Copy the inside pages on plain paper and glue inside the cover.
4. Have students color in the front cover and add their names, ages and home countries.
5. On the inside, they can place a small sticker or rubber stamp in a different box for each country they have visited, studied about or written to a pen pal.
6. The country names can be written at the bottom of each box.

Teaching Unity, Additional Activities, p. 197

Back cover

fold

Front cover

World Citizen Passport

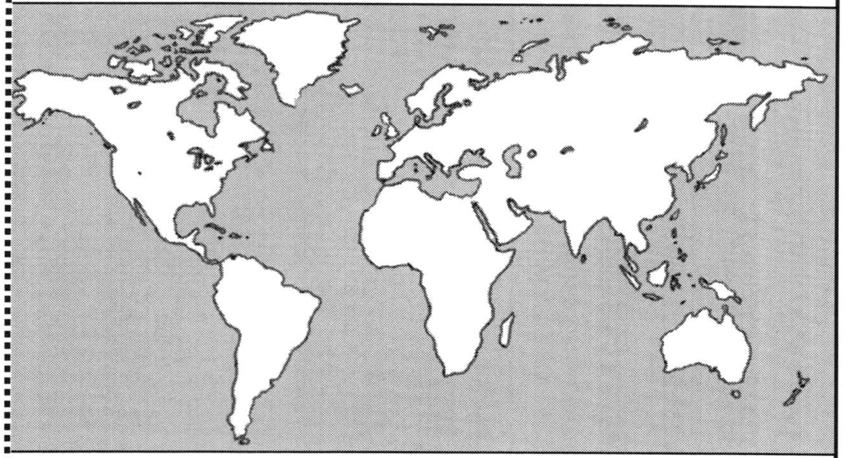

Name: _____
Home country: _____ Age: _____

www.TeachingUnity.com

Teaching Unity, Additional Activities, p. 198

Countries I have visited, read about or written to:

Countries I have visited, read about or written to:

inside pages

Teaching Unity, Additional Activities, p. 199

Further Reading and Research

Some students may be interested in exploring the themes presented in more detail. Below is a small sampling of books for further reading and research. The stories can also be read to the class, or one or more students might put together a book report to share with their peers. See Appendix G for additional resources for teachers and parents.

1. ***People,*** by Peter Spier, 1988 (ISBN: 978-0385244695). In this encyclopedic picture book, the author celebrates human similarities and differences, in what we wear, how we eat, speak, worship and play. This book portrays something of the amazing variety of human life on Earth. Suitable for all ages. Also available in Spanish from www.Amazon.com (enter *gente* and *spier* in the search box).

2. ***Children Just Like Me,*** by Barnabas and Anabel Kindersley in association with UNICEF, 1995 (ISBN: 978-0789402011). A delightful look at children from around the world. The authors spent two years meeting and photographing youngsters from every continent and more than 140 countries. The volume is divided by continent, each of which is introduced with photos of children, their names and nationalities. Then a double-page spread features pictures of each child's food, eating utensils, housing, school, friends and family. The children also comment on their favorite games, friends and hopes for the future.

3. ***All The Colors We Are / Todos los Colores de Nuestra Piel*** (English and Spanish), by Katie Kissinger and Wernher Krutein, 1994 (ISBN: 0-934140-80-4). This bilingual children's book explains how we get our skin color. It offers scientifically accurate explanations, written in simple language and illustrated with beautiful photographs.

4. ***Stephen Biesty's Incredible Body,*** by Stephen Biesty and Richard Platt, 1998 (ISBN: 9780789434241). A fascinating journey through the inner workings of the human body, this oversized volume features cross-sectional illustrations of various organs and systems. Young readers are taken on a tour of the eye, brain, spinal cord, muscles, mouth and gut. The detailed pen-and-ink color drawings are remarkable. As a follow-up to the felt lesson on "The Human Body," this book can serve to deepen children's understanding of the concept of unity in diversity.

5. ***Two Eyes, a Nose and a Mouth / Dos ojos, una nariz y una boca*** (English and Spanish), by Roberta Grobel Intrater, 2000 (ASIN: B000XHRXO6). The book is a celebration of people's similarities and differences with wonderful rhyming text and brilliant colorful photographs of multicultural and multigenerational faces.

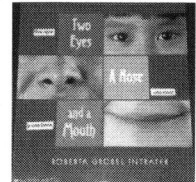

6. ***The Sneetches and Other Stories,*** Dr. Seuss, 1961 (ISBN: 978-0394800899). This collection of four of Dr. Seuss's most charming stories begins with the unforgettable tale of the unfortunate Sneetches, bamboozled by one Sylvester McMonkey McBean who teaches them that prejudice can be costly.

7. ***Through My Eyes,*** by Ruby Bridges, 1999 (ISBN: 978-0590189231). In November 1960, all of America watched as a tiny six-year-old Black girl, surrounded by federal marshals, walked through a mob of screaming segregationists and into her school. An icon of the civil rights movement, the author chronicles each dramatic step of this pivotal event in American history. A beautiful story of courage and faith.

8. ***Sister Ann's Hands,*** by Marybeth Lorbiecki and Wendy Popp, 2000 (ISBN-10: 0140565345). A gifted African-American teacher is just a little too unique for some of the students and parents in a parochial school in the 1960s. The teacher finds a way to educate the children about racism.

9. ***Black Is Brown Is Tan,*** by Arnold Adoff and Emily Arnold Mccully, 1973 and 2004 (ISBN: 9780064432696). Now a classic, this is a beloved story of an African-American mother, a white father, and their two "tan" children in a loving extended family. Softly-colored pictures with poetic, rhyming text sing the joys of family life and appreciate the many skin tones in their biracial family. The language is as magical as the message.

10. ***Two Mrs. Gibsons,*** by Toyomi Igus, 2001 (ISBN: 9780892391707). There are two Mrs. Gibsons in this young girl's life and she remembers both of them with love. The older Mrs. Gibson has skin the color of chocolate, big hands and a big voice, and she gives big hugs. The younger Mrs. Gibson has skin the color of vanilla, writes Japanese and cooks Japanese food. It is not until the end of the book that readers discover that the first Mrs. Gibson is the girl's grandmother, while the second Mrs. Gibson is her mother.

PART IV

Children's Performance

Children's Performance

The children's performance is designed to provide students with an opportunity to demonstrate and reinforce what they have learned. This is often the highlight for children and adults as well. The fact that students will be performing in front of a live audience serves as excellent motivation for them to learn the material presented in class. The program can include songs, memorized passages, short talks, demonstrations to illustrate various concepts, a display of crafts, poetry, skits and a mini-opera. The following pages include a sample agenda for the event, rehearsal instructions, scripts and other materials. Feel free to modify the program to suit the needs of the participants.

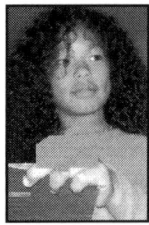 

If you are coordinating this event, it will be helpful to sit in on classes and take notes on which children might be best suited for which presentations. Some students will memorize quotes easily, some may be good at explaining a concept, and others might enjoy acting or presenting one of the felt lessons. Assign parts or ask for volunteers. Be sure everyone is included.

One or two children should be asked to serve as Master or Mistress of Ceremonies (MC). Select children who are responsible, who have strong voices and stage presence, and who can keep the program moving forward. This places children center stage and in charge of the show.

Before the rehearsal, gather any props and costumes, line up assistants and determine their preferences for rehearsal groups. A copy of the agenda and the rehearsal groups should be given to each assistant. Copies of the relevant scripts and readings should be given to the assistants and children who will be working on those parts.

Rehearsal for the Show

During rehearsal time, the coordinator's tasks include:

- ❏ Meet together with all the participants to explain the nature of the program.
- ❏ Talk about program order, where to sit, use of strong voices so the audience can hear, eye contact, learning the parts rather than reading them, and how to use a microphone if needed.
- ❏ Select assistants to work with each rehearsal group.
- ❏ Assign parts to each child depending on interest and ability.
- ❏ Distribute costumes and props as appropriate.
- ❏ Inform groups when the rehearsal time is almost over.
- ❏ Collect all props and set them out for the show.

> Note: While our children's performance has typically been scheduled for the evening, the program could be held at any time. During a weekend retreat, Saturday evening is often the most convenient time for inviting neighbors and friends. This means that activities from the fourth class on Sunday morning will not be included in the presentation.

Materials Needed

Note: Items in italics are included in this section. This list of materials, the sample agenda, rehearsal groups and program for the audience are included as editable Word documents in the downloads for this book.

- ❑ *Agenda*
- ❑ *Rehearsal groups* and *Rehearsal notes*
- ❑ Welcome sign (if desired)
- ❑ *Sample program* (for distributing to the audience)
- ❑ Background music (to be played as people are arriving)
- ❑ Microphone and sound system (if needed)
- ❑ Art exhibit (children's art can be hung from a clothesline or displayed on the wall)
- ❑ Song sheets for all (including audience) and music (for song leader)
- ❑ Felt board and easel
- ❑ Memory quotes
- ❑ Stick and bundle of sticks for skit
- ❑ Sturdy chair for skit
- ❑ *The Eye* (script and felt pieces)
- ❑ *Hooray for Skin* (poem)
- ❑ Colors of Our World (four color pictures)
- ❑ *How We Got Our Skin Color* (script and props for skit)
- ❑ *Barriers into Bonds* (script and felt pieces)
- ❑ *We Can Build a Beautiful World* (song sheet and costumes for mini-opera)
- ❑ Craft samples:
  - __ Lanyards
  - __ Flowers of One Garden
  - __ Leaf Laminate
  - __ Diversity Streamer
  - __ Personal Poster
  - __ Barriers into Bonds design
- ❑ Refreshments

> Note: If you have time for a longer program, you can also include some of the craft projects, skits and demonstrations from the "Additional Activities" section.

Sample Agenda for MC (90 min.)

(1) **Welcome guests** to our program on **"THE LIGHT OF UNITY"** (cell phones off)

(2) **Opening music** _____

(3) **Intro** (don't read): There is only one race of people in the world, the human race, and we all belong to it. We come in different shapes, sizes and colors, but we are one human family. Our world will be a better place when all people learn to live and work together in unity. We have been studying about unity all week, and tonight we are pleased to present what we have learned.

(4) **Introduce** each section and each presenter and thank them afterwards.

THE LIGHT OF UNITY (15 min.)
- ❑ Song: One Planet, One People (ALL)
- ❑ **Say**: With all of the problems facing the world today, one of our most important needs is unity. These next two skits will help us understand why.
- ❑ Stick and bundle demo _____
- ❑ Heavy chair skit _____
- ❑ Craft: Lanyards _____
- ❑ Memory quote: "So powerful is the light of unity…"_____

UNITY IN DIVERSITY (20 min.)
- ❑ Song: Hawaiian Unity Song (ALL)
- ❑ Memory quote: "We are all the fruits…" _____
- ❑ Short talk: Unity in Diversity _____
- ❑ Crafts: Flower poster _____ Leaf laminate_____ Diversity streamer_____
- ❑ Musical demo: Row Your Boat _____
- ❑ Felt lesson: The Eye _____
- ❑ Song: Rapp Song (ALL)

THE COLORS WE ARE (20 min.)
- ❑ Poem: Hooray for Skin _____
- ❑ Craft: Personal poster _____
- ❑ Memory quote: "What should it matter…" _____
- ❑ Short talk: Colors of Our World _____ _____
- ❑ Skit: How We Got Our Skin Color ─────────▶
- ❑ Song: Good Neighbors (ALL)

1. _____
2. _____
3. _____
4. _____
5. _____
6. _____
7. _____

OVERCOMING PREJUDICE (30 min.)
- ❑ Poem: Sneetches excerpt
- ❑ Felt lesson: Barriers into Bonds _____
- ❑ Song: What Mankind Has to Learn (ALL)
- ❑ Memory quote: "Darkness cannot drive out darkness…" _____
- ❑ Mini-opera: We Can Build a Beautiful World
- ❑ Craft: Barriers into Bonds_____ _____
- ❑ Song: Listen (ALL STAND)
- ❑ **Say**: We hope you liked our program. Please join us for refreshments!

Teaching Unity, Children's Performance, p. 207

Rehearsal Groups

Scripts and instructions are included on the following pages.

PROGRAM COORDINATOR: _____

- ❑ Select and orient 1 or 2 MCs. Provide each with a clipboard, pencil and copy of the agenda.
- ❑ Divide children into 3 groups and assign assistants to each group (7-8 assistants total).
- ❑ Make sure each child has at least one part in addition to the group songs.
- ❑ The songs can be practiced all together at the end of the group rehearsal.
- ❑ One or two children can be asked to play a short musical selection to begin the program.

Rehearse each part below with the children. The order will be different during the show.

GROUP #1: Demonstrations and Skit (very little speaking, easiest parts)
(2 adults + 7 children)

- ❑ Stick and Bundle Demo *(see rehearsal notes)*
- ❑ Chair Lift Skit *(see rehearsal notes)*
- ❑ Skit: "How We Got Our Skin Color"

1. _____
2. _____
3. _____
4. _____
5. _____
6. _____
7. _____

GROUP #2: Singing (singing and acting, medium difficulty)
(2-3 adults + 9 or more children)

- ❑ Musical Demo *(see rehearsal notes)*
- ❑ Mini-opera: "We Can Build A Beautiful World"

GROUP #3: Speaking (variety of parts, medium difficulty and above)
If necessary, use children from the other groups after they have finished.
(3-4 adults + 5 or more children)

- ❑ Poem: "Hooray for Skin" _____ _____ _____ _____
  (as an individual or a choral reading)
- ❑ Memory quotes _____ _____ _____ _____
- ❑ Show each craft, explain how you made it and what it means (2-3 children each):

Lanyards	_____	_____	_____
Flowers of One Garden	_____	_____	_____
Leaf Laminate	_____	_____	_____
Diversity Streamer	_____	_____	_____
Personal Posters	_____	_____	_____
Barriers into Bonds	_____	_____	_____

1. _____
2. _____
3. _____
4. _____
5. _____
6. _____
7. _____
8. _____
9. _____

- ❑ Short talk on "Unity in Diversity" (1 or 2 children) _____ _____
- ❑ Short talk on "Colors of Our World" *(see rehearsal notes)* _____ _____
- ❑ Felt lesson: "The Eye" _____ _____
- ❑ Felt lesson: "Barriers into Bonds" _____ _____

Rehearsal Notes

Stick and Bundle Demo *(1 child)* _____

Materials: One thin stick, a lot of thin sticks tied together in a bundle

1. Ask an audience member to come up and try to break the stick. (It should be easy.)
2. Then give the same person the bundle of sticks to break. (This should be impossible.)
3. Ask: What can we learn from this? (There is strength in unity.)

Chair Lift Skit *(5 children)* _____ _____ _____ _____ _____

Materials: A sturdy chair

1. Have one child sit silently in a sturdy chair at the front of the room.
2. Four other children enter and, one by one, each tries to lift the chair without success. (They should struggle and grunt, hamming it up to show how difficult it is.)
3. Then the children consult, decide to work together to lift the chair with its occupant, carry it a few steps, gently set it down, congratulate each other and take a bow.

Musical Demo *(1 child who can lead a song)* _____

1. Hum a single musical note and ask the audience to hum it with you. Then sing "Row, row, row your boat" (or other common song) with the audience, but tell them they can only use that one note. (The song will sound rather dull.) Explain that this is a demonstration of **sameness**. Bo-ring!

2. Next, tell the audience that when you give the signal, they should loudly make as many different noises as they can. You should hear screeching, squawking, cackling, hooting, hissing, howling, barking and other discordant sounds. Stop them after a few seconds, and explain that this is a demonstration of **diversity without unity**. It's what we see in the world today.

3. Then quickly divide the audience into three groups (about equal in size), and give each group one note of a three-note chord. The music leader can help with this. Have each group hum its note separately, then have all sing together for (hopefully) a pleasing sound. Explain that this is a demonstration of **unity in diversity**, and it takes practice.

Colors of Our World *(2 children)* _____ _____

Materials: Four color pictures (see Unit 3, activity #4)

1. Explain to the audience that there are many types of pigments or colorings that brighten our world:

   - **Carotene** pigment makes carrots and pumpkins orange.
   - **Chlorophyll** pigment makes leaves and grass green.
   - **Hemoglobin** pigment makes our blood red.
   - **Melanin** pigment makes our skin brown.

   While speaking, hold up a large color picture of each item. See examples below.

2. All people have melanin in their skin. Melanin protects us from the sun's harmful rays—as you will see in our next skit!

Short Talk on "Unity in Diversity" *(1 or 2 children)* _____ _____

Materials: The children can review their handouts on "Unity" and "Unity in Diversity" for ideas. Encourage them to speak naturally using their own words rather than reading. They can make a sketch or write a few key words on a card as a memory aid.

Skit: "How We Got Our Skin Color" *(1 narrator + 6 easy parts = 7 children)*

_____ + _____ _____ _____ _____ _____ _____

1. Read through the skit with the group. (See following pages.)
2. Ask for volunteers, audition the narrator and assign parts.
3. Distribute costumes and props. (See script for list of materials.)
4. Rehearse the skit. (The narrator should practice with a microphone if needed.)

– Sample program for the audience –

Children's Performance

The Light of Unity

Welcome and opening music

The Light of Unity
- One Planet, One People (song)
- Stick and Bundle (demo)
- The Heavy Chair (skit)
- Lanyards (craft)
- Memory quote

Unity in Diversity
- Hawaiian Unity Song
- Memory quote
- Unity in Diversity (speech)
- Flowers of one garden (craft)
- Leaf laminate (craft)
- Diversity streamer (craft)
- Musical demonstration
- The Eye (felt lesson)
- Rapp Song

The Colors We Are
- Hooray for Skin (poem)
- Personal posters
- Memory quote
- Colors of Our World
- How We Got Our Skin Color (skit)
- Good Neighbors Come in All Colors (song)

Overcoming Prejudice
- The Sneetches (poem)
- Barriers into Bonds (felt lesson)
- What Mankind Has to Learn (song)
- Memory quote
- We Can Build a Beautiful World (mini-opera)
- Barriers into Bonds (craft)
- Listen (song)

Refreshments

– Script for felt lesson –

"The Eye"

Note: One student reads the narration while a second student places the felt pieces.

	NARRATION	ACTION	
1	The eye is an example of unity in diversity.	Place large white eye in center of felt board.	
2	Each part of the eye has a different job, but they all work together for the same goal.	Place blue circle in center of eye; then add black circle on top.	
3	For example, the pupil is the black opening in front of the eye that admits light, so we can see.	Point to black pupil.	
4	The iris opens and closes, changing the size of the pupil to let in just the right amount of light.	Point to blue iris.	
5	What would happen if all the parts of the eye were the same?	Place white circle over other circles.	

The parts of the eye are different, but they all work together, and all are necessary for sight.

Teaching Unity, Children's Performance, p. 212

HOORAY FOR SKIN
by Susan Engle

Rejoice and celebrate the skin
That keeps the veins and muscles in,
That keeps the cold and germies out.
That is what skin is all about.

Suppose that when you got your skin,
You found the skin side outside-in.
So when you talk to Mrs. Jones,
Your eyes meet over fat and bones,
And tissues, blue and white and red,
That stretch from toe to hand to head.
It makes me glad to have a skin
To keep the outside boneside-in.

Now there are folks who would be mad
If our insides were all they had
To tell all kinds of folks apart.
Maybe they'd learn to read the heart
Instead of judging from a hue
If one man's false and one man's true.

Let's all join hands and feast our eyes
On skins of every shape and size,
Of every tone of gold or white,
Of luscious black, of dark or light,
Of every shade that folks come in.
Rejoice and celebrate the skin.

© 1986, Susan Engle. Used with permission.

Note: For the performance, this poem can be recited by a single child, by two children alternating verses or lines, or by a group of children as a choral reading.

How We Got Our Skin Color

<u>Materials</u>
- ❑ Knee-high women's nylon stockings or socks (3 of medium shade, 1 dark, 1 light)
- ❑ Paper sun on pole (see next page)
- ❑ Strip of red cloth

<u>Characters</u> *(7 children)*
1. Narrator
2. Sun (child holding up sun on pole)
3. Sunburn Kid (with red cloth wrapped around one arm)
4. Weakbone Kid (walks slowly, bent over)
5. Three Melanin Kids (Each wears a medium shade nylon stocking on the right arm. In addition, the first child carries a dark nylon, and the third child wears a light nylon under the medium one.)

1. _____
2. _____
3. _____
4. _____
5. _____
6. _____
7. _____

Note: All characters enter from stage right (actor's right when facing audience) and exit stage left.

	NARRATION	ACTION
1	How did we get our skin color? We all need just the right amount of sunlight in order to survive.	Sun enters, moves to center stage.
2	Too much sun can cause sunburn, skin cancer or heatstroke.	Sunburn Kid enters with red arm hidden at first. Sun touches kid's arm, kid says *ouch!* and shows the "burn," then exits frowning.
3	Too little sun can cause weak bones.	Sun sets. Weakbone Kid limps across stage and exits frowning.
4	Melanin, the coloring in our skin, helps to block the sun's rays.	Sun rises. Melanin Kids enter together, line up in front of sun facing audience, with right arms out, smiling.
5	If your ancestors lived in a very warm climate, they developed more melanin in their skin to protect them from the hot sun.	Sun moves close to and "shines" on first kid who adds a dark nylon over the medium nylon on right arm.
6	If your ancestors lived in a very cold climate, they developed less melanin in their skin so more sunlight could enter.	Third kid (farthest from the sun) removes medium nylon to reveal a light one underneath.
7	And that's how we got the colors of our skin.	Kids proudly show off their skin colors to the audience, then exit smiling.

Skit is based on concepts from the book, *All the Colors We Are* by Katie Kissinger.

Teaching Unity – Children's Performance

Sun pattern for skit on "How We Got Our Skin Color"

Cut from yellow paper.

1. Trace around this circle on bright yellow paper and cut it out to make the sun. You can also trace a dinner plate or other large circular object.
2. Cut 8-10 yellow triangles to make the sun's rays.
3. Glue the sun and its rays onto the inside of a blue manila folder or blue poster board to represent the sky.
4. Using a permanent marker, draw a nose and a mouth on the sun.
5. Using a sharp point, poke two holes through the sun approximately where eyes would be, and insert the arms of a real pair of sunglasses. (Use the glasses to measure for correct spacing of the holes.)
6. Add masking tape to the back of the poster to reinforce the holes.
7. Tape the poster to a yardstick, broom handle or other lightweight pole.
8. To store, remove the stick and glasses and close the folder.

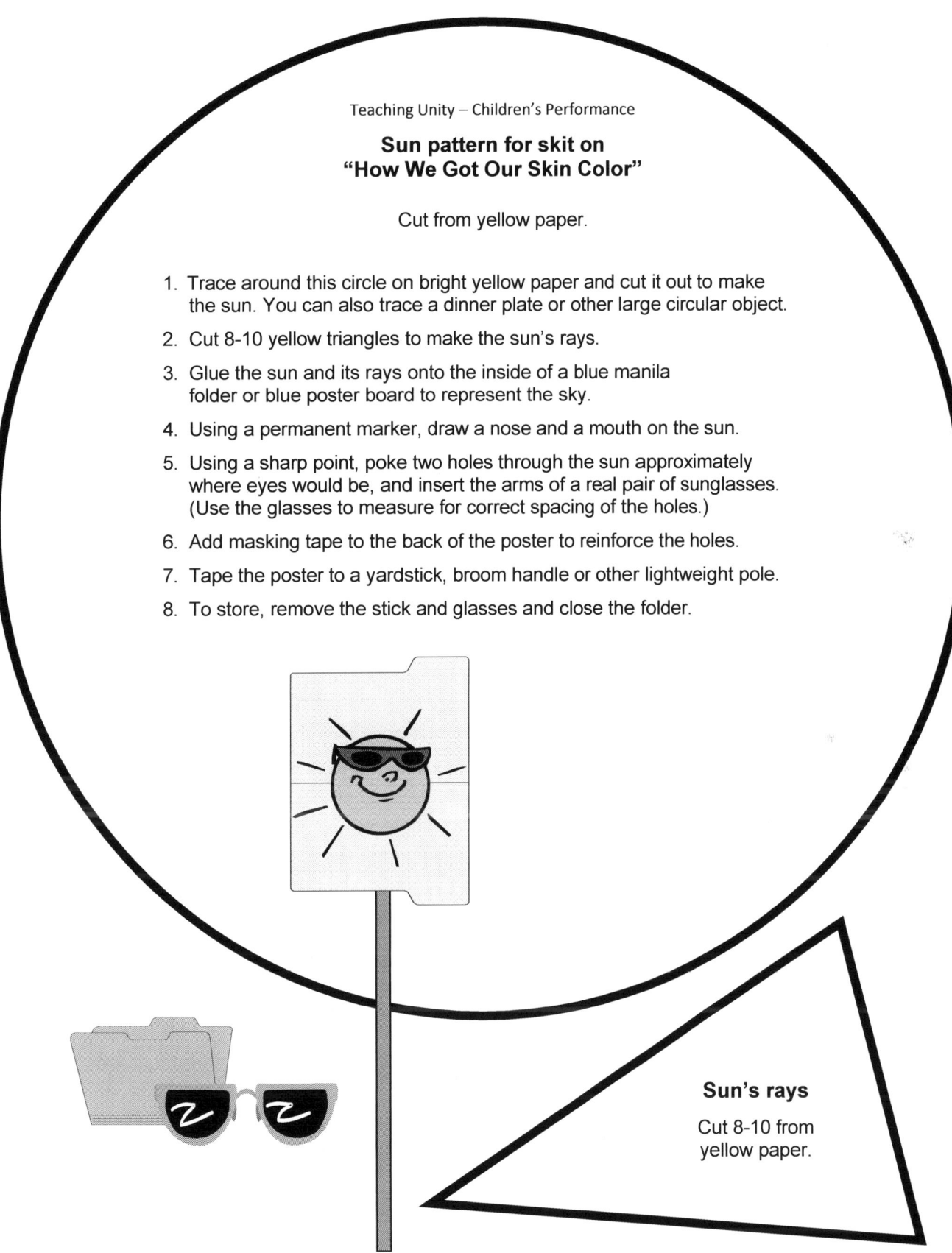

Sun's rays

Cut 8-10 from yellow paper.

– Script for felt lesson –

"Barriers into Bonds"

Note: One student reads the narration while a second student places the felt pieces.

	NARRATION	ACTION
1	All around the world people are different in many ways.	Place globe in center of felt board and add the people around it in a circle. 
2	We have different skin colors, speak different languages, come from different cultures, live in different countries, and practice different religions.	As each difference is mentioned, place it above one of the people.
3	Some people dislike others without even knowing them just because of these differences. This is called prejudice. Because of prejudice, our differences have become barriers between us.	Place the barriers between the people. 
4	But we can overcome these prejudices through the power of unity.	Clasp your hands together.
5	When we realize that we all belong to the same human family, we will see our differences as a source of beauty and strength. Then these barriers will become bonds.	Flip the barriers over and turn them sideways to form bonds. 
6	When the human family is united, the world will finally be at peace.	Add the dove above the earth. 

Teaching Unity, Children's Performance, p. 216

 # We Can Build a Beautiful World

© Russ Garcia. Music excerpted and simplified.
Used with permission. See music section for sheet music.

Divide children into three groups with costumes as indicated below. Include choreographed gestures if desired. The audience can also be divided into three groups, given the words, and asked to join in.

Group A: Green people are the best. Far better than the rest.
We hate you because you're different!
We are superior, you are inferior.
We love us and we hate you, my friend.

Group B: Purple people are the best. Far better than the rest.
We hate you because you're different!
We are superior, you are inferior.
We love us and we hate you, my friend.

(Sung in a round)

A: Green people are the best. Far better than the rest.
B: (silent)

A: We hate you because you're different!
B: Purple people are the best. Far better than the rest.

A: We are superior, you are inferior.
B: We hate you because you're different!

A: We love us and we hate you, my...
B: We are superior, you are inferior.

A: ...friend.
B: We love us and we hate you, my...
C: **We can build a ...**

A: We love us and we hate you.
B: ...friend.
C: **...beautiful world...**

A: (silent)
B: We love us and we hate you.
C: **...when we learn that...**

A: (silent)
B: (silent)
C: **...mankind is one.**

Costumes

Group A: Green T-shirts
Group B: Purple T-shirts
Group C: Red or multi-colored T-shirts

Sample Gestures

For Us: Thumbs up, pat heart, thumbs in lapels

For Them: Thumbs down, press palm out, hold nose

Unifiers: Help all join hands.

All: We can have a wonderful world, when we learn to love.

We can build a beautiful world,
When we learn the earth is one land.
We can have a wonderful world,
When we learn to love.

We can build a beautiful world,
When we learn to love all mankind.
We can have a wonderful world,
**WHEN WE LEARN TO LOVE!
LOVE!! LOVE!!! LOVE!!!! LOVE!!!!!**

A few photos from our children's performance

Closing Activities

At the end of the event or after the final class session on this theme, the organizers may wish to plan some closing activities for the participants. We have found the following schedule to be very effective. After the cleanup, call everyone together for a celebration of their achievements.

1. **Opening:** Begin with a welcome and some group singing.

2. **Thought for the Day:** Ask for individual volunteers to recite any of the memory quotes they have learned, or have the students recite them together as a group:

   > So powerful is the light of unity
   > that it can illuminate the whole earth.
   >
   > We are all the fruits of one tree,
   > the flowers of one garden, the waves of one sea.
   >
   > What should it matter that one bowl is dark and the other is pale,
   > if each is of good design and serves its purpose well?
   >
   > Darkness cannot drive out darkness; only light can do that.
   > Hate cannot drive out hate; only love can do that.

3. **Evaluation:** Conduct a short oral evaluation of the activities. Ask each child, youth and adult to share brief thoughts on the three items to the right. These should be written on the board. Anyone may pass his or her turn. Suggestions can be considered in planning for the next class or event. An adult should take notes.

   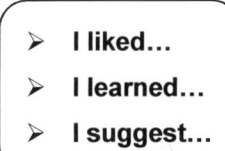
   - I liked...
   - I learned...
   - I suggest...

4. **Appreciations:** The organizers can then share any closing comments and present small gifts of appreciation to the teachers, assistants, musicians, cooks and other helpers.

5. **Follow-up:** Any follow-up suggestions and messages from the sponsoring institution can be shared at this time (see the following page for ideas).

6. **Certificates:** Certificates can be presented during a simple ceremony to recognize those students who have completed a weeklong unity camp or similar event.

7. **Announcements:** Share logistical information (lost-and-found items, rides home, etc.).

8. **Song:** Close with a sing-along, for example, "One Planet" or "Hawaiian Unity Song."

9. **Group photo:** Be sure everyone is included!

10. **Dessert:** We have a much-appreciated tradition of serve-yourself ice cream sundaes.

Follow-up Ideas

> Sponsoring organizations, teachers and parents can help children apply their new knowledge and skills by providing a variety of opportunities for practice.

A few examples are listed below:

1. During an all-school assembly, parent night or open house, encourage the children to share what they have learned about unity, diversity and overcoming prejudice.

2. During show-and-tell, students can be asked to do the skin-color demonstration and explain how we got our skin colors.

3. Invite them to visit a class for younger children to present one of the felt lessons about unity (*The Eye, Barriers into Bonds, The Human Body*).

4. Arrange for them to sing at the year-end concert (*One Planet, Hawaiian Unity Song, Good Neighbors, What Mankind Has to Learn, Listen, Multicultural Rapp Song*).

5. Prepare a library display of their craft projects (lanyards, flowers of one garden collage, leaf laminates, diversity streamers, personal posters, barriers into bonds design).

6. Have them perform some of the skits on unity (bundle of sticks, chair lift, donkey tug o' war) during a fund-raising event or special holiday celebration.

7. Invite them to recite their memorized passages or perform a choral reading of the *Hooray for Skin* poem during a local community observance, for example, Martin Luther King Day or Race Unity Day.

8. Assist them to form an after-school Unity Club or Multicultural Club, so they can continue to discuss and apply what they have learned.

9. Teachers can also write a brief report on the children's class activities and submit this with photos to the school newsletter or the local paper.

PART V
Planning a Retreat or Camp

Planning a Children's Retreat or Camp

Planning Committee

If you are planning an event such as a children's retreat or vacation camp, one or more responsible individuals will be needed to handle all the details, including finances, scheduling, publicity, registration, record-keeping, menu planning, purchase of supplies and craft materials, correspondence, staff orientation and preparation of the facility.

A committee could be appointed by the host organization or a group of parents could handle the arrangements. In either case, planning should begin several months in advance. (See checklist, pages 249-250.)

The committee will need to select a general coordinator to oversee the entire event. The coordinator can be responsible for conducting an orientation meeting, introducing the teachers, supervising key personnel (including cooks if meals or snacks will be served), general problem-solving, thanking any volunteers, and facilitating an evaluation session at the end.

Participants

The activities in this book are designed for children ages 8–12 (grades 3-7). Many activities can also be adapted for older or younger children.

In addition to establishing age limits, you may want to set a firm minimum and maximum number of participants who can attend. With just a handful of children, it is hard to establish the desired spirit and sense of community. With more than 25 children, the dynamic changes and the event may not run as smoothly. Larger groups can therefore be organized into two or more smaller groups—each with its own meeting space and teachers. Aim for a roughly equal number of girls and boys. Additional names can be put on a waiting list and contacted in the event of a cancellation.

Teachers

One individual could teach all of the lessons, the classes can be team-taught, or a different person might be asked to lead each activity. This book contains detailed lesson plans which should be copied for the teachers well in advance, giving them time to prepare. Teachers may need a small budget for supplies.

The quality of the teacher is critical to the success of the class. Teachers do not need to have professional training since the lesson plans have clear step-by-step instructions, easy-to-use patterns for producing the classroom materials, and ready-to-copy student handouts. However, teachers and their assistants should be patient, encouraging, enthusiastic, reliable, organized, able to lead class discussions, and comfortable with participatory teaching methods.

We have found capable assistant teachers from among the parents and older siblings of the participating children. With a brief orientation, they proved to be very effective and greatly enjoyed the experience.

As a general precaution, the sponsoring organization may wish to require background checks or other advance clearance for those who will be working with children, including teachers, chaperones, parents, recreation leaders and youth volunteers.

Special Role of Youth

Capable youth can be invited to assist with teaching and mentoring the children. We have found that many former participants are eager to return as volunteers. They have been a great help to the adults and a joy for the younger children. This hands-on experience also offers the youth an opportunity to be of service to their community and to acquire new skills and confidence. In addition, a unified family atmosphere is created with all age groups working together to educate the children.

Kierra, Alex, Yuri, Brynne, Alonso, Carew, Layli

Kierra records ideas from her discussion group

In the words of one youth:

> *"The retreats have been an integral part of my growing up experience, and I'm so grateful for the opportunity to come and help out now as a youth. It's really special to see my brothers and cousins and their friends, and know that they'll grow up with the same wonderful friendships and learning experiences and shared memories that my generation of youth gained.*
>
> *"I learned a lot about myself and discovered how to help kids learn and grow, and ways to make their experience happy. Although I went through all the same lessons myself, it's still great to hear and see the lessons again. Us kids have so much fun every time and I am always looking forward to the next retreat."* (Brynne H., age 16)

Other Personnel

A variety of volunteers or paid staff may be needed for the smooth functioning of your event. Volunteers can handle registration, greet children as they arrive, and show them to their sleeping quarters if they will be staying overnight. Volunteers can assist with classroom management—for example, by removing a disruptive child if necessary or by working one-on-one with those who need extra help. Volunteers can assist with craft projects and recreational activities. They can be put in charge of discussion groups, lead the singing and organize the children's performance. A special coordinator can also be selected to supervise the volunteers.

All assistants should be carefully chosen since they will act as role models for the children. They will work with them during classes, eat with them during meals, supervise them during free time and chaperone them in the dorms at night.

Brynne works with Grayson and Raul

It is important to emphasize that people should only volunteer if they truly intend to be of service. When volunteers come primarily to socialize with their peers, it can make the teacher's job more difficult and detract from the children's experience.

Facility

Your event can be held in a home, community center, campground, school, retreat center or other suitable facility. There should be sufficient parking space and access to public transportation if necessary, adequate kitchen and bathroom facilities, a classroom, dining area, place for arts and crafts, space for outdoor activities, and separate sleeping areas for males and females if children will be staying overnight. Our community uses a large private home for its children's retreats. Classes are held in the living room, folding tables are set up in the garage for meals and craft activities, and the tables are replaced with rows of chairs for the children's performance at the end of the event.

Finances

Food, craft supplies, instructional materials and other items must be purchased for the event. The host agency might decide to cover these expenses, donations can be requested, a special fund-raising event could be organized, or a fee can be charged to participants. If a fee is charged, full or partial scholarships can be offered based on need. We usually give a discount for families with two or more children attending, and volunteers are not charged. A sample budget for a weekend retreat is provided below.

* For a typical two-day retreat with 20 children and 10 volunteers, average food costs (for six meals plus snacks), runs about $10 per person for the weekend.

SAMPLE RETREAT BUDGET

Income
Participant fees $400.00
Donations 150.00

TOTAL INCOME $550.00

Expenses
Food 300.00*
Craft supplies 185.00
Costumes 40.00
Photocopies 25.00

TOTAL EXPENSES $550.00

Schedule

Sample schedules for a two-day weekend retreat, a three-day retreat, and a week-long Unity Camp are included below. The two-day schedule offers participants a choice of some of the crafts and classroom activities. The three-day schedule includes more of the crafts and activities, an evening talent show, and a group consultation on how to share with others the concepts learned at the retreat. The week-long camp allows for additional learning activities.

If these lessons are being used on a regular weekly basis, for example, as part of an after-school club, or Saturday or Sunday school, you might begin each meeting with a welcome for new children, followed by songs, prayers (if yours is a religious group), and a review of the previous lesson (including any student presentations), followed by the selected activities. At the beginning of each meeting, consider scheduling "circle time" to give children an opportunity to share news of interest to the group or to consult on pressing concerns. End each session with a review, recitation of any memory quotes, more singing, and refreshments.

– Sample 2-day schedule –

Children's Retreat
Our Town Community Center, May 4-6

"The Power of Unity"

FRIDAY
5:30 pm	Check in and decorate folders
6:00	Dinner
7:30	Group singing and orientation
8:00	**Evening program**
9:00	Volunteer briefing
9:30	Closing song and bedtime
10:00	Lights out

SATURDAY
7:30 am	Wake-up call
8:00	Breakfast
8:30	Singing
8:45	**Class #1: The Light of Unity** (75 min.)
10:00	Break
10:30	**Class #2: Unity in Diversity** (1 hr. 45 min.)
12:15 pm	Lunch and quiet time
1:30	**Class #3: The Colors We Are** (90 min.)
3:00	Snack and outdoor activities
4:30	Rehearsal for children's performance
6:00	Dinner
7:00	Prepare refreshments, rehearse songs
8:00	**Children's performance**
9:15	Refreshments and socializing
10:00	Closing song and bedtime
10:30	Lights out

SUNDAY
8:00 am	Wake-up call
8:30	Breakfast
9:00	Singing
9:15	**Class #4: Overcoming Prejudice** (1 hr. 45 min.)
11:00	Outdoor activities
12:00 pm	Lunch
12:30	Clean-up
1:00	Closing activities, evaluation, recognitions
1:30	Group photo
1:45	Dessert
2:00	Check lost-and-found; farewells

Teaching Unity, Planning a Retreat or Camp, p. 227

– Sample 3-day schedule –

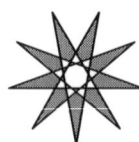

Children's Retreat
Our Town Community Center, May 4-7

"The Power of Unity"

FRIDAY
- 5:30 pm — Check in and decorate folders
- 6:00 — Dinner
- 7:30 — Group singing and orientation
- **8:00** — **Evening program**
- 9:00 — Volunteer briefing
- 9:30 — Closing song and bedtime
- 10:00 — Lights out

SATURDAY
- 7:30 am — Wake-up call
- 8:00 — Breakfast
- 8:30 — Singing
- **8:45** — **Class #1: The Light of Unity** (75 min.)
- 10:00 — Break
- **10:30** — **Class #2: Unity in Diversity** (1 hr. 45 min.)
- 12:15 pm — Lunch and quiet time
- 1:30 — Craft activities
- 3:00 — Snack and outdoor activities
- 4:30 — Memorization practice (alone, pairs or groups)
- 5:15 — Group singing practice or free time
- 6:00 — Dinner
- 7:15 — Singing and share memorized quotes
- **8:00** — **Evening program** (children's video, talent show, etc.)
- 9:15 — Evening snack
- 9:30 — Closing song and bedtime
- 10:00 — Lights out

SUNDAY
- 8:00 am — Wake-up call
- 8:30 — Breakfast
- 9:00 — Singing
- **9:15** — **Class #3: The Colors We Are** (90 min.)
- 10:45 — Outdoor activities
- 12:00 pm — Lunch and quiet time
- **1:30** — **Class #4: Overcoming Prejudice** (1 hr. 45 min.)
- 3:15 — Snack and outdoor activities
- 4:15 — Rehearsal for children's performance
- 6:00 — Dinner

– Sample 3-day schedule, continued –

SUNDAY
- 7:00 pm — Prepare refreshments, rehearse songs
- **8:00 — Children's performance**
- 9:15 — Refreshments and socializing
- 10:00 — Closing song and bedtime
- 10:30 — Lights out

MONDAY
- 8:30 am — Wake-up call
- 9:00 — Breakfast
- 9:30 — Singing
- **9:45 — Group consultation on how to share what we learned**
- 10:30 — Outdoor activities
- 12:00 pm — Lunch
- 12:30 — Clean-up
- 1:00 — Closing activities, evaluation, recognitions
- 1:30 — Group photo
- 1:45 — Dessert
- 2:00 — Check lost-and-found; farewells

During the volunteer briefing at the start of the retreat, children should be given a simultaneous activity such as watching an appropriate video, playing a game or singing. We often put out puzzles for the children to work on. If schedules permit, the volunteer briefing can be held prior to the retreat.

Indoor games

Marshmallow roast

Parachute challenge

Note: The sample newsletter announcement, flier with registration form, daily and weekend schedules (pages 227, 230–232) are included as editable Word documents in the downloads for this book.

– Sample daily schedule –

UNITY CAMP

Day camp sponsored by the Harmony Park Association

	MONDAY	TUESDAY	WEDNESDAY	THURSDAY	FRIDAY
8:00-9:00	Before-care (by arrangement with additional fee)				
9:00	Welcome and sign in (folder decorating)	Welcome and sign in (rainbow chain)	Welcome and sign in (ribbon of hearts)	Welcome and sign in (paper people)	Welcome and sign in (free drawing)
9:30	Morning circle: orientation, rules, singing, discussion on ways to share what we learned				
10:00	Warm-up activities (unity bingo)	Warm-up activities (group match)	Warm-up activities (link-ups)	Warm-up activities (human knot)	Instructions for children's performance
10:30	Snack (light snack provided)				
10:45	Class #1 The Light of Unity	Class #2 Unity in Diversity	Class #3 The Colors We Are	Class #4 Overcoming Prejudice	Rehearsal for children's performance
12:00	Lunch and quiet time (campers bring own lunch)				
1:30	Art project (flowers of one garden)	Art project (diversity streamers)	Art project (personal poster)	Art project (barriers into bonds)	Final rehearsal
3:00	Snack (light snack provided)				**Children's performance** Recognitions, group photo, evaluations, refreshments, lost and found, farewells
3:15	Outdoor activities (all aboard)	Outdoor activities (lava island)	Outdoor activities (trust walk)	Outdoor activities (tug of peace)	
3:45	Clean up and prepare for departure				
4:00	Departure				
4:00-5:00	After-care (by arrangement with additional fee)				

Publicity

Once you have selected a date, obtained a facility, confirmed the teachers and finalized the schedule, you will need to publicize your event. The sample newsletter announcement below, and the sample fliers on the following pages, will give you some ideas.

– Sample newsletter announcement –

UNITY CAMP PLANNED

Save the date!

A weeklong Unity Camp for children ages 8-12, is scheduled for August 5-9 at Harmony Park. The camp will run Monday through Friday, from 9:00 a.m. – 4:00 p.m., with a children's performance on Friday starting at 3:00 p.m.

The program is designed to teach kids about the oneness of humanity, the value of diversity and the need for unity.

We will be learning about:

- The Light of Unity
- Unity in Diversity
- The Colors We Are
- Overcoming Prejudice

Your child will participate in a variety of activities including music, arts and crafts, drama, reading, group discussion and outdoor games.

Unity Camp is a safe place to learn and grow while having fun!

Phone: (805) 555-2244
Email: HarmonyPark@yahoo.com

– Sample flier with registration form –

UNITY CAMP

for kids ages 8–12

Sponsored by the Harmony Park Association

Join us for a week of learning and fun with music, arts & crafts, drama, games, storytelling, snacks, new friends & more!

August 5-9, 20____
Harmony Park, 1863 Peace Street
Harmony, CA 93428 - (805) 555-2244

COST: $150 per child ($99 if paid before June 15). Scholarships available.
Make checks payable to: Harmony Park Association. Space is limited; please apply early.

Participants should bring a sack lunch and any medicines with clear instructions. Wear play clothes, sturdy shoes and sunscreen. Please do NOT bring electronic games, radios, CDs, iPods, etc.

Monday through Friday, 9:00 a.m. – 4:00 p.m.
Children's performance Friday starting at 3:00 p.m.
Ask us about extended care before and after camp.

- -

 UNITY CAMP

Mail this form to the address above. For questions, email: HarmonyPark@yahoo.com

Child's name (print): _____ Age: _____ Sex: _____

Address: _____ Phone: _____

Email: _____ Fee enclosed: $ _____ Partial scholarship requested: $ _____

Emergency contact: _____ Phone: _____

Medical or dietary information: _____

The child named above has my permission to attend the Unity Camp on August 5-9, 20____ at Harmony Park. I understand that s/he is participating at her/his own risk. I hereby give the event organizers permission to administer first aid and obtain emergency medical treatment if necessary.

_____   _____   _____
Parent or Guardian (print name)   Signature   Date

Teaching Unity, Planning a Retreat or Camp, p. 232

– Sample flier with registration form –

Children's Retreat

for kids ages 8–12

Sponsored by Our Town Community Center

Join us for a weekend of learning and fun with music, arts & crafts, drama, games, storytelling, tasty meals, new friends & more!

May 4-6, 20___
Community Center, 1919 Unity Lane
Our Town, WA 98765 - (987) 123-4567

COST: $40 per child ($35 if paid before March 15). Additional children from same family, $30 each. Scholarships available. Make checks payable to: Our Town Center. Space is limited; please apply early.

Participants should bring: sleeping bag, pillow, towel, toothbrush and toothpaste, comb, any medicines with clear instructions, bathing suit, sturdy shoes, pajamas and change of clothes. Put child's name on everything. Please do NOT bring electronic games, radios, CDs, iPods, etc.

Starts Friday at 5:30 p.m. with check-in and dinner. Ends Sunday at 2:00 p.m.

✂ -

Children's Retreat

Mail this form to the address above. For questions, email: center@gmail.com

Child's name (print): _____ Age: _____ Sex: _____

Address: _____ Phone: _____

Email: _____ Fee enclosed: $ _____ Partial scholarship requested: $_____

Emergency contact: _____ Phone: _____

Medical or dietary information: _____

The child named above has my permission to attend the Children's Retreat on May 4-6, 20____ at the Our Town Community Center. I understand that s/he is participating at her/his own risk. I hereby give the event organizers permission to administer first aid and obtain emergency medical treatment if necessary.

_____ _____ _____
Parent or Guardian (print name) Signature Date

Teaching Unity, Planning a Retreat or Camp, p. 233

As part of your publicity efforts, you can also invite the children's families and any interested friends, neighbors and co-workers to the children's performance at the end of the event. (See sample invitation below.) Several reminders may be necessary to ensure a good turnout.

– Sample invitation to the children's performance –

Children's Performance

"The Light of Unity"

All welcome!

Dear Friends and Neighbors,

Our Scout troop is sponsoring a children's retreat to be held at our house this weekend, May 4-6, so there will be a lot of youngsters in the area and a few more cars than usual.

On Saturday evening, the children will be presenting a short program to share what they have learned. The program will consist of songs, demonstrations to illustrate various concepts, some memorized passages, a showing of arts and crafts, some skits and a mini-opera. The show will be followed by refreshments and (weather permitting) a marshmallow roast.

We warmly invite you to join us for the program this Saturday, at our home at 7:55 p.m. Please bring a sweater as the evenings can be chilly.

We look forward to seeing you there!

Your neighbors,
Steve and Randie
999-1919

Registration

Once the registration forms have been received, the names of the children can be added to a master list in alphabetical order (see sample below). A separate list of teachers and other staff will be needed as well. If an Excel spreadsheet is used, it will be easy to make changes and to print out separate lists by last name, gender, age, payment status or other variable if desired.

Based on experience, aim for a roughly equal number of boys and girls. After the maximum number of children have registered, additional names can be put on a waiting list and contacted if there are any cancellations.

– Sample registration list –

	Child's Name	Age	Sex	Form	Paid	Check	Health Info	Contact	Phone	Email
1	Alex King	8	M	√	$40	#1234	---	Lisa King	342-9876	lk@king.net
2	Angela Lee	11	F	√	$15	cash	no eggs			
3	Jamal Mohajer	9	M	√			---			
4	Maria Ramirez	12	F	√	$40	#456	no peanuts			
5	Teresa Ramirez	10	F	√	$30	#456	inhaler			
↓										

Table title: **Children's Retreat, Our Town Community Center, May 4-6**

A few weeks before the event, send a note to all participants to confirm their attendance and remind them of what to bring. (See sample on following page.) If the event is being sponsored by a local church or other membership organization, you might include the list of names (without the health and payment information), so families can arrange to share transportation if desired.

Retreat photo by Bahíyyih Hansen, used with permission.

– Sample letter of confirmation –

Dear Mrs. Mohajer,

We are pleased to confirm registration of: <u>Jamal Mohajer</u> for the upcoming Children's Retreat to be held at the Our Town Community Center on May 4-6.

The weather is still cool, so a jacket or sweater will be needed. In addition, children should bring a sleeping bag, pillow, towel, toothbrush, toothpaste, comb, any medicines with clear instructtions, bathing suit, sturdy shoes, pajamas and a change of clothes. *Please do NOT bring electronic games, iPods, CDs, etc.*

Write your child's name or initials on anything that could end up in the lost-and-found box. Youth and adult volunteers will also need to bring their own bedding.

We look forward to seeing you all in just a few weeks!

With warmest greetings,

Children's Retreat Planning Committee

It is also a good idea to send a brief reminder just before the event. (See sample below.)

– Sample last-minute reminder –

Dear friends,

The Children's Retreat is just around the corner. We look forward to welcoming you this Friday, May 4, at 5:30 p.m. for check-in and dinner. A schedule of events and directions to the Our Town Community Center are enclosed. We have a full weekend of activities planned and look forward to seeing you in just a few days!

With warmest greetings,

Children's Retreat Planning Committee

One year, a serious flu outbreak necessitated the following communication:

– Sample health advisory –

To parents and volunteers
for the Children's Retreat at the
Our Town Community Center

Dear friends,

We look forward to welcoming you to the retreat in just over two weeks.

Please be aware that influenza viruses are circulating in Our Town and in the region. If you or your child have signs of flu-like illness (for example, fever, cough, sore throat, vomiting, body aches) or an obvious respiratory infection (runny nose, nasal congestion, cough, etc.), you may need to stay home in order to protect the health of all involved.

If this is the case, please let us know as soon as possible, so we may contact the next person on the waiting list. Also, if someone becomes ill during the retreat, s/he may need to return home.

Each person should consider getting a flu vaccine now—at least 2 weeks before the retreat. If you have any questions, please contact your doctor.

We hope that everyone will be able to attend.

With warmest greetings,

Children's Retreat Planning Committee

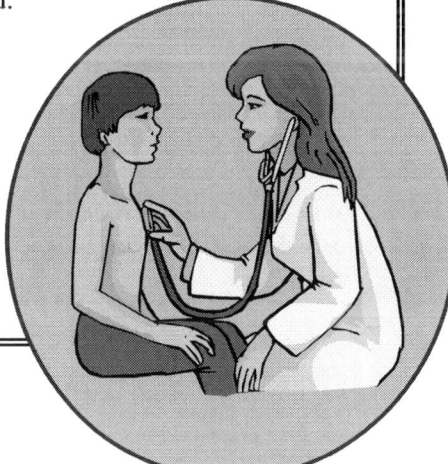

✓ Materials

Before the event, all the materials should be prepared for each activity. The teachers should make or purchase the instructional materials and photocopy the handouts for their own classes. In addition, you may need some of the following items:

Publicity
[ ] Publicity fliers and registration forms
[ ] Newsletter announcements
[ ] Invitations for children's performance

Registration
[ ] Welcome sign
[ ] Registration sign
[ ] Registration list
[ ] Name tags
[ ] Bookkeeping ledger
[ ] Dorm assignment list
[ ] Volunteer service lists
[ ] Student folders with storage box
[ ] Materials for decorating folders

Orientation
[ ] Orientation checklist and materials
[ ] Message from sponsoring agency

Classes
[ ] Lesson plans and handouts
[ ] Whiteboard, easel, markers, eraser
[ ] Notebook paper, pencils, pens
[ ] Song sheets
[ ] Dictionary
[ ] Map or globe
[ ] Craft supplies

Meals
[ ] Menus, recipes, shopping lists
[ ] Large pots, pans, serving utensils
[ ] Food, drinks, snacks
[ ] Plates, bowls, cups
[ ] Napkins, cutlery

Supplies
[ ] Dish soap
[ ] Hand soap
[ ] Sponges
[ ] Trash bags
[ ] Paper towels
[ ] Toilet paper

Children's Performance
[ ] Scripts and felt lessons
[ ] Costumes and props
    (thrift shops can be a great
    source for these items)
[ ] Microphone and amplifier
[ ] Power strips, extension cords
[ ] Extra lighting

Miscellaneous
[ ] First aid kit
[ ] Tape or tacks for posting items
[ ] Clipboards for activity coordinators
[ ] Alarm clock for morning wake-up
[ ] Enough tables and chairs
[ ] Sports and recreational equipment
[ ] Quiet time materials
    (chess, board games, puzzles, etc.)
[ ] Portable music player
[ ] Music CDs or audio files
[ ] Musical instruments
[ ] Camera with extra memory card
[ ] Extra batteries for AV equipment

Closing Activities
[ ] Certificates of completion
[ ] Gifts for staff and volunteers

Site Preparation

Before people arrive, the site needs to be prepared for the activities. Consider the following:

Facility

[ ] Set up the registration area.

[ ] Prepare separate sleeping areas for girls and boys.

[ ] Remove throw rugs or other obstacles for wheelchairs.

[ ] Store expensive or breakable items.

[ ] Put night lights in the halls and bathrooms.

[ ] Stock bathrooms with extra toilet paper.

[ ] Set out brooms, dustpans, sponges and mops.

[ ] Arrange spaces for any outdoor activities.

[ ] Have extra towels and blankets on hand.

Postings

[ ] Put a note on rooms or items that are off limits.

[ ] Post any class materials (maps, charts, pictures).

[ ] Post copies of the retreat schedule in different rooms, including dorms.

[ ] Post the meal schedule and menus in the kitchen.

[ ] Post signs for registration, bathrooms, etc.

[ ] Display photographs from the previous retreat.

Tables and Chairs

[ ] Set up a table for children to decorate their folders.

[ ] Set up tables and chairs for meals and craft activities.

[ ] Cover tables with protective tarps if needed.

[ ] Prepare the classroom and arrange seating for orientation.

Check-in Process

For an Overnight Retreat

It is helpful to have two people in charge of check-in on the first day of the retreat. They should arrive about 15 minutes early to set up. Provide them with a list of the children who will be attending, a file with their registration forms in alphabetical order, a few blank forms, name tags and markers, and a folder for each participant.

Registration Tasks

1. Welcome people as they arrive.
2. Be sure each child has a signed registration form.
3. Make each person a name tag.
4. Give everyone a folder and have them write their name on it.
5. Show them where to decorate their folders if desired.
6. Have a volunteer show them to the dorm to drop off their things.

Name Tags

For convenience, you may wish to use self-stick mailing labels for name tags. These can be printed in advance using large bold letters. The name tags will be more legible if they are prepared by an adult, rather than letting children print their own names when they arrive. We use first names only, but you may wish to use last names or titles for the adults.

Folders

We use colored folders for the children and plain manila folders for the adults. This allows children to select a preferred color and to quickly identify their own folder from among the pile during class times. The folders are stuffed beforehand with:

- ❑ Letter from the sponsoring institution (see page 276)
- ❑ Retreat schedule
- ❑ Song sheet
- ❑ Class handouts
- ❑ Two sheets of blank notebook paper
- ❑ Instructions for crafts and other activities (adult folders only)

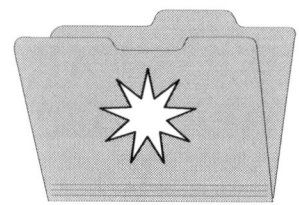

During the check-in period, those who wish to decorate their folders can be invited to a table that has been prepared with markers, stickers, construction paper, scissors, glue, glitter and similar materials. Once decorated, the folders are collected and stored upright in a box for use during class sessions. The folders are collected again at the end of each class. If children are asked to hold on to their own folders during the retreat, some children will misplace them or forget to bring them to class.

For a Day Camp

For a weeklong day camp, the process is essentially the same except that children should be signed in and out each day. For safety reasons, you will need a list of those people who are authorized to pick up each child. During the registration process, parents can be asked to fill out a pickup authorization form (see sample below).

– Sample pickup form –

UNITY CAMP
Pickup Authorization Form

Please return this form before the first day of camp to:
Harmony Park, 1863 Peace Street, Harmony, CA 93428

Child's Name: _____ Age: _____ Sex: _____

Child's Name: _____ Age: _____ Sex: _____

For the safety of your child(ren), they may be picked up from camp ONLY by those individuals specified by you in writing on this authorization form. All authorized persons must show photo ID or other type of valid identification which may be requested by our staff. In an emergency, authorization by phone may be accepted.

Please print the name and phone number of those individuals authorized to pick up your child. You will be notified if anyone else attempts to pick up your child. Print legibly to complete the form and return it prior to the first day of camp.

Name	**Phone**	**Relationship to Child**
_____	_____	_____
_____	_____	_____
_____	_____	_____

Name of child's parent or guardian: _____

Phone: _____ Additional phone: _____

Signature: _____ Date: _____

Teaching Unity, Planning a Retreat or Camp, p. 241

In addition to the authorization form mentioned above, you will need a daily sign-in / sign-out sheet like the one below.

– Sample sheet for signing in and out –

UNITY CAMP ~ Monday, August 5					
Please sign your child in and out each day					
	Child's Name	Time In	Signature	Time Out	Signature
1	Alex King				
2	Angela Lee				
3	Jamal Mohajer				
4	Maria Ramirez				
5	Teresa Ramirez				
↓					

Meals and Snacks

If food will be served, a schedule of meals and snacks can be posted in the kitchen as a guide for the cooks. If meals are ready on time, classes and other activities will not be delayed. Information on food allergies should also be readily available (see example below).

– Sample allergy alert –

* Angela Lee (age 11), **eggs,** phone: 321-2202
* Maria Ramirez (age 12), **peanuts,** phone: 321-3304

Signs and Certificates

A few signs will help to orient arriving campers and direct the flow of traffic, for example: Welcome to Unity Camp, Registration, Wheelchair Access, Parking, Cabins and Bathrooms. Signs can be printed on cardstock and laminated for repeated use. You might also wish to prepare a certificate of completion for those children who attend the weeklong Unity Camp.

Note: Welcome and registration signs and a blank certificate are available online as part of the downloads for this book:

< www.TeachingUnity.com >.

Teaching Unity, Planning a Retreat or Camp, p. 243

Opening Activities

If these lessons are being used as part of an intensive program, such as a summer camp or weekend retreat, it is a good idea to provide some self-directed activities for children while they are waiting for others to arrive. After checking in, for example, they can be shown to a table to decorate their folders, to work on simple puzzles or other small projects. If desired, a separate table with the appropriate materials can be set up for each project. The instructions can be posted and assistants asked to supervise the children. These activities can also be incorporated into an ongoing weekly class.

Orientation Program

The orientation program on the first day is designed to make everyone feel welcome and to help them get to know each other. Explain to the group that we will be learning about **UNITY**, something the world greatly needs today. We will focus on four main topics:

1. The Light of Unity
2. Unity in Diversity
3. The Colors We Are
4. Overcoming Prejudice

– Sample orientation program –

1. **Opening music**
2. **Welcome**
3. **Message from sponsor**
4. **Introductions**
5. **Review of schedule**
6. **Event guidelines**
7. **Warm-up activities**
8. **Group singing**

A sample orientation program is outlined here. We begin with music and an official welcome on behalf of the sponsoring body. This is followed by introductions where all participants are asked to state their name, age (children only), town, and one interesting personal fact—for example, a favorite hobby, a special skill or unusual pet. As a variation, people can be asked to act out their hobby or skill without using words, and the group can guess what it is.

We also introduce the teachers and other key staff at this time, including the Service Coordinator. The Service Coordinator oversees any volunteers, making sure they know what to do, have the necessary tools and are at their posts on time.

After introductions, we distribute the schedule and review it carefully with the group, emphasizing class times, quiet time and bedtime. During the orientation we also cover the list of guidelines on the following pages. These can be modified to fit your own circumstances. The orientation goes more smoothly if children are asked to save their questions until the end.

– Sample event guidelines for orientation –

Event Guidelines

Safety and Supervision

- Wear your name tags every day.
- All the youth and adults are like your aunts and uncles; please listen to them.
- All assistants are needed to help with all classes, recreation and craft activities.
- If someone is sick or doing something unsafe, tell an adult right away.

Classes

- Classes are not optional. Please show up on time, ready to learn.
- The crafts, songs, skits and games are also part of class.
- Store your folders in the box and take them out at the start of each class.

Recreation

- The foosball game can be used during breaks but not during meals or quiet time.
- The hot tub can only be used during outdoor activities with an adult present.
- It is okay to play on the lawn but avoid the flower beds.
- No television, computers or electronic games.

Facility

- Please walk and use quiet voices inside the house.
- Take shoes off inside the house unless clean and dry.
- Girls' and boys' dorms are off limits to the opposite sex.
- Showers should be short to allow time and hot water for all.
- Don't touch thermostats; inform the host if you are too hot or cold.
- Be gentle with faucets, handles, shower curtains, chairs, etc.
- Clean up after yourself and others.
- Park cars in designated areas only.

Food

- No food or drinks in carpeted areas.
- Put your name on your cup, rinse and re-use it.
- Vegetarian food can be eaten by others after the vegetarians have been served.
- Scrape dirty dishes and stack them next to the sink.
- Don't throw out the silverware.
- Use the recycling bins.

Relating to Others

- What are some of the virtues we should practice here?
  (Courtesy, cooperation, patience, sharing, respect, honesty, service…)

- No backbiting, putdowns, mean teasing or roughhousing.

- If someone is in a wheelchair, how can you include them in the activities?
  (Rather than telling them they can't do something, try to think of a way that they can participate.)

- If you see someone who seems sad, what can you do?

- If you see someone who is alone, or not part of an established group, how can you make that person feel included?

- Are there any questions?

After reviewing the guidelines, you can organize one or more warm-up activities (see pages 13-20 and 149). These ice-breakers will help children get to know each other and will serve to introduce the theme of unity. This can be followed by group singing and a light snack.

During the briefing for volunteers, children can be shown a short video relating to the theme (see following page). They might also enjoy seeing photos from a previous retreat.

As an alternative, a few jigsaw puzzles of various levels of difficulty can be set out for the children to work on. Puzzles provide an opportunity for teamwork and collaborative problem solving. They are inexpensive and fun, and can be enjoyed by all ages.

Videos on Unity

During the volunteer orientation, the children may wish to watch excerpts from one of the following videos which are related to the theme of unity.

Starting Small: Teaching Children Tolerance

This 1997 video by Margie McGovern, profiles seven exemplary classrooms in which teachers are helping children learn about tolerance and respect. Of particular relevance is the first segment which shows elementary school children finding out about their own skin colors and painting their multicultural portraits. The video comes with a teacher's guide and is free to schools, home school networks, religious groups and non-profit organizations working with children or youth. Free orders must be authorized by the organization's director. Download order forms from: < **www.tolerance.org/kit/starting-small** >. Mail to the address below. Allow 8 weeks for delivery. Amazon.com also carries the DVD.

> Teaching Tolerance Order Department
> 400 Washington Ave.
> Montgomery, AL 36104 USA

The Power of Race Unity

This 1998 documentary was produced by the Bahá'ís of the United States. Of particular interest is the 3-minute segment which profiles Anisa Kintz, who at the age of eight, founded the "Calling All Colors Conference," a kids' program to combat racism and prejudice. This is a forceful example of what a single child can do to advance the cause of unity. The video can be viewed online. Turn up the sound and click the first segment after the introduction.

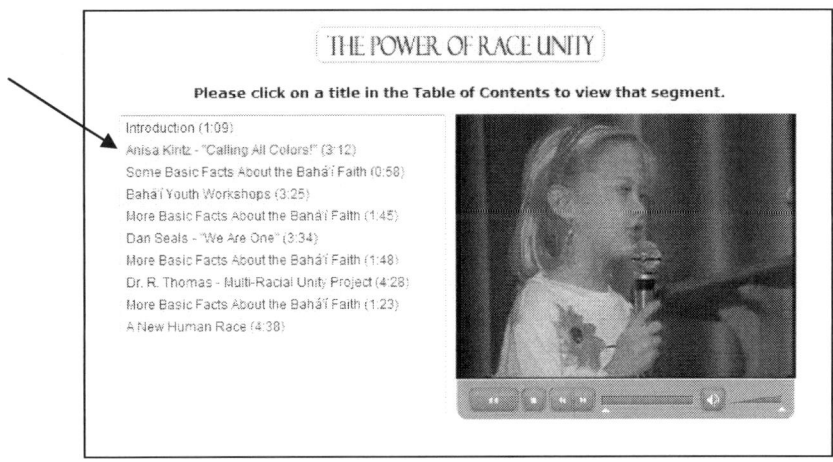

www.bahaiprinciples.org/videos (or)
www.bahaiprinciples.org/videos/powerraceunity/broadband/powerraceunity.html

Volunteer Orientation

For our retreats, if we haven't yet had an opportunity to meet with the volunteers, we gather them immediately following the general orientation for a briefing of their own. We begin by thanking everyone for their willingness to serve, then quickly review the following topics:

1. Overall goals of the event
2. Creating an inclusive atmosphere and a sense of community
3. Types of assistance needed for each activity (classes, crafts, meals, recreation, singing, bedtimes)
4. Specific duties of each volunteer
5. Positive discipline techniques (see below)
6. Safety concerns, allergies, emergency phone numbers
7. Location and use of any special equipment that will be needed
8. Location of recycling bins, cleaning supplies, plunger, ibuprofen
9. Questions from the group

Positive Discipline

With regard to discipline, volunteers are asked to "catch the children being good," so that positive behavior is recognized and reinforced. This may be more effective if done in private. *("Juan, I noticed you found Katrina's folder after she lost it. That was very helpful of you.")*

If you wish to make these good deeds more visible, consider setting up a **"virtues tree"** that will be on display during the entire event. Children and adults can attach pre-cut paper leaves and flowers to the tree to symbolize good deeds. A personal good deed can be represented by a flower; the positive action of another can be represented by a leaf with that person's name written on it. (The tree can be made from brown construction paper taped to the wall, or a bare branch set in a bucket of stones or sand.)

For negative behaviors, it may be useful to role play a few common situations during the briefing, so the volunteers will have practice resolving them beforehand.

Big Brothers and Sisters

A few children may have behavioral issues or may feel shy and uncomfortable in a large group. We ask specific youth to "adopt" one of these children throughout the event. Some of the older children can be enlisted to act as buddies for new kids as well.

✓ Planning Checklist

Four to Six Months in Advance
[ ] Determine the sponsor.
[ ] Appoint a planning committee.
[ ] Set the dates and times.
[ ] Decide on a minimum and maximum number of participants.
[ ] Prepare a budget.
[ ] Determine what fees will be charged and how funds will be raised.
[ ] Obtain a suitable facility.
[ ] Select a general coordinator to oversee the event.

Three to Four Months in Advance
[ ] Determine the daily schedule.
[ ] Obtain teachers for each class, craft and special activity.
[ ] Provide teachers with lesson plans and a budget for materials.
[ ] Find a song leader and provide song sheets and musical scores.
[ ] Send out a "save the date" notice to potential participants.
[ ] Implement any fund-raising plans.

Two to Three Months in Advance
[ ] Design a flyer, registration form and other publicity materials.
[ ] Appoint a registrar and set up a registration list.
[ ] Appoint a treasurer and set up a ledger to account for income and expenses.
[ ] Publicize the event to your local community.
[ ] Publicize the event to a wider area if desired.
[ ] Inform parents when their registration form has been received.
[ ] Start a waiting list if necessary.

One Month in Advance
[ ] Ask the sponsoring institution for a message to the children.
[ ] Obtain any scholarship funds and donations.
[ ] Plan the orientation program.
[ ] Obtain the items needed for each activity (see materials checklist).
[ ] Check with teachers and other key personnel to be sure they are getting ready.
[ ] Ask teachers to make demonstration models of each craft.
[ ] Invite parents and the community to the children's performance.

Two to Three Weeks in Advance
[ ] Send a letter of confirmation to the participants.
[ ] Inform teachers how many copies will be needed for student handouts.
[ ] Make sure there will be enough tables and chairs for the event.
[ ] Prepare all additional forms, signs and certificates as needed.
[ ] Obtain small gifts for the teachers and their assistants.
[ ] Arrange to have photos taken if desired.
[ ] Prepare menus and shopping lists.

A Few Days in Advance
[ ] Select a volunteer coordinator if needed.
[ ] Contact key personnel to be sure they are prepared.
[ ] Inform cooks re: number of participants, meal times and special dietary needs.
[ ] Purchase paper goods and cleaning supplies.
[ ] Finalize sleeping arrangements and inform the registrars.
[ ] Remind people about the children's performance.
[ ] Alert neighbors that young children will be in the area.

The Day Before
[ ] Stuff participant folders and place in storage box.
[ ] Prepare the site and post signs and schedules.
[ ] Set out materials for quiet-time activities.
[ ] Purchase and store the food.

The Day After
[ ] Congratulations! You did it!
[ ] Schedule a massage.

Some of the children and volunteers from our retreats in Yakima.

PART VI

Appendices

Appendices

A. Words of Wisdom 257

B. Memorization Techniques 268

C. Help with Reading 271

D. Think-Pair-Share 273

E. Speed Discussions 275

F. Sample Letter from Sponsor 276

G. Additional Resources 277

H. Bibliography 280

I. About the Author 281

APPENDIX A

Words of Wisdom

A quotation or thought-for-the-day has been included with each unit for students to memorize. Some of the quotes have been simplified for use with children. Those four quotations are included here along with additional words of wisdom drawn from various cultures and religious traditions, from scientists and philosophers, statesmen and women, poets and Nobel Peace Prize winners, writers, musicians and others. Brief biographical notes about the author of each quote are found at the end of this section.

The teacher may select a different quotation from this compilation for the students to memorize or another quote of their own choosing which reinforces the key concepts in each unit. Appendix B describes a number of effective memorization techniques.

As an additional activity with older children who are fluent readers, the class may wish to develop and present a program of dramatic readings for an audience of family and friends (see p. 193). Have each student select one or more favorite quotations to read or recite. Alternatively, students can be divided into four groups (one for each theme below), and each group can then select their favorite quotations, arrange them in order, and decide who will recite each one.

Provide scripts with individual parts numbered and highlighted, so each student knows when it is his/her turn. Microphones should be used if needed, and background music or special lighting added if desired.

When rehearsing with the children, encourage them to speak slowly and clearly in a strong voice that can be heard on the other side of the room. They should also wait a moment before speaking to leave a brief silence between them and the previous reader, so the words are not all crowded together. The children may need help with the pronunciation of certain words.

Note: In some religious traditions, it would be considered disrespectful to portray specific religious figures. Their words can be recited, but students would not dress up as those individuals.

The Light of Unity

1) "So powerful is the light of unity that it can illuminate the whole earth." (Bahá'u'lláh, *Gleanings*, p. 288)

2) "Behold, how good and how pleasant it is for brethren to dwell together in unity!" (*The Bible,* Psalms 133:1)

3) "In union there is strength." (Aesop, "The Bundle of Sticks" from *Aesop's Fables*)

4) "A single twig breaks, but the bundle of twigs is strong." (Tecumseh, quoted in *Touch the Earth: A Self-portrait of Indian Existence*, by T. C. McLuhan, 1973)

5) "He who experiences the unity of life sees his own self in all beings, and all beings in his own self…" (Krishna, from *The Bhagavad-Gita*, VI, 29)

6) "All men were made by the same Great Spirit Chief. They are all brothers." (Chief Joseph, Lincoln Hall speech, Washington D.C., 14 January 1879)

7) "The fact that all peoples can intermarry and have healthy children proves that we all remain members of the same species. Our differences are trivial in a biological sense." (Boyce Rensberger, "Forget the Old Labels: Here's a New Way to Look at Race," Washington Post, 16 November 1994)

8) "Have we not all one father? Hath not one God created us?" (Hebrew scriptures, Malachi 2:10)

9) "God hath made of one blood all nations of men for to dwell on all the face of the earth." (*The Bible,* Acts 17:26)

10) "O mankind! We created you from a single pair of a male and a female and made you into nations and tribes." (*Qur'an* 49.13)

11) "The earth is but one country, and mankind its citizens." (Bahá'u'lláh, *Gleanings*, p. 250)

12) "Our true nationality is mankind." (H. G. Wells, *The Outline of History*, 1920, p. 644)

13) "The World is my country, all mankind are my brethren, and to do good is my religion." (Thomas Paine, *The Age of Reason*, 1794, quoted in the Oxford Dictionary of American Quotations, p. 235)

14) "I am not an Athenian, nor a Greek, but a citizen of the world." (Socrates, quoted by Plutarch, *Of Banishment: A Greek philosopher in Athens,* wikiquote.org)

15) "Internal peace is an essential first step to achieving peace in the world. How do you cultivate it? It's very simple. In the first place by realizing clearly that all mankind is one, that human beings in every country are members of one and the same family." (Tenzin Gyatso, the Dalai Lama, www.betterworld.net/quotes)

16) "Mitakuye oyasin" (we are all related). (Traditional Lakota Sioux prayer, wikipedia.org)

17) "The love of one's country is a splendid thing. But why should love stop at the border? There is a brotherhood among all men." (Pablo Casals, quoted in *Joys and Sorrows: Reflections by Pablo Casals*, by Albert E. Kahn, 1974)

18) "We may have all come on different ships, but we're in the same boat now." (Martin Luther King, Jr., Washington, D.C. speech, 27 August 1963)

19) "Through our scientific genius, we have made of this world a neighborhood. Now through our ethical and moral commitment, we must make of it a brotherhood." (Martin Luther King, Jr., Western Michigan University speech, 18 December 1963)

20) "We must learn to live together as brothers, or perish together as fools." (Martin Luther King, Jr., Western Michigan University speech, 18 December 1963)

21) "We shall survive only together, black and white. We can be human only together, black and white." (Desmond Tutu, Nobel Peace Prize acceptance speech, 1984)

22) "A house divided against itself cannot stand." (Abraham Lincoln, from a Republican State Convention speech, Illinois, 16 June 1858. The quotation is a paraphrase of the Bible, Mark 3:25)

23) "The well-being of mankind, its peace and security, are unattainable unless and until its unity is firmly established." (Bahá'u'lláh, *Gleanings,* p. 286)

24) "Instead of fighting with each other, can we all, united, fight poverty and disease and illiteracy? Is it possible for us to put all our efforts and all our energy into one single purpose, the betterment and progress and development of all our lands and all our peoples?" (Golda Meir, United Nations speech, 1 March 1957)

25) "The day will come when men will recognize woman as his peer, not only at the fireside, but in councils of the nation. Then, and not until then, will there be the perfect comradeship, the ideal union between the sexes that shall result in the highest development of the race." (Susan B. Anthony, International Council of Women speech, London, 27 June 1899, quoted in *Life and Work of Susan B. Anthony, vol. 3*, by Ida Husted Harper, 1908)

26) "You may say that I'm a dreamer, but I'm not the only one. I hope someday you'll join us, and the world will be as one." (John Lennon, from the song "Imagine," 1971)

* * * * *

Unity in Diversity

1) "All mankind are the fruits of one tree, flowers of the same garden, waves of one sea." ('Abdu'l-Bahá, *Foundations of World Unity*, p. 23)

2) "We may have different religions, different languages, different colored skin, but we all belong to one human race." (Kofi Annan, quoted in *Simply Living: The Spirit of the Indigenous People,* Shirley Jones, ed., 1999, wikiquote.org)

3) "We're one, but we're not the same." (Bono, from the song "One," 1991)

4) "People have one thing in common; they are all different." (Robert Zend, quotes.ubr.com)

5) "Each man is good in the sight of the Great Spirit. It is not necessary for eagles to be crows." (Sitting Bull, www.indigenouspeople.net. See p. 262, #2 for full quote.)

6) "Differences of habit and language are nothing at all if our aims are identical and our hearts are open." (J. K. Rowling, *Harry Potter and the Goblet of Fire*, words of the fictional character Dumbledore)

7) "The diversity in the human family should be the cause of love and harmony, as it is in music where many different notes blend together in the making of a perfect chord. If you meet those of a different race and color from yourself...think of them as different colored roses growing in the beautiful garden of humanity, and rejoice to be among them." ('Abdu'l-Bahá, *Paris Talks,* 1912, p. 52-53)

8) "In diversity there is beauty and there is strength." (Maya Angelou, www.goodreads.com)

9) "I was seeing in a sacred manner the shapes of all things in the spirit…And I saw that the sacred hoop of my people was one of many hoops that made one circle…and in the center grew one mighty flowering tree to shelter all children of one mother and one father. And I saw that it was holy…" (Black Elk, quoted in *Black Elk Speaks*, John Neihardt, 1932)

10) "No leader surveying the world scene today can doubt that the achievement of wholeness incorporating diversity is one of the transcendent goals of our time…" (John W. Gardener, *On Leadership,* 1990)

11) "Peace is not unity in similarity but unity in diversity, in the comparison and conciliation of differences." (Mikhail Gorbachev, Nobel Peace Prize acceptance speech, 5 June 1991)

12) "If we cannot end now our differences, at least we can help make the world safe for diversity. For, in the final analysis, our most basic common link is that we all inhabit this small planet. We all breathe the same air. We all cherish our children's future. And we are all mortal." (John F. Kennedy, American University commencement address, 10 June 1963)

13) "Difference is of the essence of humanity. Difference is an accident of birth and it should therefore never be the source of hatred or conflict. The answer to difference is to respect it. Therein lies a most fundamental principle of peace: respect for diversity." (John Hume, Nobel Peace Prize acceptance speech, December 10, 1998)

14) "We live now in a global village and we are in one single family. It's our responsibility to bring friendship and love from all different places around the world and to live together in peace." (Jackie Chan, www.betterworld.net/quotes)

15) "...when the will and the determination exist, nations and peoples of diverse backgrounds can and will work together, in unity, to the achievement of common goals and the assurance of that equality and brotherhood which we desire." (Haile Selassie, English translation of a 1963 speech to the United Nations, www.nazret.com/history/him_un.php)

16) "We have the ability to achieve, if we master the necessary goodwill, a common global society blessed with a shared culture of peace that is nourished by the ethnic, national and local diversities that enrich our lives." (Mahnaz Afkhami, www.betterworld.net/quotes/diversity-quotes.htm)

17) "Human diversity makes tolerance more than a virtue; it makes it a requirement for survival." (René Dubos, www.betterworld.net/quotes)

18) "Every view of the world that becomes extinct, every culture that disappears, diminishes a possibility of life." (Octavio Paz, http://news.bbc.co.uk/2/hi/europe/5019582.stm)

19) "We could learn a lot from crayons; some are sharp, some are pretty, some are dull, while others bright, some have weird names, but they all have learned to live together in the same box." (Robert Fulghum, www.goodreads.com)

20) "The one thing that unites all human beings, regardless of age, gender, religion, economic status or ethnic background, is that deep, down inside we ALL believe that we are above average drivers." (Dave Barry, *Dave Barry Turns Fifty*, p. 182)

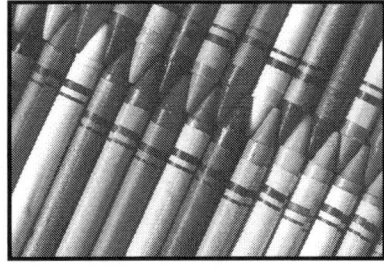

The Colors We Are

1) "We, who are clay blended by the Master Potter, come from the kiln of Creation in many hues. How can people say one skin is colored, when each has its own coloration? What should it matter that one bowl is dark and the other is pale, if each is of good design and serves it purpose well?" (Polingaysi Qoyawayma, *No Turning Back: A Hopi Indian Woman's Struggle to Live in Two Worlds,* 1978)

2) "I am a red man. If the Great Spirit had desired me to be a white man he would have made me so in the first place. He put in your heart certain wishes and plans, in my heart he put other and different desires. Each man is good in his sight. It is not necessary for eagles to be crows." (Sitting Bull, www.brainyquote.com)

3) "One of my theories is that the hearts of men are about alike, no matter what their skin color." (Mark Twain, www.famousquotes.com)

4) "…beneath the skin, beyond the differing features and into the true heart of being, fundamentally, we are more alike my friend, than we are unalike."
(Maya Angelou, from her poem "The Human Family")

5) "…the human 'races' are remarkably alike under the skin. The variation among individuals is much greater than the differences among groups. In fact, the diversity among individuals is so enormous that the whole concept of race becomes meaningless at the genetic level." (Sribala Subramanian, "The Story in Our Genes," *Time Magazine,* 16 January 1995, in a review of *The History and Geography of Human Genes,* by Luca Cavalli-Sforza, et al., a synthesis of over 50 years of research in population genetics.)

6) "Diversity makes for a rich tapestry, and…all the threads of the tapestry are equal in value no matter what their color." (Maya Angelou, www.goodreads.com)

7) "The mineral kingdom abounds with many-colored substances...but we find no strife among them on that account. In the kingdom of the plant and vegetable, distinct...hues exist but the fruit and flowers are not in conflict for that reason...Throughout the animal kingdom we do not find the creatures separated because of color. They recognize unity of species and oneness of kind. If we do not find color distinction drawn in a kingdom of lower intelligence and reason, how can it be justified among human beings?" ('Abdu'l-Bahá, *Foundations of World Unity,* p. 34, from a talk given prior to 1921)

8) "I have a dream that my four little children will one day live in a nation where they will not be judged by the color of their skin but by the content of their character." (Martin Luther King, Jr., speech from the steps of the Lincoln Memorial, 28 August 1963)

9) "That until the philosophy which holds one race superior and another inferior is finally and permanently discredited and abandoned; That until there are no longer first-class and second-class citizens of any nation; That until the color of a man's skin is of no more significance than the color of his eyes; That until the basic human rights are equally guaranteed to all without regard to race; That until that day, the dream of lasting peace and world citizenship and the rule of international morality will remain but a fleeting illusion..." (Haile Selassie, English translation of a 1963 speech to the United Nations, popularized in the song "War" by Bob Marley, www.ethiopiancrown.org/address.html)

10) "If we say we do not see color…we fool ourselves. We are all different…But that's what makes us beautiful as a human race." (C. JoyBell C., http://cjoybellc.com)

11) "Racial superiority is a *pigment* of the imagination." (Author unknown)

* * * * *

Overcoming Prejudice

1) "Darkness cannot drive out darkness; only light can do that. Hate cannot drive out hate; only love can do that." (Martin Luther King, Jr., *Where Do We Go from Here: Chaos or Community?*, 1967, p. 62)

2) "Love is the cause of unity in all things." (Aristotle, *The Beginning of All Wisdom*, by Steven Stavropoulos, p. 103, http://blog.gaiam.com/quotes)

3) "Hatred does not cease by hatred, but only by love; this is the eternal rule." (Buddha, *The Dhammapada: The Sayings of the Buddha*, translated by Balangoda Ananda Maitreya Maitreya)

4) "This is my commandment, that ye love one another, as I have loved you." (Jesus, *The Bible*, John 15:12)

5) "…be a friend to the whole human race." ('Abdu'l-Bahá, *Selections from the Writings of 'Abdu'l-Bahá*, p. 169)

6) "Tret pepel as good as you kan." (Andrew, age 7, written during class)

7) "Close your eyes to racial differences and welcome all with the light of oneness." (Bahá'u'lláh, *Bahá'í Scriptures*, p. 157)

8) "If you judge people, you have no time to love them." (Mother Teresa, www.goodreads.com)

9) "All prejudices, whether of religion, race, politics or nation, must be renounced, for these prejudices have caused the world's sickness." ('Abdu'l-Bahá, *Paris Talks*, p. 146)

10) "It is never too late to give up our prejudices." (Henry David Thoreau, *Walden*, 1854)

11) "I am against every form of racism and segregation, every form of discrimination. I believe in human beings, and that all human beings should be respected as such, regardless of their color." (Malcolm X, from a January 1965 interview, wikiquote.org)

12) "Let us all hope that the dark clouds of racial prejudice will soon pass away…and in some not too distant tomorrow the radiant stars of love and brotherhood will shine over our great nation with all of their scintillating beauty." (Martin Luther King, Jr., "Letter from Birmingham Jail," 16 April 1963)

13) "I have no color prejudices nor caste prejudices nor creed prejudices. All I care to know is that a man is a human being, and that is enough for me; he can't be any worse." (Mark Twain, www.searchquotes.com)

14) "*Ecidujerp* is prejudice spelled backwards. Either way, it makes no sense."
    (Author unknown)

15) "Hatred…never failed to destroy the man who hated..."
    (James Baldwin, *The Fire Next Time*, 1964)

16) "You can't hold a man down without staying down with him."
    (Booker T. Washington, wikiquote.org)

17) "You've got to be taught to be afraid, of people whose eyes are oddly made, and people whose skin is a different shade, you've got to be carefully taught."
    (Oscar Hammerstein II, lyrics from the 1949 Broadway musical *South Pacific*)

18) "No one is born hating another person because of the color of his skin, or his background, or his religion. People must learn to hate, and if they can learn to hate, they can be taught to love..." (Nelson Mandela, *Long Walk to Freedom*, 2000)

19) "Everybody thinks of changing humanity and nobody thinks of changing himself."
    (Leo Tolstoy, "Three Methods of Reform" in *Pamphlets Translated from the Russian*, by Aylmer Maude, p. 29; wikiquote.org)

20) "You cannot control how diverse any room is, or any institution, or any policy. But you can control how diverse you are, and who you love and who you listen to."
    (Sherman Alexie, Rutgers University speech, 10 October 2001, http://blog.gaiam.com/quotes)

21) "If you don't like the way the world is, you change it. You have an obligation to change it. You just do it one step at a time." (Marian Wright Edelman, www.encyclopedia.com)

22) "You must be the change you wish to see in the world." (Mahatma Gandhi, as paraphrased by his grandson Arun Gandhi, www.gandhitopia.org/forum/topics/a-gandhi-quote)

* * * * *

Author Notes for Words of Wisdom

(Alphabetized by first name or title)

'Abdu'l-Bahá (1844-1921), born 'Abbás Effendí. Oldest son of and appointed successor to Bahá'u'lláh.

Abraham Lincoln (1809-1865), 16th President of the United States.

Aesop, ancient Greek storyteller credited with hundreds of morality tales now collectively known as *Aesop's Fables*.

Andrew (age 7), second-grade student from Moses Lake, Washington, USA.

Aristotle (384-322 BC), ancient Greek philosopher, a founder of Western philosophy, who wrote on government, ethics, science, logic, metaphysics, linguistics, morality and more.

Bahá'u'lláh (1817-1892), Persian nobleman, born Mírzá Ḥusayn-'Alí. Founder of the Bahá'í Faith.

Bhagavad-Gita, 700-verse poem containing the core beliefs of Hinduism, part of the ancient Sanskrit epic Mahabharata.

Bible, King James version. Contains the Jewish and Christian scriptures.

Black Elk (1863-1950), Oglala Sioux warrior and medicine man.

Bono (1960-), born Paul Hewson. Humanitarian and lead singer for the Irish rock band U2.

Booker T. Washington (1856-1915), African-American author, orator and presidential advisor.

Boyce Rensberger (1942-), U.S. science writer and editor, director of the Knight Science Journalism Fellowships program at MIT.

Buddha (563-483 BC), Hindu prince, born Siddhartha Gautama. Founder of Buddhism.

C. JoyBell C., contemporary author and poet.

Chief Joseph (1840-1904), Native American leader of the Nez Pierce tribe.

Dave Barry (1947-), Pulitzer Prize-winning American author, columnist and humorist.

Desmond Tutu (1931-), South African civil rights activist, Anglican archbishop, Nobel laureate.

Golda Meir (1898-1978), born Golda Mabovich. Fourth prime minister of the State of Israel.

Haile Selassie (1892-1975), born Tafari Makonnen. Emperor of Ethiopia, presided over formation of the Organisation of African Unity (OAU), promoted international collective security.

Hebrew scriptures. Malachi was a minor prophet in the *Tanakh*—the Jewish Bible. The Book of Malachi is the last book in the Old Testament of the Christian Bible.

Henry David Thoreau (1817-1862), U.S. author, poet, philosopher and naturalist.

Herbert George (H. G.) Wells (1866-1946), English author best known for science fiction.

J. K. (Joanne) Rowling (1965-), British novelist, best known for the Harry Potter fantasy series.

Jackie Chan (1954-), born Chan Kong-sang. Chinese actor, martial artist, director, producer, screenwriter, singer, comedian, philanthropist and UNICEF Goodwill Ambassador.

James Baldwin (1924-1987), American novelist, playwright, poet and social critic.

Jesus of Nazareth (approx. 4 BC-33 AD), founder of Christianity.

John F. Kennedy (1917-1963), 35th President of the United States.

John Hume (1937-), Irish politician, member of the European Parliament, Nobel laureate, recipient of the Defender of Democracy Award and the Gandhi Peace Prize.

John Lennon (1940-1980), English singer-songwriter, member of the Beatles rock band.

John W. Gardner (1912-2002), U.S. social reformer, author, and Secretary of Health, Education and Welfare under President Johnson.

Kofi Annan (1938-), Ghanaian diplomat, 7th secretary-general of the U.N., Nobel laureate.

Krishna, central figure of the Hindu religion, born a prince in India about 5,000 years ago.

Lakota Sioux, indigenous people of the Great Plains in North and South Dakota, USA.

Leo Tolstoy (1828-1910), Russian novelist, philosopher and social activist credited as a major influence on Gandhi and Martin Luther King, Jr., for his views on pacifism and non-violence.

Luca Cavalli-Sforza (1922-), Italian population geneticist, author and professor.

Mahatma Gandhi (1869-1948), Indian political and spiritual leader who led India to independence and inspired movements for non-violence and civil rights across the world.

Mahnaz Afkhami (1941-), Iranian-born author, leading advocate for women's rights, former Minister of Women's Affairs in Iran.

Malcolm X (1925-1965), born Malcolm Little, controversial African-American Muslim minister, orator and human rights activist who later in life embraced the cause of race unity.

Marian Wright Edelman (1939-), U.S. activist for children's rights, lawyer, founder and president of the Children's Defense Fund.

Mark Twain (1835-1910), born Samuel Clemens. American author and humorist, public speaker and master riverboat pilot.

Martin Luther King, Jr. (1929-1968), U.S. civil rights leader, Baptist minister.

Maya Angelou (1928-), born Marguerite Ann Johnson. African-American author, poet, teacher, performer and civil rights activist.

Mikhail Gorbachev (1931-), former president of the Soviet Union, social activist, environmentalist and Nobel laureate.

Mother Teresa (1910-1997), born Agnes Gonxha Bojaxhiu in Albania. Catholic nun who devoted her life to the poor and sick of Calcutta. Nobel laureate, many other awards.

Nelson Mandela (1918-), South African politician and president, anti-apartheid activist, Nobel laureate, numerous other awards.

Octavio Paz Lozano (1914-1998), Mexican author, poet, professor, diplomat, Nobel Prize for Literature, many other awards.

Oscar Hammerstein (1895-1960), American librettist, playwright, theatrical producer and director, recipient of multiple Tony and Academy Awards.

Pablo Casals (1876-1973), born Pau Casals i Defilló. Renowned Spanish cellist, wrote music for the U.N. Anthem for World Peace, received U.S. Presidential Medal of Freedom.

Polingaysi Qoyawayma (1892-1990), also known as Elizabeth Q. White, Hopi Indian teacher, author, artist.

Qur'án, the sacred scripture of Islam.

René Dubos (1901-1982), French-born American microbiologist, environmentalist, Harvard Medical School professor and Pulitzer Prize winner.

Robert Fulghum (1937-), American author, speaker and Unitarian Universalist minister.

Robert Zend (1929-1985), Hungarian-born Canadian documentary producer, novelist, poet, composer, playwright, filmmaker, artist.

Sherman Alexie, Jr. (1966-), Native American author, poet, filmmaker and performer, recipient of multiple writing awards, Spokane/Coeur d'Alene tribal member.

Sitting Bull (1831-1890), born Tatanka Iyotake, Hunkpapa Sioux holy man and tribal chief.

Socrates (c. 470-399 BC), ancient Greek philosopher, credited as a founder of Western philosophy, renowned for his contributions to ethics, pedagogy and logic.

Sribala Subramanian (1962-), Indian-born American journalist and advocate for children's issues, education and health care.

Susan B. Anthony (1820-1906), U.S. women's suffrage leader and newspaper publisher.

Tecumseh (1768-1813), Native American chief of the Shawnee tribe.

Tenzin Gyatso (1935-), 14th and current Dalai Lama, Tibetan Buddhist spiritual leader, social activist and Nobel laureate.

Thomas Paine (1737-1809), English-American political activist and author whose writings helped inspire the American Revolution.

APPENDIX B

Memorization Techniques

A quotation or thought-for-the-day has been included with each unit for students to memorize. This will focus their thinking and help them to better remember the lesson. Memorization is done by linking information and by fitting new ideas into existing mental frameworks. A variety of techniques have been developed to help us recall information more easily. A few basic strategies are described below.

Simple Repetition

Read the passage out loud from start to finish. Repeat until it is memorized. Students can work alone, in pairs or in groups repeating after the teacher. Another method is to record the passage and replay it until it is learned.

Forward Buildup

Start at the beginning and recite the first phrase. Repeat until it is memorized, then add the second phrase. Continue in this manner until you have reached the end. Break a long selection into smaller parts and learn each part separately; then connect them.

Backward Buildup

Start at the end and recite the last few words. Repeat until they are memorized. Then add the previous phrase and read through to the end. Continue in this manner until you have reached the beginning and have learned the entire passage.

Disappearing Act

Write a passage on the board and have students read it aloud several times. Then, using an eraser, swipe a diagonal path through the entire passage. This will leave a blank space on each line. Ask for student volunteers to read the passage again. Let everyone take a turn. Then make another eraser swipe and ask for another round of volunteers. Continue until the passage has completely disappeared.

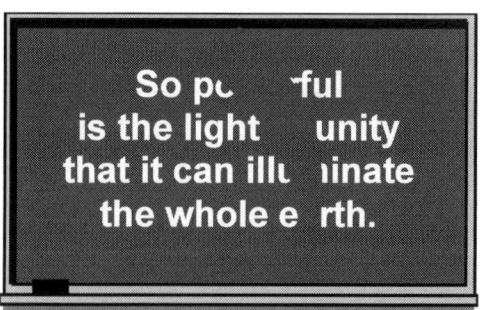

Acronyms

An acronym is a word formed by combining the first letters of a series of words, for example, SCUBA (**S**elf **C**ontained **U**nderwater **B**reathing **A**pparatus) or LASER (**L**ight **A**mplification by **S**timulated **E**mission of **R**adiation). Acronyms are useful for remembering a group of words or topics in a particular order.

Melodies

Music is a powerful aid to memory. For example, many of us learned the letters of the alphabet to the tune of "Twinkle, Twinkle, Little Star." Some passages will be easier to remember if set to music.

Logical Patterns

Information can sometimes be organized into a logical pattern to make memorization easier, for example, from small to large, simple to complex, old to new, or by chronological order.

Visualization

Words can be tied to visual cues to aid recall. One method of visualization is called "chaining," where each image is used as a trigger to help you remember the next item on the list. The task is often easier if the items on the chain are linked in a story. For example, if you are memorizing a grocery list (bananas, bread, cheese, milk, paper towels, etc.), you might create a string of mental images beginning with a monkey as your shopping assistant. Of course, the monkey wants a *banana*. After finishing the banana, she is still hungry and asks for a sandwich (*bread* and *cheese*), which makes her thirsty so you give her a glass of *milk*, which she spills on the floor, so a *paper towel* is needed to clean up the mess, and so forth.

Journey

This is another form of visualization. Imagine yourself walking along a familiar path, perhaps from your bedroom to the kitchen, or from your classroom to the cafeteria. Identify a number of landmarks along the way, for example, a certain tree, a bench, a flower garden. Use the path to remember your material by associating each landmark with one item you wish to recall. For example, if you are trying to memorize a list of people, you might visualize the first person climbing the tree, the second person sitting on the bench, and the third person weeding the flower garden. See each person in your mind as you "walk" along the path. The more unusual the image, the easier it will be to remember. Use exaggeration, humor, silly movements and vivid pictures to spice up your journey. For example, the first person might be cutting down the tree; the second person, balancing the bench on his nose; and the third person, growing like a flower in the garden.

Memory Maps

This is another technique that uses visualization and association. The items to be recalled are mentally plugged into a familiar pattern such as a car or a human face. With a face, use the eyes to remind you of the first topic, the ears for the second and the mouth for the third. For example, for a talk on unity in diversity, the eyes could remind you to share the explanation given in Unit 2 (page 44). The nose (with two essentially identical nostrils), could help you to recall that unity is not sameness. The mouth could remind you of singing from the musical demonstration (page 39).

Mnemonic Devices

Pronounced "neh-MON-ic," this is a memory trick that helps you remember something difficult by associating it with a phrase that is easier to remember. For example, many budding musicians have learned the lines of the treble clef in music (E-G-B-D-F) by associating them with the phrase: **E**very **G**ood **B**oy **D**oes **F**ine. The taxonomic order for our system of biological classification (Kingdom, Phylum, Class, Order, Family, Genus, Species) is easily remembered with the phrase: **K**ing **P**hilip **C**ome **O**ut **F**or **G**oodness **S**ake!

Pictures

As another form of visualization, students can draw or cut and paste representative pictures on top of the written words. For example, this quote by Tecumseh from page 258, "A single twig breaks but the bundle of twigs is strong," might be illustrated as follows:

A 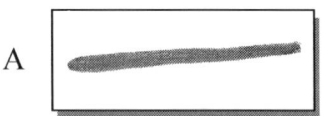 breaks but 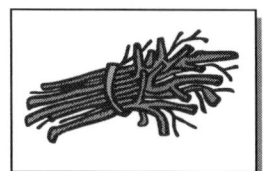 is

Gestures

Gestures can also be used as a memory aid. For example, when teaching the quote in Unit 1 (page 27), flex your arm muscle when saying the word *"powerful,"* clasp your hands together when saying *"unity,"* and spread your fingers wide with palms out for *"illuminate."* Students can perform the movements as they recite the passage. If you or an assistant knows sign language, you can teach children the correct signs to accompany the words.

Card Trick

Print each word of the quote on a separate large card. Give one card to each student. If there are more students than words, two students can hold the same card. If there are fewer students than words, some can hold two cards. Mix the students up and tell them to arrange themselves in order without speaking. Then have each child read his or her word in order, holding up the card up as they speak.

Two useful websites on memory:

www.geosoc.org/schools/pass/memory/memindex.htm

www.studygs.net/memory

APPENDIX C

Help with Reading

The lessons in this book include a number of opportunities for students to read aloud. Some students may need outside assistance with reading skills and comprehension. The following techniques for tutoring reading are designed to help students who already speak the language of instruction and who have a basic knowledge of letters and sounds.

Assign a tutor to each student. They should arrange to meet (in person or by phone) on a regular basis for 30-45 minutes each time. More frequent meetings (even daily) will produce faster results.

For the Tutor

The student will need several short books or pamphlets on topics of interest. Try out reading material at different levels of difficulty to determine where the student feels comfortable. Your school librarian or public library should be able to assist with recommendations.

Select something just above the student's reading level, so there is some challenge. While the student listens, you should read the entire booklet or selection (about five minutes' worth) using a normal speaking voice. Ask the student for a brief summary to ensure comprehension. Then read only the first paragraph or section out loud while the student follows along on the page. Next, have the student read the paragraph once silently.

Repeat this cycle until the student feels ready to read the paragraph out loud fluently in a normal conversational voice. Have the student read the passage out loud. If you both agree that it was read well (so the passage sounds right and makes sense), proceed to the next paragraph. If not, repeat steps 2 and 3 (below) until the student is ready to read the passage aloud perfectly. Then go on to the next paragraph until the book or selection is completed. If the student is able to read the passage fluently after only one reading, the book is too easy. If the student is still unable to read the passage smoothly after about five attempts, the book may be too difficult.

You can check for comprehension by occasionally having students give a brief summary. Work for about thirty minutes at a time.

1	2	3	4

Teacher reads book; student listens	**Teacher reads passage; student follows with eyes**	**Student reads same passage silently**	**Student reads passage aloud to teacher**

You can work with several students at once if each student has an audio player with headphones. Make an audio recording of each book. Then follow the same tutoring method outlined above, with students listening to your voice on the recording. They can replay the recording to hear the paragraph again. Have them inform you when they are ready to read out loud.

When reading, students should not point at words, track sentences with their fingers, or cover the text with frames or rulers. This prevents the eye from taking in larger quantities of print. It also prevents students from glancing ahead for context clues and slows them down. They should not move their lips while reading silently, as this also tends to decrease reading speed.

Leave about ten minutes at the end of every tutoring session for new reading. Have each student choose a new book at their current reading level and read aloud one paragraph at a time. If a student gets stuck on a word, do not tell her/him to sound it out phonetically if s/he has already tried to do so unsuccessfully. Many words have the same letter groups but are quite irregular in their pronunciation. For example, try sounding out the "ea" in heal, bread, break, reality, bear, earth, heart, theater and beauty. Instead, respond with the following strategy:

1. Ask the student to figure out the word using context clues. This means skipping the word and reading to the next punctuation mark, re-reading the sentence to determine the meaning, and identifying the unknown word.

2. If unable to identify the word by context, give the student a hint such as the definition of the word, a synonym or a fill-in-the-blank sentence.

3. If the student is still stuck, pronounce the word and give its meaning.

4. Always have the student re-read the sentence.

When students are able to read at a given grade level with minimal repetition on their main selection and almost no errors on their new reading, they are ready to advance to the next level. Your students might also enjoy some take-home reading at an easier level. You can provide them with appropriate material and should spend a few minutes at the beginning of the next session discussing it with them.

You might find it useful to make an audio recording of each student reading on the first and last days of your tutoring program in order to measure progress. Good luck!

Note: Ideas for this section were taken from several excellent web sites, including http://ToRead.com, www.ed.gov/insts/americareads, ReadingRecovery.org, ReadRight.com, ReadingExchange.com, EduPlace.com and ncrel.org/sdrs/timely/britoc.htm, and from formal observation and evaluation of students in the ReadRight program at Union Gap School in Washington State.

APPENDIX D

Educational Strategy
Think-Pair-Share

Think-Pair-Share is a cooperative discussion strategy formalized by Professor Frank Lyman at the University of Maryland in 1981. Its name derives from the three steps of student action:

1. Think: The teacher poses an open-ended, thought-provoking question (not something with a simple *yes* or *no* answer). Students are given a brief period (anywhere from 10 seconds to about 5 minutes, depending on the complexity of the topic) to think individually about their responses.

2. Pair: Students pair up with a partner to discuss their answers and, based on their collective insights, identify the ones they think are best. This interaction also provides an opportunity to clarify difficult words and challenging concepts. Students are given 1 to 10 minutes to work depending on the difficulty of the question. More time will be needed if students are asked to produce a chart or diagram of their thinking. With a large class and a complex topic, the teacher may wish to add an additional step: Ask the pairs to regroup into fours in order to further refine their thoughts before sharing with the entire class.

If there is not an even number of students, one of them can partner with the teacher or join one of the pairs.

3. Share: The teacher asks each pair to share its thinking with the class. With a large group, the teacher might only call on some of the pairs. Responses can be noted on the board. If desired, one or two students can also be called upon to summarize the entire discussion. The quality of the activity will largely depend upon the quality of the question posed in step one.

Some Benefits of Think-Pair-Share

Think-Pair-Share has many advantages over the traditional classroom practice of the teacher asking a question and calling on one or two students to answer. In the traditional classroom, as soon as the first individual is called upon, the others often stop thinking about the question. Think-Pair-Share is a valuable educational strategy for the following reasons:

- It allows everyone to participate equally including those who never volunteer in class or who might be slower to respond. Increased student participation leads to improved learning and retention of information.

- It structures the discussion, promotes focused student conversations and limits off-task behavior.

- It develops thinking and communication skills through speaking, listening, asking questions, analyzing and summarizing others' ideas.

- It allows concepts to be presented in the language of the students in addition to the language of the textbook or teacher.

- It improves the quality of class discussions by giving students a chance to think about and discuss their answers rather than blurting out the first thing that comes to mind. Teachers often wait less than a second before calling on students. With silent "wait time" built in, responses will have better explanations and greater detail.

- It is a low-risk strategy, allowing students to try out ideas on a partner and refine their thoughts before sharing with the group at large. This is less threatening than speaking in front of the entire class with an untested answer.

- It allows students to learn from each other and to see the same concepts expressed in a variety of ways, as different individuals develop answers to the same question.

- It ensures a high level of student engagement in a cooperative process.

- It is an effective strategy for children, youth and adults in classes of any size.

APPENDIX E

Speed Discussions

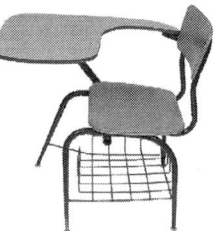

A speed discussion is an educational strategy used to foster dialogue and to quickly help the class develop a collective understanding of the topic at hand.

Procedure: Students meet in pairs for a series of short discussions lasting 1 to 5 minutes, depending on the complexity of the topic. At the end of each interval, the teacher rings a bell or uses another signal, cueing students to move on to the next partner. The discussions are guided by a list of questions that can be printed on a handout, written on the board, projected on a screen, spoken by the teacher or posted on the wall. Answers can be shared with the class after each round or after all of the questions have been discussed.

To make this work smoothly, the first pairs can be assigned in advance, or students can be asked to turn in a specific direction in the seating arrangement, in order to not waste time finding a partner. If space is available, one easy way to organize the discussion is to arrange the classroom chairs in two concentric circles with the same number of chairs in each circle. When the signal is given, students in the outer circle remain in their seats, while students in the inner circle rotate one move in the same direction, e.g., to their right. This can also be done with students standing—without chairs.

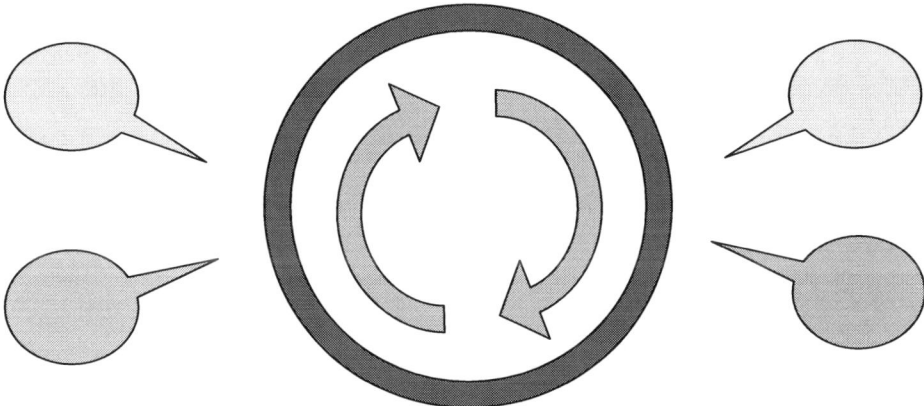

Variation: If time is available, rather than considering a new question with each new partner, you could have each pair answer the question, then change partners and discuss the same question again. After the third round, tell the class to move on to the next question. Continue in this manner until each question has been discussed with three different people. This allows for a more thorough consideration of the topic and gives students an opportunity to refine their own thinking during the process.

Benefits: The movement and excitement of a speed discussion can quickly get students talking about the topic. It draws the entire class into thinking about each question rather than letting one student give an answer while the rest sit passively in their seats. Additional benefits are similar to those of Think-Pair-Share (see previous page).

APPENDIX F

Sample Letter from Sponsor

August 5

Dear young friends,

How happy we are that you have gathered together this week to learn about unity! We know you will enjoy all of the fun activities your teachers have planned.

Unity is one of the most important challenges facing our world today. Unity Camp will help to prepare you for life as global citizens, respectful of the differences between people and learning how to work together for a more peaceful world.

We would like to learn about your experiences this week. Please feel free to write to us and tell us what you have learned.

With warm greetings,

Harmony Park Association
Board of Directors

APPENDIX G
Additional Resources

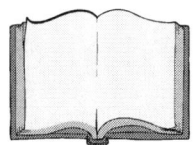

Books for Teachers and Parents

Anti-Bias Curriculum: *Tools for Empowering Young Children,* by Louise Derman-Sparks and the A.B.C. Task Force. National Association for the Education of Young Children: Washington, D.C., 1989.

Because We Can Change the World: *A Practical Guide to Building Cooperative, Inclusive Classroom Communities,* by Mara Sapon-Shevin. Allyn and Bacon: Boston, rev. 2010.

Beyond Heroes and Holidays: *A Practical Guide to K-12 Anti-Racist, Multicultural Education and Staff Development,* by Enid Lee, Deborah Menkart, Margo Okazawa-Rey. Teaching for Change: Washington, D.C., rev. 2007.

The Color of Words: *An Encyclopedic Dictionary of Ethnic Bias in the United States,* by Phillip H. Herbst. Intercultural Press: Boston, 1997.

Culturally Responsive Teaching: *Theory, Research and Practice,* by Geneva Gay. Teacher's College Press: New York, 2000.

Multiracial Child Resource Book: *Living Complex Realities,* by Maria P. P. Root and Matt Kelley. MAVIN Foundation: Seattle, 2003.

Navigating Diversity: *An Advocate's Guide Through the Maze of Race, Gender, Religion and More,* by Patty Bates-Ballard and Gregory Smith. BookSurge: Charleston, SC, 2008.

Planning for Effective and Culturally Responsive Teaching and Learning: *Strategies That Ensure Equity and High Achievement for All Students,* by Johnnie McKinley. BookSurge: Charleston, SC, 2009.

Rethinking Our Classrooms: *Teaching for Equity and Justice.* Volume 1 by Wayne Au, Bill Bigelow, Stan Karp; rev. 2007. Volume 2 edited by Bill Bigelow, 2001. Rethinking Schools, Ltd.: Milwaukee, Wisconsin.

Roots and Wings: *Affirming Culture in Early Childhood Programs,* by Stacey York. Redleaf Press: St. Paul, MN, rev. 2003.

The Virtues Guide: *A Handbook for Parents Teaching Virtues,* by Linda Kavelin Popov. The Virtues Project: www.virtuesproject.com, WellSpring International, Canada, 1995.

We Can't Teach What We Don't Know: *White Teachers, Multiracial Schools,* by Gary Howard. Teacher's College Press: New York, rev. 2006.

Online Resources

Addressing Student Diversity. List of web resources on all aspects of diversity.
< *www.mhhe.com/socscience/education/diverse.mhtml#addressing* >

Awesome Library. Extensive compilation of multicultural links.
< *www.awesomelibrary.org/Classroom/Social_Studies/Multicultural/Multicultural.html* >

Center for the Study of White American Culture. A multiracial organization that encourages dialogue among all racial and cultural groups. < *www.euroamerican.org* >

Culture for Kids. Great source of bilingual and multicultural books, videos, music, posters and software. < *www.cultureforkids.com* >

Diversity Links. Multicultural groups, organizations and web links.
< *www.wesleyan.edu* > enter *"diversity resources"* in the search box.

EdChange. Comprehensive multicultural site with articles, links, classroom activities, lesson plans, research, historic collections, quizzes, fact sheets, film reviews, poetry journal and more.
< *www.edchange.org/projects.html* >

Intercultural Press. Books, training DVDs and simulations on cross-cultural communication.
< *www.interculturalpress.com* > enter *"intercultural"* in the search box.

MAVIN. Organization that celebrates the mixed heritage experience and raises awareness through educational resources, programs and research. *Mavin* means "one who understands" in Yiddish. < *www.mavinfoundation.org* >

Multicultural Lesson Plans and Resources. Hundreds of links to lessons for all grade levels and subjects: math, music, history, religion and more.
< *www.cloudnet.com/~edrbsass/edmulticult.htm* >

National Association for Multicultural Education. NAME provides leadership in equity, diversity and multicultural education, from pre-school through higher education.
< *www.nameorg.org* >

National Forum on People's Differences. Questions and answers about human differences: everything you wanted to know but were afraid to ask. < *www.yforum.com* >

Ocean. Free download of the world's religious literature, for the purpose of promoting greater understanding. Over 1,000 books in English, plus collections in 6 other languages.
< *www.bahai-education.org/ocean* >

Race Relations. Articles, resources, discussion groups. < *http://racerelations.about.com* >

Rethinking Schools. Produces educational materials committed to equity and the vision of a multiracial democracy. Focus on problems facing urban schools, particularly issues of race. < *www.rethinkingschools.org* >

Social Studies School Service. Multicultural posters, lesson plans, poetry, stories, songs and more. < *www.socialstudies.com* > *enter "multicultural" in the search box.*

Society for Intercultural Education, Training and Research. SIETAR is a membership organization for students and professionals concerned with intercultural relations in the U.S. and worldwide. < *www.sietarusa.org* >

Teaching for Change. Provides resources for teachers and parents to transform schools, to build a more equitable multicultural society, and to help students become active global citizens. Includes an annotated list of multicultural children's literature. < *www.TeachingForChange.org* >

Teaching Tolerance. A wealth of free anti-bias lessons, videos, books and other resources for teachers. < *www.tolerance.org* >

Understanding Prejudice. Interactive exercises, searchable databases and over 2,000 links on prejudice, stereotyping and discrimination. < *www.understandingprejudice.org* >

* * * * *

APPENDIX H
Bibliography

All the Colors We Are / Todos los Colores de Nuestra Piel: *The Story of How We Get Our Skin Color,* by Katie Kissinger and Wernher Krutein. Redleaf Press: Minnesota, 1994.

Because We Can Change the World: *A Practical Guide to Building Cooperative, Inclusive Classroom Communities,* by Mara Sapon-Shevin. Allyn and Bacon: Boston, 1999.

The Power of Unity, by Randie Gottlieb. UnityWorks: Yakima, WA, 2005.

The Sneetches, by Theodor Geisel, a.k.a. Dr. Seuss. Random House Books: New York, 1961.

APPENDIX I

About the Author

Randie Gottlieb is the head of UnityWorks, an international diversity training firm, and adjunct professor of multicultural education at Heritage University on the Yakama Nation Reservation in central Washington State, USA. She is also co-founder of the Mona Foundation, a non-profit supporting grassroots educational development worldwide. She earned degrees in education from Cal State, Boston University and Harvard.

The author of eight other books and a frequent presenter, Dr. Gottlieb has worked as a school principal, curriculum developer and college administrator, and has served as a teacher at every level— from pre-school through post-graduate. Her work has taken her to over 30 countries, including 11 years in Puerto Rico, where she managed an international training center, and with her husband, founded a Montessori-based elementary school.

During that time, she also traveled repeatedly to rural Panama, helping to train indigenous Ngöbe-Bugle school teachers who in turn provided basic education for hundreds of isolated and impoverished children lacking access to government schools. Her work was featured in *Montessori Leadership Magazine*.

After returning to the United States, Dr. Gottlieb served for 10 years as Executive Director of the EMPIRE Consortium, providing assistance with multicultural program planning, implementation and assessment for K-12 schools in central Washington State. Under her direction, EMPIRE was highlighted as a model program by President Clinton's National Initiative on Race, and awarded best program of the year by the National Association for Multicultural Education.

In addition to her work in education, Randie earned a bachelor's degree in wood design; played volleyball on the U.S. women's national team, and continues to win awards for her humorous poetry. With her husband Steven, a pediatrician, she has raised two wonderful sons and has been organizing and teaching children's classes on unity for many years.

PART VII
Index of Activities

List of Activities in Each Unit

Opening Activities   **Page**

1. Unity bingo (ice-breaker) 13
2. Room mixer (ice-breaker) 16
3. Group match (ice-breaker) 16
4. Circle diagram (ice-breaker) 17
5. Getting to know you (ice-breaker) 19
6. Videos (introducing the theme) 247

UNIT 1: The Light of Unity

1. Introduction 22
2. One Planet, One People (song) 22, 28
3. Definitions of "unity" and "disunity" (pairs brainstorm) 22
4. Unity is / Disunity is (reading with questions) 23, 29
5. Pantomime (movement activity) 23
6. The benefits of unity (demonstrations) 23-26
    A. Bundle of sticks 23
    B. Chair lift 24
    C. Donkey tug o' war 24
    D. Hot and cold 24
    E. Shoe demo 25
    F. Word puzzle 26
    G. Summary 26
7. Unity (reading with student questions) 26, 30
8. Thought for the day: "So powerful is the light" (memorization) 27
9. Closing questions (review) 28
10. Lanyards (craft) 28, 31

UNIT 2: Unity in Diversity

1. Introduction and review 36
2. Similarities and differences (brainstorming and movement activity) 37-38
3. Leaves of one tree (class discussion) 38
4. Unity in diversity (reading with student questions) 38, 42
5. Musical demonstration (singing) 39
6. The eye (felt lesson) 39, 43-47
7. Machines in motion (worksheet with discussion questions) 39-40, 48

Teaching Unity: List of Activities by Unit, p. 285

List of Activities by Unit (continued)

   8. Unity in diversity (small group discussion) 41, 49
   9. Thought for the day: "We are all the fruits" (memorization) 41
 10. Hawaiian Unity Song (song) 41
 11. Craft activities 41, 50-57
      A. Flowers of one garden (cut-and-paste collage) 51-52
      B. Leaf laminates (lamination using hot iron) 53-55
      C. Diversity streamers (hanging decoration with ribbons and tin can) 56-57

UNIT 3: The Colors We Are
   1. Introduction and review 60
   2. Thought for the day: "What should it matter" (memorization) 61
   3. Skin color (demonstration and discussion) 61-62
   4. Colors of our world (teacher talk with pictures) 62
   5. How we got our skin color (story with questions) 63-64
   6. Class features chart (groups investigate and report back) 64, 66-67
   7. Hooray for Skin (poem) 65, 68
   8. Good Neighbors (song) 65
   9. Personal poster (write, trace, paint, cut and paste) 65, 69-72

UNIT 4: Overcoming Prejudice
   1. Introduction and review 78-79
   2. Bridges and barriers (brainstorming and word wall) 80
   3. Prejudice (class discussion) 81
   4. The Sneetches (poem with comprehension questions) 82, 90
   5. The Sneetches (simulation) 82-83
   6. Putdowns (brainstorming and class discussion) 84
   7. Personal stories (small group sharing) 85, 91
   8. Put-ups (brainstorming and writing) 85
   9. Dealing with putdowns and prejudice (reading) 86, 92
 10. Name it, claim it (worksheet and skits) 86, 93
 11. Creating unity (role plays) 87, 94-95
 12. Thought for the day: "Darkness cannot" (memorization) 87
 13. Barriers into bonds (felt lesson) 88, 96-102
 14. Barriers into bonds (worksheet) 88, 103
 15. Barriers into bonds (craft) 88, 104-108
 16. The Light of Unity (final review) 88
 17. What Mankind Has to Learn (song) 89
 18. Circle of unity (visualization) 89, 109

List of Activities by Unit (continued)

Music
1. Instructions for group singing 114-115
2. Song sheet 116-117
3. Musical scores 119-124
   A. Good Neighbors 119
   B. Hawaiian Unity Song 120
   C. One Planet, One People 121
   D. What Mankind Has to Learn 122
   E. We Can Build a Beautiful World 123-124

Additional Activities
1. Complete listing of additional activities 147-148
   A. Warm-ups 149
   B. Craft projects 150-167
   C. Outdoor games 168-176
   D. Skits, demonstrations and puzzles 177-192
   E. Speaking, reading, writing and research 193-199
2. Further reading and research 200-201

Children's Performance
1. Songs, memory quotes, presentation of crafts 141-143, 207-208
2. Stick and bundle (demo) 209
3. Chair lift (skit) 209
4. Musical demo 209
5. Colors of our world (demo) 210
6. Unity in diversity (talk) 210
7. How we got our skin color (skit) 210, 214-215
8. The eye (felt lesson) 212
9. Hooray for Skin (poem) 213
10. Barriers into bonds (felt lesson) 216
11. We Can Build a Beautiful World (mini-opera) 217

Closing and Follow-up Activities 219-220

Index of Activities by Category

(Note: Some items are listed in more than one category.)

Arts and Crafts   Page

- Barriers into bonds (paper or vinyl diagram) 88, 104-108
- Chalk mural (freehand group drawing) 151
- Children's performance (project presentations) 207
- Diversity streamers (hanging decoration with ribbons and tin can) 56-57
- Felt lesson design (topics chosen by students) 177
- Flowers of one garden (cut-and-paste collage) 51-52
- Folder decorations (draw, cut and paste) 240
- Friendship bracelets (hand weaving) 156
- Hands of humanity (cut-out cookies) 160-161
- Lanyards (braiding with flat plastic lacing) 28, 31
- Leaf laminates (lamination using hot iron) 53-55
- Leaves of one tree (trace, cut and write) 151-152
- Leaves of one tree poster (trace, cut and paste) 153
- Light switch covers (modeling clay) 157
- Mosaic art (design created using small pieces) 158-159
- Paper carnations (tissue paper flowers) 155
- Paper people (draw, cut and paste) 150
- Patchwork quilt (class project with fabric squares) 162-167
- Personal poster (write, trace, paint, cut and paste) 65, 69-72
- Pigment posters (cut and paste) 154
- Rainbow chain (cut and paste) 150
- Ribbon of hearts (draw, cut and paste) 150
- Virtues tree (write and tape) 248

Demonstrations, Skits and Role Plays

- Apple turnovers (demonstration) 181
- Bundle of sticks (strength in unity) 23, 209
- Chair lift (strength in unity) 24, 209
- Circle of unity (visualization) 89, 109
- Colors of our world (teacher talk with pictures) 62, 210
- Colors of the heart (skit) 177
- Cooperation (skit) 179-180
- Creating unity (role plays) 87, 94-95

Donkey tug o' war (cooperation) 24
Felt lesson design (topics chosen by students) 177
Flower garden (skit) 178
Hot and cold (cooperation) 24
How we got our skin color (short play) 210, 214-215
Musical demonstration (sameness, diversity, unity) 39, 209
Name it, claim it (worksheet with role plays) 86, 93
Pantomime of unity and disunity (creative movement) 23
Shoe demo (interdependence) 25
Similarities and differences (brainstorming and movement activity) 37-38
Skin color (demonstration and discussion) 61-62
The Sneetches (simulation) 82-83
We Can Build a Beautiful World (mini-opera) 123-124, 217
Word puzzle (two heads better than one) 26

Discussions, Questions and Brainstorming

Bridges and barriers (brainstorming and word wall) 80
Definitions of "unity" and "disunity" (pairs brainstorm) 22
How we got our skin color (storybook with questions) 63, 64
Leaves of one tree (class discussion) 38
Machines in motion (worksheet and discussion) 39-40, 48
Personal stories (small group sharing) 85, 91
Prejudice (class discussion) 81
Putdowns (brainstorming and class discussion) 84
Put-ups (brainstorming and writing) 85
Similarities and differences (brainstorming and movement activity) 37-38
Skin color demo (demonstration and discussion) 61-62
The Sneetches (poem with questions) 82, 90
Think-Pair-Share (educational strategy) 274-275
Unity (reading with student questions) 26, 30
Unity in diversity (reading with student questions) 38, 42
Unity in diversity (small group discussion) 41, 49
Unity is / Disunity is (reading with questions) 23, 29

Felt Lessons

Barriers into bonds (overcoming prejudice) 88, 96-102, 216
The eye (unity is not sameness) 39, 43-47, 212
Felt lesson design (topics chosen by students) 177
The human body (unity in diversity) 186, 187-192

Introductions, Ice-breakers and Warm-ups

Birthday line-up	149
Circle diagram	17-18
Getting to know you chart	19-20
Group match	16
Human knot	149
Jigsaw puzzles	246
Link-ups	149
Room mixer	16
Unit introductions	
1. The Light of Unity	22
2. Unity in Diversity	36
3. The Colors We Are	60
4. Overcoming Prejudice	78-79
Unity bingo	13-15
Videos introducing the theme of unity	247
1. Starting Small: Teaching Children Tolerance	247
2. The Power of Race Unity	247

Music

Children's performance	207
Instructions for group singing	114-115
List of songs	118
1. Good Neighbors	65, 119
2. Hawaiian Unity Song	41, 120
3. One Planet, One People	22, 28, 121
4. We Can Build a Beautiful World (mini-opera)	123-124, 217
5. What Mankind Has to Learn	89, 122
Musical demonstration (sameness, diversity, unity)	39, 209
Musical scores	119-124
Song sheet	116-117, 142-143

Outdoor Games

All aboard	170
Beach ball volley	169
Centipede	172
Cooperative musical chairs	168-169
Electric fence	172
Fingertip touchdown	171

    Freeze dance 169
    Hoop game 170
    Human knot 149
    Lava island 170
    Maypole dance 173-175
    Parachute games 173
    Trust walk 171
    Tug of peace 168

Puzzles

    Jigsaw puzzles 246
    Tangrams 181-186
    Word puzzle 26, 130

Readings, Stories and Poems

    The Cold Within (poem) 195
    Dealing with putdowns and prejudice 86, 92
    Hooray for Skin (poem) 65, 68, 213
    How we got our skin color 63-64
    The Sneetches (poem excerpt) 82, 90
    Unity 26, 30
    Unity in diversity 38, 42
    Unity is / Disunity is 23, 29

Review

    Benefits of unity 26, 28
    Questions about unity 36
    Questions about unity in diversity 60
    Questions about unity, diversity, race and skin color 78-79
    Questions for final review 88

Speaking, Reading, Writing and Research

    The Cold Within (poem) 195
    Famous figures monologues 194
    Felt lesson design 177
    Further reading and research 200-201, 277-279
    International pen pals 193
    Letters from history 194

Memorization techniques 268-270
Personal interview 196
Personal poster 65, 69-72
Public presentations 194
Quotation recitation 193
Tutoring reading 271-272
Unity in diversity (student presentation) 210
What's in a name? 195
World citizen passport 197

Thought for the Day

Children's performance 207-208
List of memory quotes 141
   1. So powerful is the light of unity 27
   2. We are all the fruits of one tree 41
   3. What should it matter that one bowl is dark 61
   4. Darkness cannot drive out darkness 87
Thought for the day (review) 36, 61, 79, 88
Words of wisdom (additional quotations) 257-267

Worksheets

Barriers into bonds (overcoming prejudice) 88, 103
Class features chart (investigating our colors) 64, 66-67
Machines in motion (unity in diversity) 39-40, 48
Name it, claim it (responding to biased remarks) 86, 93

* * * * *

Made in the USA
San Bernardino, CA
15 May 2018

Made in the USA
San Bernardino, CA
15 May 2018